'This is an exceptionally sensitive and creati̶͟ ̶̶̶̶̶ drama as an articulation of how grace and ̶̶̶̶̶̶̶̶̶guage. Full of fresh insight and wide-ranging ̶̶̶̶̶̶̶ity and energy, it will send us back to the pla̶̶̶̶̶̶.'

Rowan Williams, Poet, Theologian and 104th Archbishop of Canterbury

'This book illuminates Shakespeare's work, and likewise illuminates the writing of the great if sometimes under-valued theologian, Nicholas Cusanus (1401–1464). The especial virtue of the volume is to demonstrate how theological conceptions of language derived from Cusanus may shed light on some of the essential characteristics of Shakespearian language. Following Gerlier, one is led to see that our God given capacity for language is fundamentally meant to identify the value of others in the divine order, and to enter into relationship, above all, through expressions of praise. Shakespeare is at one and the same time devoted to this understanding and aware of how easily it may be corrupted – and with what tragic consequences.

There is no strained suggestion here that Shakespeare had been directly influenced by Cusanus. But there is skill, even virtuosity, in the way that Gerlier elicits the concept of praise from Cusanus's writing and then, through a very detailed analysis of two plays – *King Lear* and *The Winter's Tale* – convincingly turns an interpretive key in the language and action of Shakespeare's drama... All of this is accomplished in exceptionally lucid and elegant prose'.

Robin Kirkpatrick, Professor of Italian and English Literature, Robinson College, University of Cambridge

'Valentin Gerlier has restored to vigour a Christian Humanist reading of Shakespeare in a more precisely theological key. He convincingly argues, through dazzlingly close readings, that *King Lear* and the late plays concern a Renaissance crisis of language: it is a human poetic construct; and yet if it is regarded as only an instrument of power and deceit, then its sacramental core as sign and gift of mediated transcendence is denied. Human trust and association become in consequence impossible, and nature herself is corrupted. Such tragic delusion means that we can only wait in hope for the divine miraculously to break through our discourse and actions if life is to be restored. Nothing could show better the new relevance of Shakespeare for our current human crisis'.

Catherine Pickstock, Norris-Hulse Professor in Divinity, University of Cambridge

Shakespeare and the Grace of Words

Crossing the boundaries between literature, philosophy and theology, *Shakespeare and the Grace of Words* pioneers a reading strategy that approaches language as grounded in praise; that is, as affirmation and articulation of the goodness of Being. Offering a metaphysically astute theology of language grounded in the thought of Renaissance theologian Nicholas of Cusa, as well as readings of Shakespeare that instantiate and complement its approach, this book shows that language in which the divine gift of Being is received, apprehended and expressed, even amidst darkness and despair, is language that can renew our relationship with one another and with the things and beings of the world. *Shakespeare and the Grace of Words* aims to engage the reader in detailed, performative close readings while exploring the metaphysical and theological contours of Shakespeare's art—as a venture into a poetic illumination of the deep grammar of the real.

Valentin Gerlier is a scholar, musician and lecturer in Theology, Philosophy and Ethics at the University of Chester, Research Associate at the Margaret Beaufort Institute of Theology, Cambridge, and tutor at the Temenos Academy. He has acted in and directed numerous Shakespeare plays, and teaches Shakespeare at the Institute of Continuing Education, University of Cambridge.

Routledge Studies in Shakespeare

The Shakespeare Multiverse
Fandom as Literary Praxis
Valerie M. Fazel and Louise Geddes

Shakespeare's Returning Warriors – and Ours
Alan Warren Friedman

Shakespeare's Influence on Karl Marx
The Shakespearean Roots of Marxism
Christian A. Smith

Shakespeare and Happiness
Kathleen French

Shakespeare and Emotional Expression
Finding Feeling through Colour
Bríd Phillips

Aemilia Lanyer as Shakespeare's Co-Author
Mark Bradbeer

Shakespeare's Law
Mark Fortier

Shakespeare and the Grace of Words
Language, Theology, Metaphysics
Valentin Gerlier

Reading Robert Greene
Recovering Shakespeare's Rival
Darren Freebury-Jones

For more information about this series, please visit: https://www.routledge.com/Routledge-Studies-in-Shakespeare/book-series/RSS

Shakespeare and the Grace of Words
Language, Theology, Metaphysics

Valentin Gerlier

NEW YORK AND LONDON

First published 2022
by Routledge
605 Third Avenue, New York, NY 10158

and by Routledge
4 Park Square, Milton Park, Abingdon, Oxon, OX14 4RN

Routledge is an imprint of the Taylor & Francis Group, an informa business

© 2022 Valentin Gerlier

The right of Valentin Gerlier to be identified as author of this work has been asserted in accordance with sections 77 and 78 of the Copyright, Designs and Patents Act 1988.

All rights reserved. No part of this book may be reprinted or reproduced or utilised in any form or by any electronic, mechanical, or other means, now known or hereafter invented, including photocopying and recording, or in any information storage or retrieval system, without permission in writing from the publishers.

Trademark notice: Product or corporate names may be trademarks or registered trademarks, and are used only for identification and explanation without intent to infringe.

Library of Congress Cataloging-in-Publication Data
A catalog record for this title has been requested

ISBN: 978-1-032-12140-6 (hbk)
ISBN: 978-1-032-12141-3 (pbk)
ISBN: 978-1-003-22327-6 (ebk)

DOI: 10.4324/9781003223276

Typeset in Sabon
by codeMantra

Dedicated to the memory of
 MARINA SOPHIE VAN HOECKE
 Loving Mother, Teacher of Wisdom.

Contents

Acknowledgements	xi
List of Abbreviations	xiii
Preface	xv

PART I
Approach   1

1 Shakespeare, Language and Religion: Problems and Possibilities   3
  Introduction: Shakespeare, Language and Religion 3
  Skepticism and Cultural Poetics: Language as Power 7
  The 'Turn to Religion' and its Ambiguities 10
  *Transition: Gadamer's Hermeneutical Philosophy of
    Language and Rowan Williams' Metaphysics* 13
  Some Theological Readings of Shakespeare 19
    Grace, Gift and Ethics in *The Winter's Tale*:
      John Milbank 19
    Nature and Forgiveness in King Lear: John Hughes 23
    Language, Acknowledgement and Forgiveness in the
      Late Plays: Sarah Beckwith 25
    Shakespeare, Cusa and Doxology: Johannes Hoff and
      Peter Hampson 27
  Theology and Literature: Issues and Insights 31
    Literature as Theology? 31
    Theology as Literature? 33

2 'A Wide and Universal Theatre': Shakespeare, Cusa and Doxology   47
  Introduction 47
  *Cusa, Theology and Language: Context and
    Background* 50

x Contents

The Limits of Language and the Crafting of Names 53
Praise, Possest and Poetics 59
Calling and Responding: The Voices of the Soliloquy 65
The Liturgical and the 'Middle-Voice' 71
Response as Responsibility: The Hospitality of Words 75
Conclusion 78

PART II
Readings 87

3 The Unsaying of the World: *King Lear* 89
Introduction 89
Spatialisation versus Symbolic Speech 91
'Nothing in the Middle': Weightless Words,
   Ponderous Silences 95
'Nature', or Creativity versus Curses 101
Swearing and Jesting in Vain 109
The Voice of the Skeleton Man 112
Nakedness in Garments, or Fiction versus Justice 117
Words without a Cause 122

4 Words of Childlike Grace: *The Winter's Tale* 134
Introduction 134
Turning the World to Stone 137
The Rescue of Words: Fools, Counsellors, Oracles 146
   Interlude: From Time to Tale 150
The Art of Storytelling; or Cutpurses,
   Courtiers and Clowns 152
The Queen of the Flowers, or the Voice of Nature 157
The Grace of Words and the Ground of Language 165

Epilogue: Shakespeare, Metaphysics and
'Theology and Literature' 181

Bibliography 187
Index 204

Acknowledgements

Friends, companions and teachers are life's great gifts, and I would like to acknowledge the tremendous gratitude I feel to those who have given me love, care and support during the completion of this project.

I would like to deeply acknowledge Brian Edwards, my first Shakespeare teacher and now lifelong friend. Immense gratitude goes to Joseph Milne, who taught me how to *read* Shakespeare in the true and deep sense. I would like to thank Duane Williams, who helped me realise and admit what I always knew in my heart: that I needed to undertake this research and write this work.

For their friendship and encouragement, I would like to thank Kamil Sawicki, Daniel Samuel, Elizabeth Powell, Sadia Abdullah, David Brazier and Ashna Sen.

I feel deeply grateful to my students, whose attentive comments, penetrating questions and poetic spirit have made rehearsals, classes and seminars such inspiring moments.

For unending support in this and many other projects and the gift of a lifelong friendship, my deep gratitude goes to Ziyah Jabbar and Amanda Spring.

I am grateful to the Temenos Academy for providing a haven for the pursuit of true and good things.

This study would not have been possible without the generous financial help provided by the Hockerill Educational Foundation, the Sir Richard Stapley Educational Trust, the St. Luke's College Foundation and the London Community Network. My gratitude goes to these institutions for their generous support.

At the Faculty of Divinity, Cambridge, I would like to thank my PhD supervisor Malcolm Guite, as well as Giles Waller, Ankur Barua and Férdia Stone-Davis for their kindness and encouragement. Heartfelt thanks go to the librarians at both the Faculty of Divinity and the Faculty of English, for their selfless and tireless work behind the scenes. I am also very grateful to my examiners Rowan Williams and Vittorio Montemaggi for their generous readings, their clarifying questions and penetrating insights.

For his wisdom and his deep understanding of Shakespeare, I would like to thank Robin Kirkpatrick. For her immense generosity, constant encouragement and inspiration, I would especially like to thank Catherine Pickstock.

Finally—for her spirit, her courage, her wisdom and her grace, I am deeply thankful to my beloved wife Anneke Dessens—the true Queen of the Flowers.

Abbreviations

AYL	*As You Like It*
CAL	*Christianity and Literature*
CUP	Cambridge University Press
DDI	*De Docta Ignorantia*
DM	*Idiota de Mente*
DP	*De Possest*
DVD	*De Visione Dei*
JMEM	*Journal of Medieval and Early Modern Studies*
KL	*King Lear*
LAT	*Literature and Theology*
MT	*Modern Theology*
OUP	Oxford University Press
RAL	*Religion and Literature*
RAR	*Renaissance and Reformation*
SUR	*Shakespeare Survey*
SQ	*Shakespeare Quarterly*
TIM	*Timon of Athens*
UCAL	University of California Press
UCP	University of Chicago Press
UP	University Press
VEN	*De Venatione Sapientiae*
WT	*The Winter's Tale*
YUP	Yale University Press

Preface

This book is about the deep and fundamental interconnectedness of word and gift. Its overall thesis is that any act of speech is always already involved in a linguistic universe, at the heart of which radiates the redemptive affirmation of the goodness of being that is the Word or *logos*. As the creative ground of all words, the *logos* makes all words potentially unique instantiations of this primordial affirmation, making all words potentially redemptive, and so potentially gifts. This is the theological grammar, underwritten by the Prologue of the Gospel of John that, I argue, mediates the encounter between theology and literature in general, and between theology and Shakespeare in particular.

The readings of Shakespeare ventured in this study are concerned with teasing out this universal linguistic phenomenon—working out how language may be inhabited by the *logos* as a primordial *call*. As this call, the *logos* invites a human *response* of affirmation, gratitude and laudation for the gift of being, even despite its most terrible vicissitudes. The key term I use to evoke this basic response is *praise*. From a theological point of view, this marks my approach as 'doxological'—a word which stems from the koiné Greek *doxa,* 'glory', 'praise' and *logos,* a term with a staggering multiplicity of connotations, from 'word', 'saying', 'speech', 'account', 'story', 'thought' and even 'harmony'. In many Christian traditions, 'doxology' is associated with hymns, prayers, psalms and devotion and alludes to the whole spirit of the liturgy. In this book, 'praise' means first of all a fundamental trait of linguistic expression, which is to *affirm* and *articulate* the good in all things and beings and, in and with such articulation, offer the gift of gratitude to their transcendent origin. If 'affirming' means a simple yet profound exaltation, a 'saying yes' to one another, to the world and to God, 'articulating' means offering, in the same instance, a creative account of what it is one is saying 'yes' to. Such an account can remain elusive, elliptical and even problematic—the point is that it has been said, been offered, or, in a theological sense, been returned as a *gift*. Accordingly, the energies of language first arise not in order to indicate, describe, signify or even to communicate: language's primal vitality is to respond, to recognise and to acknowledge, to give thanks and to celebrate, and by celebrating and giving thanks also saying, unfolding, poetically revealing something of the divinely given gift for which and to which gratitude is given.

Because word and gift are two fundamental theological categories, the book is also, as I have suggested above, an attempt to explore the interconnectedness of theology and literature. My approach suggests that there is something irreducibly poetic, or indeed literary, in theology, just as there is something irreducibly theological—in the sense of an orientation towards 'ultimate concerns' mediated by the symbols, tropes and motifs of a religious culture, understood broadly—in literature. By this, I do not mean to analyse Shakespearean text as simply influenced by, or as a by-product of, the complex religio-political contexts of his day—nor will I take a rhetorical approach which draws comparison with figures also present in the Bible or the Book of Common Prayer, for example. Instead, I understand the two disciplines as mutually illuminating and in mutual dialogue insofar as they share the common primordial conviction that the phenomenon of language *itself* can be illuminating, meaningful and revelatory.

Throughout the book, and taking my cue from Shakespeare, I attempt to sketch out a metaphysical approach that depicts reality as originally and fundamentally linguistic, and productive of ever new ways of expression, a process that is both open ended yet also oriented to the divine. My key theological partner is the philosopher, mystical theologian, mathematician, astronomer and lawyer Nicholas of Cusa (1401–1464). Cusa wrote at the close of the Middle Ages and is seen by many as a liminal figure between two epochs, perhaps in the same manner in which Shakespeare can be understood as writing at the close of the Renaissance and the onset of modernity. Both, I suggest, share a concern with the deep cultural and spiritual crisis of their day in which, to briefly summarise, the interwoven connections between language, reality and God had been severed. As God increasingly became understood as a radically transcendent being removed from a terminally fallen world, new notions of material reality transformed the world into a purely objective realm, divorced from transcendence and with no spiritual possibilities of its own. This split between God and the world also produced a split at the heart of language: what had once ensured the principle of spiritual intelligibility of all things and beings with and for one another became seen as a merely conventional, limited and metaphysically deficient system of human communication. Words became distrusted, suspect, stripped from their fundamental potentialities as truth-bearers.

Both Shakespeare and Cusa, I argue, sensed that if words do not touch the world and cannot reach to God, then all of our expressions of trust in and love for one another, all our cultural symbolic acts, all our attempts to acknowledge, recognise and understand nature are potentially without force and without meaning. Could language be understood as human artefact, as poetic production, as it was in the

Renaissance, without being a *mere* cultural construct? This is the situation that motivated some of Cusa's writings and, I suggest, some of Shakespeare's. In his late writings, Cusa explores what he calls *scientia laudis*, 'the science of praise', as a way out of this cultural and spiritual deadlock. Simply put, praise, for him, is a mode of genuine contact with reality because it responds to the lure of the goodness of being, 'always already' participating in it, and thus also 'articulating' it. To expand on some of the metaphysical outcomes that emanate from Cusa's intuition, which, in turn, allow me to read Shakespeare in a theological key, I draw on some contemporary phenomenology (Hans-Georg Gadamer, Jean-Louis Chrétien), metaphysics and theology (Rowan Williams, John Milbank, Catherine Pickstock) as well as numerous literary sources and Shakespearean critics. I try to venture in these ambitious metaphysical directions without ever leaving reflection on Shakespeare' art behind; hence, the second part of this book engages in detailed exploratory readings of two plays, remaining in creative conversation with the critical literary tradition throughout.

Reading Shakespeare in the light of doxology provides specially compelling instances of seeing language as theologically grounded in praise, gratitude, offering and affirmation without having to culminate in overt, univocal or transparent expressions of laudation to God. There is a difference between suggesting language is grounded in praise, as I do, and mere *overt* acts of praise, which often can be perfunctory or obsequious. I suggest rather that the creative wellspring of language as praise is potentially infinite: every linguistic resource can potentially turn into a gift; every linguistic form can be 'requisitioned' by the *logos* in its outpouring at the heart of the real. There is no privileging of the lofty over the mundane, no favouring of religious over ambiguous, pleonastic, ironic or even bawdy expression. Indeed, instances when language shatters the norms of ordinary utterance in an attempt to express what is beyond them—such as, for example, in the tormented yet deeply revealing linguistic creativity of Tom O' Bedlam in *King Lear*— become especially felicitous for my doxological reading.

Likewise, to see language as grounded in praise creates as special, productive tension when language's primary purpose is deviated from. Indeed, drama begins when speakers deny the vulnerable preciousness of the gift of words, and become engaged in dissimulations, duplicities and even outright opposition to and rejection of the vital energies of language. Reading Shakespeare, I argue that the 'tragic' aspects of drama coincide with a movement away from language's origins, from the call that is at the heart of linguistic expression. Such a movement breaks the primordial bond between words, world and Word, or language, cosmos and God. Conversely, a movement beyond the tragic, such as one encounters in *The Winter's Tale*, corresponds also to the recovering of something of the miracle of language as such, re-forging human relationships as well as relationships with nature through ritual, song, poetry, prayer and linguistic creativity. Indeed, doxology might be seen to correspond with the primordial energies and original instances of the theatre itself, insofar as they were indeed 'rituals that made the invisible incarnate' as the great Shakespearean director Peter Brook puts it.[1]

There has been, in the last two decades, a 'religious turn' with regard to Shakespeare scholarship. The scholarly ambience, moving beyond the hegemony of the 'hermeneutics of suspicion', has now somewhat warmed to religion; literary critics have been more interested in or at least willing to work with Shakespeare's own religious culture. Even so, an overtly theological reading might still be regarded with reserve: at best, it is felt, one can attempt to explore religion as an aspect of Shakespeare's hybrid and transitional proto-modern culture, and to do so one must restrain oneself to the methodological tools preferred by secular scholarship. Out-and-out 'theology' is perhaps felt as an unwelcome trespassing of the disciplinary boundaries, enforcing an ideological 'conversion' on Shakespeare that does not seem substantiated in any unambiguous ways by the primary sources and that is certainly out of tune with academia's standards of objectivity. Yet, this book does not seek to unambiguously 'theologise' Shakespeare. Readers primarily interested in Shakespeare will find no attempt to 'baptize' his works, no apologetics, and no 'Christ figures'; readers primarily interested in theology will find no easy harmonisations with the scriptures. I take no position on, nor am I interested in, Shakespeare's own confessional convictions. Numerous works, some of which are discussed in this book, have attempted to discern theological traits in Shakespeare's work. This study has, in a sense, tried to do the opposite: to draw out a Shakespearean component to theology—to show that learning from, attending to and wrestling with the literary, in all its unpredictable vitality, its porous and ambiguous meanings and especially its character as being ever incomplete, ever underway, always moving towards new expression and new meaning, is a vital component of theological reflection. This is also the sense in which the book explores the notion of 'grace': as an allusion to the unforeseen, surprising and redeeming vitalities of language itself, to its creative and healing potencies. Throughout, I try to show that grace coincides with a creative orientation to the order of words as aligned with gratitude, with offering and with praise: in other words, 'the grace of words' becomes possible once the linguistic cosmos is felt and understood to be creatively open to its gift.

I have chosen to focus on detailed close readings of two plays only: *King Lear* and *The Winter's Tale*. I read these plays in terms of a transition from the tragic to the post-tragic, beginning in a situation in which the roots of language in love and praise are lost and the world is in prey to an ontology of power, to a post-tragic gesture towards the re-founding of genuine community beyond sorrow and loss, which is synonymous with a rediscovering of the roots of language itself.

The book is in two parts. The first part delineates the metaphysics and theology latent in my doxological approach and explores the Renaissance theo-literary contexts alluded to above. Chapter 1, 'Shakespeare, Language and Religion: Problems and Possibilities', engages in a creative dialogue with literary scholarship on Shakespeare and religion; with philosophy, metaphysics and the burgeoning academic area termed 'theology and literature'. I suggest that some difficulties for a study of Shakespeare and religion from the point of view of the literary tradition have arisen because of the implicit hegemony of a kind of criticism that looks on religion and language alike as players in a 'secular' ontology of power. Instead, reading Shakespeare theologically requires a more supple and patient metaphysics of language, a heuristic approach that takes into account a sense of human language's creative participation in the Word. This, I argue in both Chapters 1 and 2, involves the revivification of an approach proper to Renaissance Christian humanism, not merely as a fixed theological 'position', but understood in the more fluid and elusive sense that human access to the divine is always already mediated by the human, thus inevitably involving language, imagination and *poesis*. I suggest that a theological reading true to this Renaissance spirit entails a foregrounding of the interplay between word and gift, showing also how language inevitably invokes and articulates deep relationships between human and material worlds. It is this connection between the gift-like character of language and the linguistic entanglement of gift that suggests my doxological approach, which forms the basis of metaphysical and theological reflection in each of the chapters to follow.

Chapter 2, 'A Wide and Universal Theatre', draws out the theoretical underpinnings of my doxological approach. Here, I focus on Nicholas of Cusa, an influential voice in Renaissance intellectual currents, whose metaphysics and theology of language show strong continuities with Shakespeare's work. As I outlined above, Cusa proposes, in his last works, the 'science of praise' as a heuristic and performative mode of apprehension of the real grounded in a metaphysics of participation. Through this doxological turn, Cusa shows that praise is a mode of speech that is also a mode of knowledge, culminating in participation with God, who is 'The First Praise'. Drawing from Cusa as well as Shakespeare scholars and contemporary philosophers and theologians, I argue that speech as praise is both a performative, poetic response to *and* voicing of 'the First Praise' that has always already called us into speech. The doxological approach culminates in 'liturgical' speech, a donative mode of language which, as 'middle-voiced', is neither fully autonomous nor fully passive, and thus able to unite theatricality and truth, art and nature, potency and being.

The second part of the book explores this doxological approach through creative, exploratory readings of the two plays, in which I outline a pattern of a falling away from and return to authentic doxological expression. In Chapter 3, 'The Unsaying of the World', I show that in *King Lear,* the transformation of the language of love into a rhetoric of power and manipulation results in tragic outcomes for the human and material world alike. The fracturing of word from gift culminates in a situation in which relationships between self, other and world are reduced to a ploy for power and control in a universe defined as fundamentally inert, dumb and hostile. To respond to this situation, the play's language creatively reaches beneath and beyond cultural limitations to find a kind of doxological expression that can re-weave a bond between human beings, words and world. Slowly and painfully, characters encounter the call present in their linguistic universe: a call to genuine utterance as a gift to affirm and articulate the goodness of being.

Chapter 4, 'Words of Childlike Grace', portrays the world of *The Winter's Tale* as strangled by a culture that encounters nature as fallen beyond redemption, and melancholically looks upon innocence as an irretrievable loss enforced by intimate relationships, in particular relationships with women, and by coming into contact with the energies of the natural world. Because innocence is seen as lost, genuine language can no longer flourish, and the agents and products of this 'infection', women and children, are looked upon with terminal, deadly suspicion. The play, I argue, stages the gradual rebirth of language beyond the deadly consequences of mistrust and beyond a death-bound culture of hostility towards the potencies of the material universe. Here, Shakespeare imbues the world with an atmosphere of innocence: he thus modulates from the courtly to the country, and from rhetorical sophistication and linguistic manipulation to the archetypal energies of a Romance-like 'tale'. By slowly reweaving the connection between word and gift and redrawing the ultimately paradoxical relationships required by doxology, the play celebrates the performative, creative and ultimately redeeming dimensions of language. In its final scenes, *The Winter's Tale* incorporates truth and fiction, art and nature into a 'middle-voiced' speech of praise—this paradoxical 'middle' being the site where the 'grace of words' can be encountered. The conditions for the redemption of human relationships as well as relationships with the material world, I show, inevitably involve a sacramental elevation of meaning—poetics and ethics, or the affirmation and articulation of the goodness of being, become truly possible when art is brought together with doxological rite and language is once again in harmony with the *logos.*

The Epilogue provides place for reflection on the method and practice that has been at work in the book and arisen out of my creative engagement with Shakespeare, and what that might mean for 'theology and literature' as an interdisciplinary venture. I summarise my position on the debate about religion in Shakespeare studies and show that the relation between poetics, dramaturgy and theology is uniquely instantiated by the plays themselves. More generally, my doxological approach, as applied to as well as developed by my close readings, allows me to show a new centrality for literature and poetics within theology: if the affirmation and articulation of the goodness of being ultimately require a theological grounding for language, it follows that theological thinking can no longer ignore the literary; that is, it can no longer do without the salutary mediation of human language, *poesis* and imagination.

Note

1 Peter Brook, *The Empty Space* (New York: Touchstone 1996), 52–53.

Part I
Approach

1 Shakespeare, Language and Religion

Problems and Possibilities

Introduction: Shakespeare, Language and Religion

This study seeks to negotiate the porous boundaries of the interdisciplinary terrain called 'theology and literature'. Its orientation is theological, in the sense that it is concerned with unravelling some of the metaphysical and poetical implications of the paradox of the incarnation, 'the Word made flesh', through looking in detail at two of Shakespeare's plays.[1] Thus, this book begins not with a claim, but with a venture: that emanating from a deep grammar of the incarnation, something of the divine can be encountered in the words we say—to ourselves, to one another, to things as well as to beings and ultimately to God. But 'the Word made flesh' also means, in a certain participatory sense, that flesh is made word, and thus my venture will probe how something of the material as such, things as well as beings, can also be encountered in speech. This elusive relationship between Word, words and flesh will be the hermeneutical key of my approach. Yet, since this relationship can only *remain* elusive, this study will not attempt conclusively to discern confessional or theological positions in Shakespeare. It will rather seek to distinguish in what way Shakespeare can be read in the light of this relationship between Word, words and flesh—and, equally importantly, how Shakespeare's plays can bring their own distinct light *to* such relationships.

This chapter explores critical debates that surround this venture, by focusing on the thematic interplay between Shakespeare, religion and the phenomenon of language. As the figure around which my argument is built traditionally has been the focus of literary studies, the exploration below begins with how these themes have been negotiated within this tradition. In transiting to a theological approach, I supplement the insights and limitations emanating from such literary studies with a metaphysical account of language that can benefit from literary scholarship while attempting to remain faithful to my initial venture. From this, I turn to theological readings of Shakespeare, focusing particularly on the twinned themes of language and gift. This discussion offers the scholarly background to what will be my 'doxological' approach, a reading of

DOI: 10.4324/9781003223276-2

Shakespeare concerned with language *as*, fundamentally, a gift or praise to God. I conclude the chapter with a consideration of some helpful hints gleaned from scholarship in the emerging scholarly category called 'theology and literature'.

It should be noted that, despite much recent interest, the study of a meaningful, mutually illuminating relationship between literature and theology is not new to theologians: this study can be read, for example, as continuous with Austin Farrer's project, as expressed in the Preface to his Bampton Lectures of 1948: 'to think about the relation borne to one another by three things—the sense of metaphysical philosophy, the sense of scriptural revelation, and the sense of poetry'.[2] But while Farrer's work went somewhat neglected by theologians, it certainly jars with recent literary scholarship which often sets theology and literature in conflict, seeing it as essential to the autonomy of literary studies that it remain liberated from any religious ideology.

Shakespeare scholarship, while seeing it as necessary to approach religion because of contextual issues, has vacillated over where exactly Shakespeare's poetics and the allusive religious contexts that surround and inform his work fit with one another. This has been further complicated by the fact that literary criticism is *itself* an interdisciplinary study and is often used as a testing ground for theoretical apparatus.[3] In recent years, approaches to Shakespeare, language and religion have been *both* extraordinarily nourished and extraordinarily determined by their relationship to theory. It may be useful to briefly outline changing trends and paradigms in 20th- and early 21st-century Shakespeare scholarship with respect to religion and to delineate a broad narrative: one beginning from the work of George Wilson Knight, who approached Shakespeare's work as spiritual writings, a kind of 'second scripture', transiting to a more detached or even hostile approach to religion coeval with the rising influence of critical theory, and concluding in an early 21st-century post-critical 'turn to religion'.

Already from his early work *Myth and Miracle* (1929), Knight proclaimed the vision at the heart of his manifesto: 'art is an extroverted expression of the creative imagination which, when introverted, becomes religion'.[4] Like Farrer, Knight worked across the senses of metaphysics, poetry and scriptural allusions, seeking to light upon the plays in terms of deep, symbolic spiritual patterns which, to him, articulated a cosmology common to Shakespeare and the Gospels.[5] Echoing the universalist tendencies of his day, Knight read Shakespeare as a writer of unusual genius rather than a mere product of his time—a sophisticated Christian humanist who poetically illuminates a religious universe without being restrained by mere didactic concerns and confessional issues. Nowhere in Shakespeare do we find moral platitudes or simplistic nods to doctrine: dramatic resolution comes about 'not through repentance but by recognition and acceptance; and in these there lies a spiritual achievement'.[6]

It is such broadly conceived spiritual achievement that allows religion and literature to throw light upon one another while remaining separate, since 'religion exists in the order of being and immediate action, drama and literature in the order of imaginative experience'.[7]

Considered by many an exceptional teacher and lecturer, Knight was undoubtedly a brilliant, highly idiosyncratic reader of Shakespeare. Nevertheless, his eclectic interests and ambitious readings have caused him to be affectionately dismissed by some as a 'classic inter-war autodidact'[8] and repudiated by others as representative of a conservative 'hegemonic Anglicanism' that stifled Shakespearean criticism.[9] To be sure, his influential work attracted fierce response. In his *Shakespeare and Christian Doctrine* (1963), Roland Frye lambasted Knight and his followers for relentlessly unearthing 'Christ-figures' in the plays and wilfully obscuring their true purpose: Shakespeare's mirror, argued Frye, was held up to nature, not to God.[10] As literary studies took an increasingly suspicious stance towards religion, Shakespeare was gradually re-imagined from a Knightean universalist to an enlightened, highly *skeptical* classicist—more in line with a Montaigne or a Bacon than a Sidney or a Spenser.[11] This optimistic classical-humanist portrayal, however, faded in the last decades of the 20th century, making way for the rise of the postmodern imaginary. Once seen as a transhistorical figure, a mystic-poet with universal insight, Shakespeare was gradually turning into a mere product of history—a literary figure not for all time, but for an age. A brief survey of scholarship regarding *King Lear*, a play around which much of this study will be built, might serve to further illustrate this change of mood, coincident, perhaps, with the cultural assimilation of the large-scale atrocities witnessed by the 20th century.[12]

The great Shakespearean scholar A. C. Bradley had portrayed *Lear* as a tale of spiritual suffering leading to redemption and, following him, readers such as R.W. Chambers (1940) and John Lothian (1949) argued that the play's central narrative patterns were constructed around Lear's own spiritual journey, a death-to-resurrection dramatic arc.[13] Perhaps justifying his later detractors, Knight (1930) had seen Cordelia as representing nothing less than 'the Principle of Love',[14] a view also espoused by scholars of a similar epoch such as S. L. Bethell (1944) and John Danby (1949).[15] But post-WW2 scholarship began to affect the change of mood already alluded to above. Eminent critics such as Maynard Mack (1965) and William Elton (1966) now openly argued against 'optimistic' readings of the play, seeing it instead as bearing witness to a breakdown of order audiences were witnessing both on the stage and in their own lives.[16] Jan Kott's seminal *Shakespeare Our Contemporary* (1967) saw *Lear* as darkly confounding eschatological hopes, 'a play about the disintegration of the world', a world which eventually is shown, through Lear and Gloucester's downfall, simply to 'cease to exist'.[17] To Kott, the 'theatre of the absurd' was the most convincing approach to the play, for it powerfully revealed the fathomlessness of the human condition already mediated by his time's political disillusionment: hence in order to make sense of *Lear*, 'it sufficed to discover Beckett in Shakespeare'.[18] Kott's politicised readings and Peter Brook's 1962 staging of the play signalled the genesis of the 'postmodern' Shakespeare, their approach becoming thereafter 'transmuted into metaphysical terms' by numerous directors and literary critics, as R. A. Foakes notes, 'with Lear progressing towards despair rather than towards redemption'.[19] This strand of radical skepticism extended into the deconstructionist readings of Malcolm Evans (1986) and Jonathan Goldberg (1988), who saw the play as loosening the biases of unitive 'logocentric' readings in favour of irreducibly primal ambiguities and duplicities.[20]

The 1980s also saw the advent of a more politically engaged Shakespeare criticism, and concerns with the play's metaphysical messages were left behind in favour of analyses bolstered by the conceptual apparatus of critical theory and post-structuralism. Jonathan Dollimore's highly influential *Radical Tragedy* (1984) portrayed the play as an all-out attack on any form of power-ideology, whether political or religious, and thus fundamentally suspicious of Christianity's ideals of charity or providence.[21] Perceptive, interdisciplinary feminist analyses such as those of Coppélia Kahn and Janet Adelman set the play's attitude to gender front and centre, shifting reading foci from a foolish and fond old father to an absent or suffocating mother.[22] The text itself, too—a notoriously composite artefact—became problematised and politicised.[23] Preoccupations with grand spiritual visions such as Knight's all but disappeared, pierced by the hermeneutics of suspicion and the influence of the various Althusser, Lacan and Foucault.[24] The first decade of the 21st century witnessed *King Lear* criticism caught between circular historicist retrospection and an escape from it in 'presentist' readings, as Kiernan Ryan (2002) diagnosed.[25] By the 2010s, the influence of theory-centred approaches had somewhat waned, giving way to a form of historicism concerned primarily with the production and transmission of texts and material artefacts—an approach that David Scott Kastan has described, only half-jokingly, as 'the New Boredom'.[26]

Thus, a short excursion into *King Lear* studies suggests the gradual abandonment of the quest for a specifically religious dimension *within* Shakespeare's works: the advent of theory-driven approaches and a predilection for historicism have primarily oriented the debate towards the contextual. Yet, Shakespeare studies have recently recovered an interest in religion, not so much through transhistorical metaphysical interpretations *à la* Knight, but through the medium of interdisciplinary approaches with a distinct cultural-historical bent. Indeed, many in Shakespeare studies now would suggest that to detach Shakespeare's work from what was still a profoundly religious culture, in an attempt to salvage it in the name of a secular aesthetics, occlude the polysemic breadth of its meanings. The following two sections discuss recent readings in the intersections between Shakespeare, language and religion, focusing particularly on retrieving some of the theoretical assumptions prevalent in such studies. This retrieval will, in turn, lead to considerations of how these theoretical assumptions delineate the study of language and religion in Shakespeare's works.

Skepticism and Cultural Poetics: Language as Power

If a religious vision in Shakespeare and the skeptical reflexes of contemporary criticism are for many in terminal opposition, one solution has been to harmonise them. Offering a nuanced historical and philosophical account, John Cox's *Seeming Knowledge* (2007) reformulates the question of Shakespeare's religious convictions by appealing to a middle ground: the 'religious skepticism' of Erasmus and Thomas More, whose own cautious attitudes to human reason derived from their deep grounding in scripture and the ecclesiastical tradition.[27] Elaborating on Stanley Cavell's reading of Shakespeare as a key figure in the tradition of skepticism, Cox argues for a version of the latter that does not boil down to a 'straightforward drowning in unbelief'.[28] Nonetheless, Shakespeare's skepticism is for him distinctly anti-humanist, sharing more with contemporary 'hermeneutics of suspicion' and its cautionary tales of 'false consciousness' in the *knower* than the early modern epistemological method of doubting the reliability of things *known* typified by Descartes.[29] This anti-humanism allows Shakespeare to portray a 'hidden God', barely perceptible amidst the fallen human condition; hence, the tragedies dwell on 'the mystery of suffering' rather than its explanation: yet to 'acknowledge suffering', for him is also 'not to negate the transcendent goodness with which such suffering inexplicably coexists'.[30] Nevertheless, there is for Cox no progression on this theological issue in Shakespeare's work. Every play yields the same result: it begins with faith and ends in doubt.[31]

Cox's view of the import of religion in Shakespeare is representative of much recent scholarship, which recognises the cultural presence of religion without necessarily highlighting its participation in meaning-making. Hence, for example, there has been, and continues to be, much debate on Shakespeare's confessional leanings.[32] Similarly, some readings have engaged in an excavation of the rich and impressive array of religious allusions in Shakespeare's language: Daniel Swift (2013) retraces a startling array of echoes of the Book of Common Prayer, and Hannibal Hamlin (2013) works similarly with the Bible—but neither concern themselves with the full theological import of these references.[33] Such caution, for Alison Shell (2011), is justified on poetic and aesthetic grounds, since for her Shakespeare's art is nowhere limited by the dogmatic concerns of theology: indeed, he 'sacrificed theological coherence at the altar of imaginary amplitude'.[34] On this view, Shakespeare is a kind of proto-romantic, who uses religious imagery but whose true religion is art. Echoing Shell, Richard McCoy's *Faith in Shakespeare* (2013) surmises that religion in Shakespeare is 'more theatrical and poetic than spiritual' and the strength and depths of his characters and narratives 'derives from no higher power than literature'.[35] His setting up of a tentative, skeptical 'poetic faith' over against what he sees as 'constant, certain and absolute' religious faith depicts a simplistic understanding of the nature of 'belief', as Claire McEachern (2018) notes.[36] Her own work explores, in a Calvinist key, the 'supple, imaginative or interrogative' nature of early modern religious commitments and the positive inclusion of doubt as an aspect of faith.[37] Yet, her hermeneutic key in reading religion in Shakespeare remains one of doubt; specifically doubt associated with the Calvinist doctrine of predestination. Here too, religion in Shakespeare is restricted to an epistemic matter. Though modulated to an affective key, McEachern's work still defers to the hegemony of critical doubt associated with the literary tradition, as indeed does McCoy, who upholds the New Historicist thesis that the anti-theatrical bent of the reformers attempted to expose the 'fraudulent' nature of Catholic ritual, thus 'emptying out' a social space that could, in turn, be occupied by the theatre.[38] On this view, Shakespeare's poetics arise contemporaneously with an emerging secular space, and the project to imagine Shakespeare's 'poetic faith' must coincide with a Weberian cultural narrative. Like religion, Shakespeare's poetic language is intelligible only in the wake of secular disenchantment.

Despite its having waned as a 'movement' then, the influence of New Historicism on issues of religion in Shakespeare is still considerable, in many ways typifying the skeptical impulses of the critical tradition. Growing up in 1980s Yale and Berkeley (and often echoing its British counterpart 'Cultural Materialism'),[39] New Historicism theorised Kott's outlooks through the works of Foucault, Lacan, Althusser and Clifford Geertz (among others).[40] For New Historicists, a hostile approach to religion as potentially oppressive ideology is married to a theory of language as power: language is largely a subset of 'discourse'—not poetical, but political. Shakespeare's poetics are a prime example of language games bearing witness to half-audible power manoeuvres.[41] In his highly influential essay, 'Learning to Curse' (1990) for example, Stephen Greenblatt argued that Caliban's comedic cursing in *The Tempest* could be read as an eminent sign of 'linguistic colonialism', a hostile take-over by Western attitudes of the New World 'Indian' that resulted in the irreversible silencing of the latter.[42] Here, the language of dramatic poetry exists as the aesthetic cover for deeper cultural, political and ideological clashes—'circulations of social energy', to use Greenblatt's own somewhat cryptic phrase.[43] Drama and poetry, in this way, are facets of 'cultural poetics': a naïve, aesthetic account of works of literature must be surrendered to the irrefutable fact that all cultural artefacts have become 'texts'.[44] Thus here, theatre, language *and* religion are all cultural epiphenomena that serve to veil, all the while half-articulating, more sinister cultural power-machinations. Richard Wilson (2016) expresses the point forcefully: to read Shakespeare's interest in religion as poetic or imaginative rather than nakedly political amounts to nothing other than 'bland Kantian critique' concerned with 'aesthetic closure and creative disinterest'.[45]

In line with Foucault's concerns for marginalised voices silenced by the discourse of reigning narratives, this reformulation of language as power, together with an abiding ethical concern for difference and alterity, have become symptomatic of the New Historicist approach to religion.[46] In fact, it is as a result of this concern with the socially repressed that some recent writers of similar theoretical predilections have argued for Shakespeare's crypto-Catholicism.[47] Yet, despite Greenblatt's own insistence that literature does also at times articulate *opposition* to power, it is still, on this view, limited to a counter-force resisting oppression stemming from reigning power paradigms.[48] Traditional religion, on such views, fulfils one of two roles: it is either a marker for political resistance or the vestige of an abandoned aesthetic, where secular theatre has taken over what was once a religious space. New Historicism's anti-humanist bias and its concern to dissolve subjectivity into 'discourse' thus subsumes theatre, language and religion alike to a more primal proto-Hobbesian 'state of violence' to which Elizabethan society (and indeed, in curious a-historical fashion, any society) can be reduced. Early 21st-century criticism saw a backlash against such politically entrenched, a-historical critiques which, as David Aers and Sarah Beckwith (2003) noted, portrayed religion as 'politics in another guise', making 'the task of political criticism… to deliver the medieval or early modern text from its own illusions, to complete the partial insights which it had not the language to say in its own time'.[49]

This approach also had consequences for language's ethical purview: for on this view, how can words ever succeed in establishing genuine relation? Not only is poetry a facet of a subliminal power-game, but linguistic efforts to reach across difference succumb, in the end, to a politics of otherness.[50] Rather than a vehicle for creation of new meanings, relations or ways of apprehending and responding to the world, linguistic expression is always in danger of becoming terminally one-sided—for, since the other always eludes us, otherness can never truly be rendered into language, and is in danger of becoming radically inarticulate. Poetry, art and religion become intertwined in a deeper struggle of force and counter-force. It is this charge of inarticulacy, grounded in a tacit assumption that earlier ages (unlike ours?) did not possess critical tools to enable cultural self-transparency, that produces terminal difficulties in allowing poetic and religious language their own modes of expressions beyond power manoeuvres.[51] Ultimately, this concern for alterity and the exposition of hostile cultural encounters between self and other ends up violently 'othering' religion itself, as Ken Jackson and Arthur Moratti argue in a seminal article (2004): 'the productive irony revealed by the turn to religion is that the dominant anthropological "self" of New Historicism tends to render religion an alien other or makes that other over in its own image', thus engaging in the very power dynamics it professes to unmask.[52]

The 'Turn to Religion' and its Ambiguities

Jackson and Moratti's article characterised a new wave of scholarship in Shakespeare and religion through the work of scholars such as Julia Reinhard Lupton, Debora Shuger, Huston Diehl, Regina Schwartz and Jeffrey Knapp.[53] These studies have brought into question the implicit 'secularisation narrative' latent in much literary scholarship.[54] Knapp's *Shakespeare's Tribe* (2002), for example, attempted to show how Shakespeare utilised the homiletic and spiritual potential of the theatre to portray and embody a Christian communitarian attitude precisely in opposition to destructive forms of sectarianism.[55] Here, dramatic poetry offers explicit ways to reach across cultural differences and evoke a Christian ideal of social inclusivity. This sort of approach also resonated with a new sensitivity to the *literary* (as opposed to didactic or doctrinal) content of religious texts which could then play as counterpart to the religious echoes sounding in literary works.[56] As Lupton (2005) discerns, 'Western literature itself emerges out of Judaism's internal rhythms of letter and spirit, prescription and prophesy, and their re-elaboration in Christianity and Islam' and literary criticism is therefore called upon to 'attend to its own exegetical foundations... in order to draw on the considerable resources of exegetical iconography and technique so as to place literature in the broadest possible scene – social thought itself'.[57] The problem remains that this 'broadest possible scene' will not be broad enough if restricted to a *secularised* version of 'social thought itself', since secular social thought does not fully mandate the 'exegetical' tools that emanate from religion itself.

In fact, Lupton's 'The Religious Turn (to theory) in Shakespeare Studies' (2006) aptly characterises the new approach: the 'turn to religion' must first of all pass through the crucible of theory. Hence, she construes religion primarily as 'a testing ground for the struggles between the universal and the particular', a 'form of thinking' that deals with 'the big questions and systematic frameworks of psychoanalysis, philosophy, theology and politics'.[58] Yet, Hammill and Lupton (2006) also recognise that there is more to religion than 'thinking'; indeed, as they put it, it would be more faithful to approach it as an archetypal and irreducible mode of *language:* 'a reservoir of foundational stories, tropes, and exegetical habits that structure and give shape to political institutions and literary forms', though nevertheless 'also manifesting a shaping power not fully reflective of the historical settings in which they are exercised'.[59]

Like the New Historicists, Lupton's work remains characterised by a concern for the 'transitional', seeing Shakespeare's work as haunted both by traditional religion as well as an emerging 'Renaissance profane',[60] representing 'a broader, more mobile, and more layered Scriptural tradition whose coordinates are existential rather than confessional'.[61] Though her work displays sophisticated interactions with religion as indissolubly linguistic, her theoretical preferences constrain it to a mode of articulating social and philosophical questions. Opposing the 'confessional' to the 'existential' misses, for example, the register of praise, prayer and devotion, each of which has a particular way of voicing an orientation to reality *inclusive of* but *irreducible to* existential questioning.

In fact, some recent scholarship has made significant moves towards a mode of engaging with religion that is also sensitive to affective, aesthetic and literary concerns. Scholars such as Phebe Jensen (2008) have explored the relationship between traditional religion and Shakespeare's poetics and aesthetics, particularly around the theme of festivity.[62] Her work is representative of a trend in scholarship that links Catholicity with the numinous, ancestral power of images, and Protestant responses with an iconoclastic skepticism, suspicious of the powers of *mimesis*.[63] Rephrasing this distinction in more ecumenical terms, Beatrice Groves (2007) constructs a persuasive argument for the imaginative attitudes stemming from *both* sides of the confessional divide; as she puts it, '[t]he lingering memory of the visual stimuli of Catholicism, and the rising literary awareness inspired by Protestantism, created a culture ripe for the most verbally sophisticated and visually affective dramaturgy'.[64] Rather than concluding in favour of a vague, generic Christianity, she sees in Shakespeare's art a dense imaginative terrain where tropes inherited from a rich, unstable religious landscape are superimposed: thus, she explores changes in literary expression *in conjunction with* changing theological horizons.[65]

This mode of scholarship, exploring the liminal spaces between categories, has also resulted in an increasing interest in religion and literature through the lens of the 'sacramental', as a non-didactive form of mutual involvement between religious and literary imaginations. Scholars such as Robert Whalen, Judith Anderson, Timothy Rosendale and Regina Schwartz, as well as Sarah Beckwith have all focused (though in different ways) on the eucharist as pivotal to their readings of changing poetic and theological sensibilities.[66] Such scholarship is perhaps characterised in Sophie Read's approach (2013) which finds 'a conviction that patterns of thought and belief are found naturally reproduced in patterns of figuration, which they anchor and animate'.[67] Her own work argues that poetic and religious language are both expressions of a 'common mental framework'; and the shape of 'theological cadences' can be encountered in the rhetorically retrievable structures of poetry.[68] Yet, if something of the sacramental glimmers in poetic language, it is nonetheless difficult to ascertain without re-introducing the secularisation thesis via the backdoor, as Brian Cummings has observed, insofar as phrases like 'sacramental poetics' or 'incarnational drama' seem already to imply a *waning* of the powers of devotional practices to bring people into communion with God.[69]

As well as this new linguistic concern, the category of the 'religious' has also bolstered Shakespeare criticism by rescuing from New Historicist cultural poetics two important concepts: 'self' and 'thought'. In terms of the former, the work of Beckwith, Lupton, Schwartz, Patrick Gray and John Cox have all explored Shakespeare's poetic imagination as a way to think about selfhood, ethics and moral action.[70] In *Shakespeare and Early Modern Religion* (2015), David Lowenstein and Michael Witmore offer a volume of essays that reaches beyond scriptural allusions and power hegemony and sees language as more than a phantom of discourse. They suggest approaching Shakespeare as a religious *thinker* for, as they point out, '[t]he Anglo-Saxon word "thought" sits some distance away from classical words like "concept," "idea," "theology," or even "culture"'. Shakespeare and his audience take things up to feel, weigh, and consider, yet thoughts 'do not always issue in something like action, and do not always show their effects in concrete position-taking'.[71] This fluid and indeterminate position is an attempt in Shakespeare studies to overcome 'the falseness of the dichotomy between the religious world and the secular world', as Brian Cummings notes in his Afterword.[72] While Shakespeare scholars seem increasingly willing to 'think' *with* religion on its own terms—rather than *against,* or simply *about*—it remains unclear what exactly they take those terms to be. The interplay between language and religion in Shakespeare, whether teased out as bearer of 'cognitive patterns', vehicle for thought or inheritor of a poetic-sacramental imagination, remains in these studies a fruitful but ambiguously defined terrain.

Some recent works, finally, have opted to elide literary scholarship's historicist tendencies and re-inaugurate a more traditional interpretive approach. Such is the case of Piero Boitani's *The Gospel According to Shakespeare* (2010), whose reading could certainly be described as 'neo-Knightean'. For Boitani, Shakespeare the playwright operates as a 'a spy of God ... who on God's behalf explores the human spirit', and seeks 'insight into God's own intimate being'.[73] Boitani identifies the late works as 'Shakespeare's own gospel' and draws a vital link between the absolute tragic attained in *King Lear* and the subsequent post-tragic narratives of the Romances.[74] To be sure, Boitani's theologically optimistic scholarship might well puzzle more cautious literary scholars and seem jarring in today's hyperconscious scholarly environment. Yet, in a sense, one can sum up the critical consensus on Shakespeare and religion as David Scott Kastan (2015) does, that even though religion is '*the* epistemological ground organizing the fundamental categories of thought', the plays seem to present 'a "big-tent Christianity"... inclusive and theologically minimalist... that resisted religious rigor and valued social accord'.[75] One senses a contradiction here: has not the centrality of a religious approach both been avowed and avoided? But perhaps these are the contradictory results of a field that, long dominated by the hegemony of critique, struggles to move beyond it while attempting to maintain its disenchanted and 'objective' posture. Is there not here the need for a 'post-critical' reading, a mode of interpretation which, as Rita Felski puts it, 'brings new things to light rather than an endless rumination on a text's hidden meanings or representational failures'?[76] Does not the question of religion in Shakespeare require a scholarship which adventures beyond the safety of critique's demystifying stance, attending instead to the religious aspects of Shakespeare's works with a generous receptivity to new *meanings*? As Shakespeare scholars have noticed, religion extends well beyond absolutist belief, confessional battle-lines, ideological hegemonies and doctrinal disagreements to fluidly and non-doctrinally interweave with the moral, philosophical, metaphysical and literary imagination. Readings in Shakespeare and religion surely require an interpretive charity that would allow these registers of the human imagination their own authentic voicings.[77]

To further discover and articulate the question of religion in Shakespeare means then to address it, beyond suspicion, as an indelible and creatively expressive aspect of the human imagination. As Rowan Williams points out in the Afterword to *The Cambridge Companion to Shakespeare and Religion* (2019), an exploration of this theme

> needs finally to look not so much at this or that specific echo and allusion, but at what the underlying myth of loss, falsehood, sacrifice, and remedy uncovers about the human imagination itself. And the theologian is left asking about the way in which this imagination can be read as the finite imprint of a free, creative intelligence of a quite other order.[78]

It is with this hint in mind that the following sections transition into a more overt metaphysical and theological approach.

Transition: Gadamer's Hermeneutical Philosophy of Language and Rowan Williams' Metaphysics

As I have noted so far, scholarship on Shakespeare and religion tends to subscribe, implicitly or explicitly, to two different accounts of language. Readings hostile to or skeptical of religion see both religion and language as facets of a power-driven ideology and read Shakespeare in

14 *Approach*

terms of a poetics of violence that privileges enclosure over encounter, rupture over reciprocity, conceit over dialogue. Beyond this approach, more synchronic reading practices have offered approaches to Shakespeare's language and its interwovenness with religious tropes as ways of thinking through and imagining human engagement with reality. These approaches suggest that what becomes significant in language is not merely the extent to which it determines or is determined, but the extent to which it *reveals*. Hence, while the previous sections have approached language in terms of an engagement with religion, the following sketches an involvement with religion *in terms of language*. This focal shift will also provide a manner of transiting towards more theologically acute readings of Shakespeare.

To do this, I propose to discuss two approaches to language that could help shed further light on my initial 'incarnational' venture: those of Hans-Georg Gadamer and Rowan Williams. The former, while secular, attends sympathetically to the religious propensities of words and offers a hermeneutic alternative to readings haunted by an ontology of power. The latter, while coming from a religious perspective, dynamically explores the glimmers of the divine amidst secular and non-secular 'habits of language'. These two approaches, generously attentive to both religious and secular aspects, gesture at the possibility of a sacred dimension glimpsed in language *as such*, and will enable me, in turn, to articulate a framework with which to approach language in Shakespeare.[79]

Hans-Georg Gadamer is relevant for early modern literary studies insofar as he saw his own hermeneutical project as being in broad sympathy with the Renaissance speculations on *verbum*—which themselves sought to bring together conceptions of language with the idea of 'the Word made flesh'.[80] Indeed, for Gadamer, the Christian formulation of *logos*, linking language with the incarnation, is crucial to a movement beyond an instrumental approach to language as pure sign and into an exploration of the *real* relation between word and being.[81] Guided by such insights, Gadamer's interpretative strategy is not one based on ontological violence or a primal 'turn to difference', but on the priority of dialogical reciprocity. This dialogical method allows, at the same time, a recovery of the meanings originally engaged with *in the text*. Gadamer's approach to text, in fact, seeks to mediate historical distance by attending to one's meaningful, conversational engagement with it. Grasping Gadamer's theory of language thus also entails an understanding of his theory of interpretation. Since my own reading practice will take its cue from his approach, some considerations of its scope are needed.

For Gadamer, to interpret a text is to be alive to two interpretive 'horizons'; that is, the world which the text negotiates *as well as* one's own. Shaping such a conversation, the dialogue between one's own horizon and that of the historical moment of the text is never closed. Neither for the interpreter nor for the text interpreted is there such a thing as a fixed

Shakespeare, Language and Religion 15

point of reference; rather, the horizon is 'something into which we move and that moves with us'.[82] If the text, or the historical moment, is an 'other', this otherness is met, for Gadamer, not as representative of an utterly alien, unreachable alterity, but as 'making its own meaning heard' within the fundamental generosity of a dialogue in which neither self nor other are 'closed'. 'In the process of understanding', writes Gadamer, 'a real fusing of horizons occurs—which means that as the historical horizon is projected, it is simultaneously superseded'.[83]

Unlike in New Historicist theory, this fusing of horizon is not an oppressive diffusing of otherness. Rather, it corresponds to the precedence of the concern for understanding, by which Gadamer means a basic attention to the 'matter-at-hand' (*die Sache*) that is at play for both text and reader (or self and other), and with which both text and reader (or self and other) are concerned. Gadamer's interpretive retrieval is thus in fact closer to the practice of translation, in which alterity and otherness are elements at play *within* the sway of language, rather than obstacles to reciprocity: '[t]hanks to the verbal nature of all interpretation, every interpretation includes the possibility of a relationship with others. There can be no speaking that does not bind the speaker and the person spoken to'.[84] Even if the speaker or the reader's language is inexact, inadequate or underway, language is always coming to an understanding. Language's failure to fully communicate otherness thus communicates first that there is something that *can be said* that has not yet been said.

For Gadamer then, understanding and interpretation are fundamentally linked to our being linguistic beings. As for his master Heidegger, to come upon language is already to be situated *within* language, to sense that something is amiss within language *as such*. When language is at work, Gadamer notes, 'it is so little an object that it seems to conceal its own being from us'.[85] Even the question 'what is language' is itself a historical question, since it presupposes a kind of consciousness that is already historically effected.[86] But in some sense, this means that transforming language as such into an object of study necessarily obscures its nature since it must be *lived* to be glimpsed: something of its essence becomes available for interpretation when we ourselves, fully engaged in speech, become language's speakers. Language is reflective, or 'speculative', in the manner of a mirror: it creates an *image*, rather than a copy; but the image *adds being* to the original, and hence both image and original belong to a deeper unity.[87] This is why for Gadamer the poetic is the instance of language *par excellence*.

Thus, for Gadamer, to address the question of language is to address ourselves a question: we, as speakers, seek 'to approach the mystery of language from the conversation that we ourselves are'.[88] In line with this dialogic approach, an 'authentic conversation' is not one that is 'led' or willed, but is itself what leads,[89] guided by concern for the 'matter-at-hand', in such a way that *it itself* can 'come to language'.[90]

16   Approach

The opposite to an authentic conversation, by contrast, is language *manipulated*, guided only by the will to control the issue—in this case, since control must prevail, the other remains unheard. Such inauthentic conversation, bereft of reciprocity, 'silences' the other by speaking *over* her—thus, somehow, making the other inarticulate. In this sense, there is no Cartesian *cogito* or Kantian transcendental subject whose mental patterns can be extracted from this dialogic realm. Language is not 'for' the self, but selves are constituted and transformed, self-reflective and self-interpretive *because* of language. Rather than the project of an a-historical subject, *saying* comes into being only in response to the always already *said*, just like the concern of an authentic conversation arises from being caught, or seized by a question, by a 'matter-at-hand': the question 'presses itself on us', notes Gadamer; we are addressed in such a way that 'we can no longer avoid it and persist in our accustomed opinion'.[91] As that within which we articulate our fundamental orientations in existence, language grasps us and addresses us in the very occasion of being. All meaning is a staking out, a tentative venture, in a linguistic universe which is always already predisposed to meaning.

Gadamer's approach offers a corrective to what in some of the scholarship reviewed above is a neglected idea: that speech, *from a religious point of view*, never occurs *in a vacuum*, but within a world that always already addresses human beings: a world that is not merely a 'text', but that also primarily *speaks*, calls, beckons and summons. Since this is a world whose ground of being and whose ultimate calling both invoke the *logos*, a theological approach to Shakespearean drama can benefit from this sense of a dialogic reality in which as Gadamer ultimately puts it, 'Being that can be understood is language'.[92]

But 'Being' surely suggests densities that seem, at first sight, beyond the reach of *logos*. At the outset of this chapter, I proposed that the incarnation intimates a linguistic encounter with the material world as such, with things and with beings. While Gadamer remains committed to a tradition stemming from German Idealism that can confidently equate language with being, Rowan Williams sustains the interweaving of words and reality by emphasising language as an embodied, material practice. Yet, like Gadamer, Williams' work, particularly *The Edge of Words*, with which I will be concerned here, attempts to explore and affirm the linguistic character of reality.[93] Taking his cue from the general remit of the Gifford Lectures from which his book stems, Williams gestures, through a series of tentative, evocative and performative strategies, towards a renewed, poetic form of 'natural theology' which looks at the philosophical and theological import of our 'habits of language', understood in the first sense as discrete, though related, material phenomena. Yet, 'natural theology' means for Williams something rather different from its traditional instances, which provided arguments for the existence of God based on the workings of nature. Here, it is not a matter of speaking *about* God so much as it is inhabiting a kind of theological 'skill', a 'a practice of thinking to the edge of what can be said'.[94] Whatever can be said about God is thus 'bound up with the scrutiny of language itself'.[95]

Similarly to Gadamer, Williams takes account of the unfinishedness of language as 'always time related...always incomplete, and in search of the perspective of another'.[96] Drama, narrative and ritual are particularly apposite ways of understanding the peculiar ongoing nature of this having-more-to-say; but they also bear witness to a common desire for recognition between speakers, a recognition which, in turn, suggests 'a point between or beyond speakers, a point to which both are gesturing'.[97] As this point-oriented, yet also unfinished and excessive phenomenon, language also articulates this sense that more can always be said in extreme situations, in which the call to communicate 'puts pressure' on the limits of words. This binds together poetry and science, imaginative fiction and realist work, insofar as they wrestle with new ways of putting insight, thus showing what it is for 'language to make us strangers to ourselves and then recognise the world afresh'.[98] Fiction, in particular, provides possibilities to imagine the impossible, allowing us to articulate patterns of forgiveness, healing or mercy beyond seemingly irreconcilable positions and sorrow.[99]

But how does this relate to the material world? Through a creative discussion of crossovers between findings in ASD therapy, neuroscience, genetics and phenomenology, Williams argues for an approach to the non-human world which takes into account its linguistical aspect all the way down.[100] Because it can be encountered as 'the natural integrating factor in the evolving material universe', an instrumental or descriptive account of language as labelling a dead or inert cosmos is inadequate even for the findings of science. For if it is true that genetic and neurological systems interact through 'negotiations', 'finding their way in interacting with one another and constantly refining and elaborating this rather than settling in eternal equilibrium', then consciousness is but another complex iteration of this phenomenon.[101] Thus, 'it would be nearer the truth to look to language to show us what matter is', since it 'exhibits a pattern of cooperative agency in which the structure of life or action in one medium is rendered afresh (translated) in another'.[102] Matter, like language, is 'inherently symbolic', a 'complex of patterns inviting recognition and constantly generating new combinations of intelligible structures'.[103] It is not merely what is peculiarly human that calls to be said, revised and said newly; rather, this movement courses in reality as such, traversing non-human as well as human fields. The real seems at once a complete utterance *and* a mysteriously incomplete, dynamic and differentiated whole, which calls ever to be uttered again.

Importantly, though perhaps challengingly, Williams uses a philosophically loaded concept—*representation*—to retrieve a meaning from it away from its restrictive uses in 'modern' epistemology. In the latter, representation might stand for the mental reproduction of sensorial or 'factual' data. For Williams, on the other hand, it is a primary operation of language that both re-founds *and* continues the iteration of the being of things in language; for, since to re-present is in a simple sense 'to present again', it is something that both makes present the thing itself *and* its specific and unique 'thereness' as articulated in words. Here, Williams echoes Gadamer: representation constitutes nothing less than 'an increase in being'.[104] Rather than a manner of abstraction, representation intimates a fundamental participation with the world, a world both in the open-ended process of speaking itself into being and by doing so, subtly and creatively iterating the 'beyond' of such speech. Representing, in this way,

> is an act which simultaneously recognizes the other, the "object", as thoroughly bound to the life of the subject, and recognizes the self, the "subject", as invested in the object—so that conventional categories of inner and outer, mind and matter, are suspended and transformed... representation *performs* what it refers to.[105]

The representation is not a secondary instance of speech which stands for an original sensorial experience, but rather constitutes a call that stems from the being of the original, 'a dimension of its reality which is *its life in speaking and thinking*'.[106]

This excessive and gratuitous quality of speech, then, is not a flourish or addendum to the real, but belongs to the essence of things. One here begins to sense registers such as invocation, summoning, prayer and praise as *ontologically prior* realities in speech, insofar as they attest both to a primordial encounter with material reality and to its linguistic, even poetic, aspects. As Catherine Pickstock puts it in her review of Williams' work: 'it is as if a seascape naturally precipitates or demands an encomium, as naturally as it is shaped by swell and wave breaking. These poetic facets of truth-making, it seems, covertly enter into our ordinary prosaic practices' without any sense of artificiality or contrivance; as she asks: '[d]o we rather feel that we are responding to the impress of reality, its imperatives?'.[107]

These two ways of approaching language, while not *overtly* theological, cross boundaries and apply pressure on biases and assumptions that, as I showed, are often encountered in scholarship in Shakespeare and religion. Both also gesture at ways of tackling my initial venture, without necessarily having recourse to forms of historicism or to tease out religious allusions in Shakespeare. They allow us too to take caution against simply 'baptising' Shakespeare's work, painting upon it particular theologies, while offering a more flexible philosophical and theological framework than the bland, unexplored universality of a 'theologically minimalist', '"big tent" Christianity'.[108]

This study will seek to take up this metaphysical approach to language. Attempting to remain sensitive to the open-ended, unfinished and essentially creative nature of words, it will also seek to mind that speech occurs in an irreducibly relational, responsorial continuum that involves the non-human as well as the human. To stay true to my initial wager, this will ultimately mean to approach Shakespeare's language as spoken in a universe that speaks, in which *both* language and matter speak. To be sure, such an endeavour is too vast for a single study, and this book will have to be selective in the materials it can address and remain provisional in its conclusions. Nevertheless, some more pertinent theological inflections of this metaphysical approach to language will be developed in the next chapter.

Bolstered by this approach, the following section returns to Shakespeare readings, this time engaging with works by writers coming mainly from a theological perspective (with one exception) who have appealed to Shakespeare as a dialogue partner to construct and develop theological arguments that can also help illuminate my primary concern for language. It explores at some length the work of John Milbank on 'the gift' in *The Winter's Tale*, John Hughes on social forgiveness and *King Lear*, Sarah Beckwith on 'the grammar of forgiveness' in Shakespeare's late works and Johannes Hoff and Peter Hampson's reading of Shakespeare in the light of Nicholas of Cusa's participatory metaphysics and doxology. They are arranged chronologically, in order to show continuities with and variations on themes to which I have already alluded.

Some Theological Readings of Shakespeare

Grace, Gift and Ethics in The Winter's Tale: *John Milbank*

The theology of John Milbank is particularly relevant to my concern, since it has from the beginning been intertwined in an engagement with the secular narratives ruling ethics, politics and social theory as well as a concern for theological poetics. His seminal essay *Theology and Social Theory* (1990) argues that the modern construal of the social is in fact complicit with an 'ontology of violence', a reading of the world in the light of power narratives. For Milbank, social theorists 'make this ontology seem coterminous with the discovery of the human construction of the cultural world', that is, secular society, the 'object' of social science.[109] These readings interpret society in the light of a 'transcendental event' which consists in a 'military ploy of assertive difference over and against "the other"'.[110] Instead, Milbank advocates a theological understanding of the social marked by a concern for an 'analogical ontology of peace which is also an ontology of the participation of the Creation in divine creativity'[111] and which 'conceives differences as analogically related, rather than equivocally at variance'.[112] On this view, it is the task of the theologian to creatively articulate and illuminate this analogical relation grounded in a participatory ontology. Indeed, in his next major work, *The Word Made Strange* (1997), Milbank shows how theology is inextricable from a reality which is fundamentally linguistically and narratively mediated.[113] This means, for him, that all human language in some way participates in divine *logos,* and that all human *poesis* is in this manner theological.

Milbank's socio-theological move beyond an 'ontology of violence' is further elaborated in *Being Reconciled* (2003), a volume which formulates much of his thinking on the 'gift'. Milbank sees the gift as 'a kind of transcendental category in relation to the other topoi of theology, in a similar fashion to "word"'.[114] This is because 'creation and grace are gifts; Incarnation is the supreme gift; the Fall, evil and violence are the refusal of gift; atonement is the renewed and hyperbolic gift that is for-giveness' and even 'the supreme name of the Holy Spirit is *donum*'.[115] If for secular theory, according to Milbank, the fundamental categories are violence and otherness, for theology they are 'gift' and 'word', *verbum* and *donum.* Here, Milbank's poetic approach to *verbum* is complemented by a notion of gift as 'participating in an infinite reciprocity which is the divine *donum*'.[116] This equation of word and gift will bear crucial importance to this study, grounding the 'doxological turn' performed in my readings of Shakespeare.

'The Midwinter Sacrifice' (2001 [1997]), a seminal essay in Milbank's early work, and republished as Chapter 8 of *Being Reconciled,* is not *primarily* a reading of Shakespeare, but contains a compelling exegesis of some aspects of *The Winter's Tale* in the light of Milbank's thinking on ethics, gift and grace. The argument of this essay attempts to demonstrate that Christianity ultimately unites poetics and ethics, because it gives *a truly moral self.* To show this, Milbank attempts to deconstruct both classical and postmodern ethics. While the former position defines ethical rectitude as imperturbability, the latter, as we saw above, makes all ethical moves impossible.[117] For Milbank, Christianity challenges these late-antique ethical ideals of the soul as an 'inner citadel' by re-articulating classical conceptions of fortune and happiness into states of the soul dependent on an bestowal from without; that is, *the arrival of grace.*[118] Similarly, Christianity overcomes a postmodern notion of gift as a unilateral sacrifice presented under the guise of an 'other-regarding' ethics. This position, for him, accounts for the gift as radically one-sided, a kind of self-dispossession that is grounded in a secret fascination with death. Though it may (and often does) pass for the Christian view, unilateral ethics are in fact secular, since one can still practice such radical self-dispossession without 'eschatological' hope.[119] Here again, the true nature of the gift is elided, or denied.

To elaborate on his own notion of gift and grace, Milbank interprets *The Winter's Tale.* As is well known, the action of the play centres on Leontes' wrongful accusation of his wife Hermione, whom he believes to be engaged in an illicit affair with his childhood friend, Polixenes, the King of Bohemia. Leontes' refusal to confront his own folly results in the death of his son Mamilius, the loss of his new-born daughter Perdita and the (ambiguous) death/disappearance of Hermione. Once come to his senses, Leontes experiences the depth of his unforgivable betrayal. For Leontes, Milbank notes, *only* reconciliation could possibly repay the deed—and such a reconciliation, in this temporal world, is impossible. If Leontes has finally learnt to love, his love comes too late—restricted, in fact, to a sterile 'gesture'.[120] Conversely, in the beginning of the play, Leontes had been overly complacent and thus had not truly known the utter 'fragility' of the gift that is love. 'Postmodern' lateness or 'classical' complacency having been the only options, there is in Leontes' life no moment for fully ethical action, no 'present' for love and thus, for Milbank, no truly 'moral self'.[121] Without this 'moment' for love, moral actions are not performable, insofar as they seek to be performed by the will alone which, due to its 'fallen' condition, is always either complacent, or too late, or both.

As an alternative to the aforementioned 'eudaimonistic' and 'other-regarding' ethics, then, Milbank proposes a third way, the 'ecstatic': 'to receive the gift of the other as something that diverts one's life, and to offer one's life in such a way that you do not know in advance what it is you will give but must reclaim it retrospectively. A total exposure to fortune, or rather to grace'.[122] *The Winter's Tale* then is for Milbank an exploration of the poetics of this ecstatic mode, which is also why this play is particularly relevant to the Shakespearean canon. After *King Lear,* Shakespeare 'had to' imagine an ecstatic middle-way, that is, a *post-tragic* world, since *Lear* is in some sense an absolute tragedy, one that can neither be fatalistically accepted ('ontologised') nor ignored and avoided, because its reality is undeniable.[123] Either positions, for Milbank, would come *to underestimate* the nature of tragedy. To make tragedy the universal condition would render morality impossible, he argues, since ethical subjects would *require* a tragic situation in order to be ethical at all. But the 'fall' makes tragedy a contingent situation rather than an ontological reality, and is the point of departure used by Shakespeare and Christianity alike 'in order to think a genuine good' which to be a genuine gift 'can only be an original plenitude'.[124]

Grounded in this plenitude which is also its *telos,* the field of the good is only mysteriously compatible with 'willed' intention, since it is primarily a *gift* given amidst 'the joyful uncertainty of faith'.[125] Sin and tragedy, on the other hand, occur with the refusal of the gift of the good—a refusal which begins with the suspicion that good action is in fact *willed* and not a gift at all. In fact, as Milbank points out, *The Winter's Tale* does begin with an account of the fall (*WT* 1.2.66–86). Polixenes and Leontes, both seeing themselves as having once been 'boys eternal' in childhood innocence, interpret the temporal arrival of 'another' (their wives) as the beginning of their decline into sin. Hermione, on the contrary, considers the gift of marriage as the arrival of grace itself, one that preserves and renews a kind of innocence. But Leontes begins to doubt this 'joyful uncertainty', this faith in the gift of the other, and thus figures the Shakespearean rendering of 'original sin': that is, 'the reading of the unknown as source of threat or poison rather than potential or gift'.[126]

According to Milbank, Shakespeare's post-tragic writings are concerned with narrating the surprising return of the gift: hence, he turns to a kind of drama that obliquely stages eschatological hope. *A full account of the 'ethical' thus includes poetics*, since it must occur in a transformed, fabulous world, a world that gestures to the 'original plenitude', the good that is the ground of gift. Hermione's return as a living statue heals a fracture between mortal life (beyond which mortality pardon cannot be sought) and lifeless artworks, which do have a kind of eternity *but* cannot, nevertheless, *give words back*; that is, forgive and acknowledge repentance.[127] In the re-animation of Hermione,

> the dead one is given back to the living as in a sense still dead, still wounded, and yet uniquely innocent, so that he or she appears in the space of living exchange as surprising gift, beyond our life now in time... In other words, Shakespeare does not articulate magic on this earth, but magic in another, transfigured earth which is the earth given back as manifest gift.[128]

Shakespeare thus shows how the ethical can only, ultimately, be construed poetically: as this unending gift-exchange, which in its turn is grounded in the eschatological hope of a second innocence.[129] His 'ecstatic' poetics thus brings to light 'the surprisingness and unpredictability of gift and counter-gift, or their character in space as *asymmetrical reciprocity*, and their character in time as *non-identical repetition*'.[130]

Several aspects of this compelling essay are particularly relevant to this study. First, it brings into alliance the creative powers of language with the ethical dimension of being. The resources of fiction are an aspect of our response to the world because only the domain of the fabulous makes ethical action truly intelligible. *The Winter's Tale* is an appropriate title, since only a 'tale' can bear witness to the 'asymmetrical reciprocity' and 'non-identical repetition' that are the true characteristics of gift. Yet, by doing so, the play also articulates something of the deeper grammar of grace. If forgiveness is ecstatically donated through language, words themselves must shine with this gift-like quality, but can do so, ultimately, as part of a reality that has been re-apprehended and re-presented as only fully intelligible in the light of *verbum* and *donum*, word and gift.[131] Further, since the ecstatic event of gift is not a 'willed' action, this occasions the suggestion that the language of grace itself must be ecstatic, partly willed and partly encountered in the surprising, non-identical manner of a gift. Such a dimension of being also suggests the mingling, mutual co-belonging of life (or 'nature') and art, as Milbank's reading of the final figure of Hermione suggests. Lastly, the mode of childlike innocence is privileged over that of suspicion: forgiveness re-articulates life not to the detriment of the tragedy, as in a delusional flight of fancy, but transcends and refigures it through a kind of 'adult' second innocence.

Since my aim is to explore *verbum* in the light of *donum*, to shed light on the interpenetration of word and gift, what remains is to develop an approach to language *as* gift, as itself touching the sphere of a 'not-willed' 'asymmetrical reciprocity' and 'non-identical repetition': in other words, to explore how speech can be heard as patterned by a Shakespearean grammar fit to bear witness to 'the arrival of grace'.

Nature and Forgiveness in King Lear: John Hughes

The progression which Milbank gleans from *Lear* to *The Winter's Tale* makes examining the relationship between the two plays suggestive, and a close reading of the plays will constitute much of the argument of this book. In fact, Milbank's thinking on the gift influenced a significant theological reading of *Lear*: John Hughes' 'The Politics of Forgiveness' (2001). Hughes takes issue with the nihilistic and 'radical' readings that permeated much of the scholarship of the later 20th century: against Jonathan Dollimore's interpretation of *Lear* as the 'demystification of Christian charity', Hughes offers a reading of the play as a debunking of the ontology of power lurking in both conservative and 'radical' critical accounts, suggesting instead a 're-mystification' of charity.[132]

Like Dollimore, Hughes reads the play's tragic action as a conflict between two forms of social order: the old feudal conservative system, embodied by characters such as Lear and Gloucester, and the emerging 17th-century bourgeois individualism, represented by some of the younger generation: Edmund, Regan and Goneril. The former affirm an archaic idea of social order ('Nature'), but *only insofar* as it validates their own privileged places in it, thus rupturing the ontological bond between earthly polities and the transcendent principles on which they depend.[133] By contrast, the 'younger' characters, who represent the other extreme, believe that laws and justice have their origins not in any kind of transcendence, but on 'the plague of custom' (*KL* 1.2.3). For Edmund, the state of things, which *he too* calls 'nature', is nothing but a battlefield ruled by selfish intentions and power struggles. Though the play has been read traditionally as an argument for both positions, Hughes interprets *Lear* as holding the mirror up to these competing ideologies because

> their apparent opposition hides a more fundamental dialectical similarity, in their dependence upon a foreclosed, materialist account of

the world, which as such, is haunted by the fear of death and thus is unable to envisage hope and unable to accommodate forgiveness.[134]

Shakespeare portrays their encounter as inevitably disastrous, since a cause of their collision is that their deeper construal of the world is in fact the same.[135] Failing to see that that the overt disagreements between the two sides conceal the same covert ontology, critics such as Dollimore end up siding with one side rather than the other.

Yet, as Hughes remarks, that human beings are 'poor, bare, forked' animals is not the play's message. Lear is not left to howl at the storm on the heath. For Hughes, this is rather a stage that signifies the dismantling of society in order to be reconstructed; Lear is made naked only to be clothed anew.[136] Echoing Milbank, he sees such transformation, rather than proceeding 'from an effort of the will', to be 'a gift painfully given by the agents of redemption—Edgar, Kent and Cordelia—who act like midwives in bringing to birth the new Lear and Gloucester'.[137] Yet, as Hughes also notes, 'the very act of forgiving is itself an imaginative positing of a particular ontology that alone makes such an act possible'.[138] Hence, the 'agents of redemption', for Hughes, are those who, through their 'constant, transformative loving-faithfulness', attempt to give birth to a new *sense of reality*, which alone can ground the socio-political dimension of forgiveness.[139] *King Lear* intimates, then, that the founding of a genuine society is bound up with a theological account of forgiveness, understood not as the result of a willed action but as bestowed by the divine, overflowing to others and thus returned as gift to its transcendent source. Only such an account of the economy of gift, Hughes argues, goes beyond the 'commodification' of finite goods that a materialist ontology underwrites (and Dollimore condemns). The tragedy in *Lear* is thus intertwined with the costly aspect of forgiveness, bound to fragility, vulnerability and openness to such a gift, in a world in which such gifts are simply unintelligible.

Hughes' reading of the implicit theological horizon in which the play is set is significant, though he does not engage in detailed exegesis. The suggestion of forgiveness as the transformative and re-generative dimension of the world—or 'Nature', to use the play's key term—as a gift bestowed in the light of a transcendent horizon sets *King Lear* in a socio-theological key. Yet, it also suggests that the category of gift extends further than as a vital aspect of human relationship: gift also pertains to the material world to which the symbolic word 'nature' gestures. Thus, the play brings into question the characters' manner of encountering and 'representing' *the world*, since their failure to transform it through forgiveness is bound up with an account of a finite reality, a given 'pure nature' bereft of an ontological dependency on 'grace' for its completeness. The fact that 'nature' is so lexically central to the play gestures precisely towards this ontological lack. The world of *Lear*, it seems, must be *re-described* or *re-presented*, from 'a place of finite scarcity' to one of 'eternal bounty'.[140]

It is thus forgiveness, Hughes suggests, as the highest gift which itself overflows from a gift given by the Divine, which can make something like an account of 'nature' truly intelligible, thus redeeming it 'from the general curse'.[141] Here again, both Gadamer's emphasis on dialogical relationality and Williams' sense of language as a material practice are significant. If language is to glimmer with gift in other words, it must also involve a *response* to the linguistic aspect of nature, one that does not freeze it into a 'foreclosed materialist account' but, heeding its voices and responding to its calls, *receives and returns it as gift*. These notions, however, are only implicit in Hughes' account of the play and require close reading for development.

Language, Acknowledgement and Forgiveness in the Late Plays: Sarah Beckwith

A preoccupation with forgiveness is, of course, central to Shakespeare's dramatic works, and scenes of repentance, forgiveness and reconciliation can be glimpsed from the *Two Gentlemen of Verona* through to *The Tempest* and beyond.[142] In her rich and influential *Shakespeare and the Grammar of Forgiveness* (2011), Sarah Beckwith marries her medievalist literary sensitivities to a philosophical approach, in order to puzzle out ethical and philosophical questions related to forgiveness. Her work is thus typical of 'turn to religion' scholarship in Shakespeare, both in the breadth of its scope and its ambitious interdisciplinary strategies. Though not overtly theological, I have chosen to discuss it in this section because of these crossovers as well as her abiding interest in the question of language.

Echoing Milbank and Boitani, Beckwith sees Shakespeare's late writing as being, essentially, reworkings of *King Lear* and thus 'post-tragic'.[143] As she puts it, *Lear*, especially in its overturning of the felicitous ending of its source-play *King Leir*, had been a conscious experiment in inverting the Romance form, a form which 'systematically converts chance into providence'.[144] Shakespeare's late work marries an interest in the post-tragic with a return to Romance, since specifically through it 'can come a restored faith in the possibilities of grace'.[145] The representation of this post-tragic world compels Shakespeare to move towards 'the structures, histories, and practices of penitence and repentance, and their available languages, languages of forgiveness and acknowledgment'.[146] Hence Beckwith's argument is also partly historical: she sees in Shakespearean late theatre a vital attempt to remedy a historical situation in which words of forgiveness had lost their sacramental context and where obligatory vows and the standardisation of worship contributed to create an infinite gap between private beliefs and public performance, or words and world.[147] His last plays, then, are an attempt to respond to a different kind of tragedy: the threat of language's failure to account for our being.

The Winter's Tale, a clear example of this 'theatrico-religious' paradigm, focuses on the quasi-miraculous power of recognition and the acknowledgement of past deeds. In this play, returns and resurrections offer the opportunity for genuine transformation in a manner that takes up and *redeems* the past: 'a new accounting in which the *responsibility* of the one who has caused harm—Leontes—is utterly bound up with the *response* to the person harmed'.[148] The return of Hermione thus also implies the redemption of Leontes, providing him with an unhoped for ability to *speak again.* Her return is also, in some sense, the return of language.

Bolstered by speech acts and 'ordinary language' theories inherited from J. L. Austin and Stanley Cavell, Beckwith's work forges an explicit link between the spirit of forgiveness and its embodiment in performative speech.[149] As she suggests, the late plays 'affirm the priority... of trust before doubt' because the tragedies have done their work: diagnosing 'the relentless costs of imagining that language can be a private property of the mind'.[150] Hence, these works articulate a sense of the divine forgiveness as primarily felt through human language; it is no longer the sacrament but '*the agency of the human voice* that is the medium of redemption'.[151] Making language the medium of authentic relation, Shakespeare in fact *re-works* both tragic and post-tragic genres which are both 'profoundly revised through the sounding of human acknowledgment as miracle'.[152] This 'miracle' depends on characters' acceptance to be bound to their utterances, allowing language to reveal their genuine commitments, repentances, vulnerabilities and recognitions. Shakespeare's solution to tragedy, then, is first of all to redeem *language*, to attempt stagings of its true function as a genuine, responsible response, a response in which human words and human being can once more coincide.

Beckwith's Cavellian account of such language of acknowledgement is, it should be said, distinctly non-theological, because it limits the reaches of response to person-to-person communication, irrespective of what are vital aspects of the practices of penance and reconciliation to which she alludes—that is, the ineliminable 'transcendent horizon' that, from a theological point of view, dwells in such speech. How might we account for such words in the light of the *already* granted divine gift, the *logos*, that is somehow creatively involved with such utterances?[153] From a theological perspective, the performative speech of forgiveness is fully intelligible not merely in the light of what it acknowledges, but also in the light of *what it reveals*. As Milbank rightly points out, the theological sense of *The Winter's Tale* invites us to read the play not so much as post-tragic ethics, but as a union of ethics and poetics.

The language of 'acknowledgement' thus calls for a theological supplementation. Can donative instances of penance, prayer, worship, adoration, devotion and forgiveness simply be classified under the rubric of 'speech-acts'? Is it not rather that such registers of speech, by being in their own way oriented 'gifts', might also signify the archetypal font of such language *in the light of which* all other speech *can* become speech-acts? Such words, it would seem, cannot merely be said without a participatory involvement in the transcendent dimension that makes them meaningful, and thus sayable.

Hence, it may be more theologically fruitful to examine an account of language in which responses and acts of acknowledgement become first intelligible *as kinds of gifts*. Following Gadamer's sense of language as speculative, Williams' explorations at the edge of words and Milbank's notion of the gift, one might add here that there is *something* which glimmers in our words when we 'exchange charity' (*KL* 5.3.164), when we speak mutual words of love, recognition and acknowledgement, that expresses not merely the 'grammar of forgiveness' but also the author of such grammar, who participates in its utterances in some mysterious and non-reducible way—*a quality in language itself that bears witness to its source*. Truly to acknowledge one another is also, implicitly, to *give* acknowledgement to the divine ground of such speech, as that which glimmers in the gift of words. As Beckwith rightly notes, the human voice is the giver of this 'miracle'. The appropriate theological register to approach language and gift in Shakespeare is, as we will see below, that which illuminates language *as such* as gift, because it can be given, received and returned as gift: in other words, it is *the doxological*.

Shakespeare, Cusa and Doxology: Johannes Hoff and Peter Hampson

So far, I have begun to delineate how a theological approach to Shakespearean language can be distinguished from the suspicious ploys of postmodern criticism, but also from more generous ethical, existential and philosophical readings discussed above. This means, as I have suggested, understanding 'word' in the light of 'gift'. For this, the appropriate theological register is the 'doxological', that is, an understanding of language through the fundamentally donative category of *praise*, understood not as an instance, but as the *heart* of human speech, as the gift somehow always already involved in *every* spoken response.

Recent scholarship within the scope of 'theology and literature' has addressed this concern for language, prompted by a more general engagement with postmodernity and its linguistic turn. In 'Cusa: A Pre-modern Postmodern Reader of Shakespeare' (2015), Johannes Hoff and Peter Hampson approach Shakespeare in the light of Nicholas of Cusa, an eminent and pivotal theologian who unified the cosmology of late medieval

Christianity with the literary concerns of the then-nascent Renaissance humanism.[154] This chapter figures in an edited volume called *Theology and Literature after Postmodernity*, which reflects concerns in *both* theological *and* literary fields to move beyond the hegemony of critique and affirm the value of the humanities.[155] The editors of this volume, thus, seek to endorse a kind of 'theology and literature' scholarship that can articulate a sense of participation in 'an enchanted or theophanic cosmos that paradoxically allows us to hold our finitude and vulnerability, and potential for transcendence together'.[156] It is in the light of this project that Hoff and Hampson's reading becomes pertinent.

But why Cusa and Shakespeare? Though there is reasonable evidence to suggest that Shakespeare might have had exposure to aspects of Cusa's thought through the influence of Ficino and Giordano Bruno in England,[157] it may be more useful to approach both as representatives of a manner of thinking that is broadly congenial to Christian Platonism, one that specifically sought to respond to specific religious and cultural difficulties.[158] Indeed, living like Shakespeare at a time when 'late medieval certainties were giving way to early modern pluralities', Cusa's theological thinking sought to preserve fundamental pre-modern theophanic cosmology while, in turn, anticipating and responding to early modern anxieties.[159]

Hoff and Hampson's thesis is that a Cusan, doxological reading, grounded on the pre-reflexive yet discerning orientation of the mind to the true, the good and the beautiful can provide a way out of the postmodern impasse. This cultural deadlock, for them, is accurately described by Charles Taylor as caught 'between the inauthentic homogenizing demand for recognition of equal worth, on the one hand, and the self-immurement within ethnocentric standards, on the other', that is, between an undiscriminating veneration of difference for its own sake and the vain traditionalism of clinging to half-extinguished cultural identity-markers.[160] Moving beyond this obstacle, a Cusan reading approaches Shakespeare and theology in a manner that is neither shaped by the critical reflexes of a culture of suspicion, nor by attempts to appropriate Shakespeare within an overly demarcated theological tradition.

In arguing for such a reading, Hoff and Hampson affirm Cusa's pre-modern 'metaphysics of participation', from which they also sketch out a Cusan vision of language as culminating in praise.[161] As life constantly but 'non-coercively' calls us to move towards the good and the true, they argue, so the mind is naturally oriented, in 'joyful pursuit' of its own plenitude, towards transcendentals such a goodness, wisdom, truth and beauty—all of which ultimately coincide in the highest good, that is 'God himself'.[162] Embracing this natural movement of the intellect means moving into 'a praxis of doxological participation that helps us recognise the desirability' of these transcendentals.[163] The lure of these principles leads to the theological underpinnings of linguistic expression as both affirmative and donative, *since to desire and recognise the true, the good and the beautiful coincides with affirming and praising them.* To praise is a *pre-reflexive* attitude, in the sense that it does not depend upon rational judgement but on instances of marvel and wonder which, being their own mode of discernment, move us to affirm the goodness of things, thus *giving* praise both to things themselves as well as to their fount and origin—and thus to align rational reflection. To praise, in this sense, both affirms and discerns the good. Thus, as Cusa writes, '[g]oodness is praised, greatness is praised, truth is praised, and each of the remaining things [is praised]. Therefore, these ... are used in praise of God and are rightly ascribed to God, because He is the Fount of praise'.[164]

Ultimately, 'all things praise God by their existence' and likewise when we truly praise one another, it is, through us, God that is praised. In fact, praise is nothing less than *scientia laudis*: it is adoratory speech that also yields, in its own special way, a kind of knowledge of God.[165] For Cusa, the cosmos is a theophany in which God is in some way manifest: thus, in the affirmative and laudatory responses that bear witness to such manifestations, something that is at once within language and beyond words is both affirmed and articulated; that is, *revealed*.[166]

This view of reality, Hampson and Hoff suggest, can engage the theologian as well as the poet. If for Cusa, 'the one who ever-praises God makes progress continually—as a cithara-player makes progress in playing the cithara—and he becomes ever more like unto God', for Shakespeare 'Sweets with sweet war not, joy delights in joy /... /Mark how one string sweet husband to another/Strikes each in each by mutual ordering'.[167] Cusa and Shakespeare read the universe as a concordance with which we can potentially be in harmony: an act of praise is thus also an act of being at home, of *dwelling* in the universe by recognising its inherent goodness.

These exalted theological considerations may seem a world away from the skeptical tendencies of scholarship in Shakespeare and religion. But as Hoff and Hampson show, such an approach, taking its cue from the pre-critical, need not result in a *non*-critical, naïve reading. In fact, a Cusan approach substitutes the postmodern radical *epoché* (understood as the suspension of judgement and meaning) with a specifically doxological one. Hoff and Hampson highlight that apophatic spiritual and mystical practices have been increasingly conflated or confused with a critical skepticism evolving from the use of *epoché* in the phenomenological tradition: in their words, 'the mystical desire for the infinite plenitude of life turned into a fictive play with the undetermined idea of a "*je ne sais quoi*"'.[168] Yet, Cusa, by contrast, clings to the pre-reflective nature of praise to develop a sophisticated science of knowing-unknowing, or 'learned ignorance'. As Hoff writes,

> We do not praise something because we judge it good. Rather, if our praise is genuine, and not just the expression of a herd instinct, we judge something to be good because it makes us wonder and praise without requiring further thought about what we are doing.[169]

But if judgement itself takes its cue from this original wonder, it is left with the sense that it cannot fully describe or apprehend the ground of this gift to which language has already responded. Yet, paradoxically, it is this impossibility that glimmers in each genuine act of praise. As Hoff puts it,

> [o]nly the impossibility of accounting for the gift to be 'one' can account for our ability to discover in finite creatures an image of the divine oneness; only our ability to 'wonder without why' can open our eyes for the praiseworthiness of created faces; only the doxological gift to estimate the inestimable can touch on the inherent perfection of finite entities, such as their 'oneness', 'goodness', 'actuality', 'beauty', etc.[170]

Through an appreciation of the Sonnets in dialogue with Helen Vendler's own readings, Hampson and Hoff note in Shakespeare a similar doxological commitment to the lure of these transcendental principles. There is in Shakespeare a poetic ability to reach both beneath and beyond discursive reason and to dwell in the *metaxu*, 'the paradoxical "space between"', where the hyper-determination of the present moment exceeds our reflexive capacities'.[171] Read in this Cusan key, then, Shakespeare's poetics carefully negotiate the hidden transcendent in the manifest and the subtle relationship between time and eternity: 'the infinite simplicity of the creator reveals itself in the mutable but unexchangeable singularity... of this contingent creature, *thou*, to the same extent that the latter participates in the universal beauty of the (negative) infinite'.[172] Reading Shakespeare in this doxological manner requires another *epoché*: 'to bracket our latemodern, stoic habits, and disciplines of detachment, to pre-reflexively "engage", and ally ourselves with the poet's speech acts, and, by extension, with his receptive reader'.[173] It is this reading practice, in conjunction with our twinned consideration of language and gift, that this study will develop further, as will become apparent in the next chapter.

***

In dialogue with more theologically inflected studies of Shakespeare, this section has singled out the interpenetration of word and *gift* as a key in understanding language as a revelatory medium of a universe that *speaks* through human voices, but also through things and beings.

These theological reading also offer ways of superseding the postmodern critical impasse, sidestepping concerns about language as power with a pre-reflective, 'doxological' reduction and moving beyond issues of radical alterity by suggesting the possible post-tragic union of ethics and poetics. The following section further defines this study's interdisciplinary method, by means of a brief survey of work concerned with 'theology and literature'.

Theology and Literature: Issues and Insights

Literature as Theology?

As I suggested above, this study can be loosely presented as a contribution to the academic interdisciplinary concern termed 'theology and literature'. This is an academic area that has largely been nurtured by theologians with an artistic background and/or literary training, rather than literary scholars whom, as I have discussed above, have understandably been more reticent to engage with theology beyond historicism or the purview of secular theory. Nevertheless, 'theology and literature', sometimes under the umbrella of 'theology and the arts', has burgeoned in recent years, becoming recognised as an interdisciplinary academic field in its own right, with courses and qualifications, numerous publications and several journals dedicated to its furthering. However, there are as yet great variations in approach, making it an as yet under-theorised field of study, which is perhaps a reason why many departments of theology have only grudgingly acknowledged it as a worthwhile field of enquiry.[174] Mark Burrows sums up the sense of hesitancy inherent in such liminal interaction: approaching theology as

> in a sense poetry [as the 9th century theologian John Scotus Eriugena suggested] need not presume that it is, as a literary form, one and the same as truths of Christian revelations. But neither is it to retreat, in the other direction, to a blunt notion of poetry as a quaint or foolish undertaking that has to do with what is *merely* human.

One can accept, suggests Burrows, a 'modest ambition', that poetry is 'a kind of revelation' that, *like* theology, re-articulates our own selves and relationships to our world.[175] Scholarship greatly varies as to how to understand both the nature of this 'likeness' and the restrictions imposed by this 'modesty'. Some theologians, keen to see literary expression as a means to deepen our understanding of the religious dimensions of life, are nonetheless anxious to keep the two disciplines crisply separate: 'Although we may start and learn from the poetic formation of artists', writes William Dyrness (2011), 'we must... have recourse to Scripture to discern their full meaning'.[176] On this 'two-truths' view, artistic expression, though helpful, must ultimately either be laid to one side or instrumentalised to serve kerygmatic ends. This, to be sure, creates the additional problem of how to encounter the 'poetic formations' and cultural and linguistic mediations that are an indelible part of 'Scripture' itself.

Thus, a disjunctive approach perhaps oversimplifies the multitudinous ways in which the two disciplines interpenetrate. Literature and theology are, after all, both culturally embedded in a manner that suggests a more primal search for meaning: something like Paul Tillich once termed an 'ultimate concern'.[177] Literature and theology both serve to clarify and articulate how such fundamental attitudes express themselves in language and are, in some sense, inescapably linguistic. As Graham Ward (2009) reminds us in a brief but helpful article, certain cultural, narrative and poetic features tie together literature and religion in a sense that never leaves literature as 'entirely' secular. If religion and literature are both 'cultural' products, it is because culture itself is rooted in the 'imaginary' which, as the realm 'out of which the symbolic is generated', is 'prior to articulation'.[178] Religion and literature operate in the field of narrative, 'within the existential horizons of anticipation and expectation, fear and hope'.[179] Ward here refers to an aspect of a Coleridgean 'poetic faith', but rather than appeal to it as liberated from the 'restraints' of traditional religion, he suggests that a deep engagement with texts also constitutes a handing over of ourselves as readers, a *trust* in narratives to re-articulate the world for us, 'world-stories' that can thus paradoxically transform us and our relation to the real.[180] Again, our deep inhabitation of language makes it a phenomenon that at once precedes and eludes us, for despite the development of rhetorical abilities, 'associations escape, rhythms beat out older and more sacred patterns, and words carry memories of previous use'.[181]

Thus, our being inescapably linguistic coincides with our being inescapably involved in religious expression. Here, Ward moves in the direction of George Steiner's thesis in *Real Presences*: 'any coherent understanding of what language is and how language performs... any coherent account of the capacity of human speech to communicate meaning and feeling is, in the final analysis, underwritten by the assumption of God's presence'.[182] Ward's appeal to the 'imaginary' also chimes with writings which have argued for the poetic imagination as a revelatory power of theological amplitude. For Malcolm Guite (2012), the poetic imagination is a 'truth-bearing' faculty that is also 'an aspect of the *Imago Dei* in humankind'.[183] Though his appeal to the imagination is also distinctly Coleridgean, Guite sees in Theseus' speech about the imagination in *A Midsummer Night's Dream* (5.1) a forerunner of this doctrine: 'an account of the poetic imagination as the bodying forth in earthly terms of heavenly apprehension', offering a way to understand the incarnation of the Word made flesh as 'the supreme act of divine *poesis*.[184] Insofar as it is grounded in the 'imaginary', human language and culture shimmer with the lustre of the incarnation, and authentic poetic words respond to its lure. On this view, 'theology and literature', as an interdisciplinary approach, can operate in a sense that takes language as its shared terrain, with the added doxological orientation towards the true, good and beautiful that Hoff and Hampson suggest.

Moreover, reading literature in the light of these transcendental co-ordinates need not result in a dispassionate theoretical approach, simply discerning 'Platonic ideas' everywhere; it is rather to be open to the possibility that such readings might be transformative of our understanding of the very relation between the two disciplines. As Regina Schwartz and Vittorio Montemaggi (2014) point out,

> to speak about the relationship between religion and literature is not simply to speak of a common ground... it is also to be open to the possibility that our conception of such common ground might be *transformed* by the light shed on it by the encounter of religion and literature.[185]

Approaching readings in this way can lead to the discovery of truth as an unpredictable *event*, 'a surprising gift, an epiphany'.[186] In developing my doxological account of language as a propitious crossover between the two disciplines, I want to highlight how this shared terrain might come to light if language is understood, in the light of the incarnation, as both mysteriously involved with the furthering of this 'bodying forth' and also made to ring with its fundamental dedication *to* things: language in other words, as always already invoking, calling upon and evoking anew a relationship to the good, beautiful and true, in its manifold articulations.

Theology as Literature?

If Graham Ward sees literature as never entirely secular, Olivier-Thomas Venard sees theology as never entirely non-literary. In his three-volume work *Thomas d'Aquin poète théologien* (2002–2009), Venard seeks to demonstrate how Thomas' theology has an irreducibly literary dimension.[187] Writing in response to the rationalising impulses of 'neo-Thomism', Venard shows how the literary strategies of the *Summa Theologiae* can be understood as *poetic* expression in their attempt to *make manifest*, in the epiphanic mode mentioned above, what cannot be directly expressed. Refreshingly, Venard compares Aquinas' prose to the fiercely secular, late-modern writings of Arthur Rimbaud, a poetry that, for all its hostility to any overt theological move, remains perpetually visited by the spectral presence of the transcendent.[188] In Rimbaud, the darkness immanent to the sublimity of poetic language as such hints

34 *Approach*

at what is, for Aquinas, the luminescent mystery of the transcendent God. In fact, Venard argues, Thomas' lapidary diction, blazing clarity and simplicity of style are *poetic* moves intended to make manifest the diamond-like brilliance and ultimate simplicity of that towards which he points. In his view, Aquinas is the composer of a poetic theology fully intelligible only within an analogical cosmos.

Venard succinctly diagnoses the problems of 'theology and literature'. First, from a secular point of view, it is impossible to distinguish something like a divinely given 'grace' from an aesthetic 'sublime'. Second, as we have already seen, the predominance of the 'hermeneutics of suspicion' has made it highly difficult to recover a pre-reflexive *naiveté* with regard to language. The 'linguistic turn' that is symptomatic of postmodern culture has inflected all academic disciplines with an anxiety at the inescapability of linguistic mediation—one which Venard aptly summarises: 'if one has to be able to word one's thought in order to be able to think one's word… any claim to know the origin of meaning seems delusive'.[189] Truth being nothing but a 'mirage', the human mind is ceaselessly bound to circularity, rupture and original difference. To be sure, this goes to the heart of a significant postmodern problem, since many postmodern thinkers claim that theirs is a 'fundamental' account of language which they inevitably must denounce as the mirage itself.[190]

Yet, for Venard, this circularity is something that both medieval and postmodern approaches also *affirm*: they both presume in some way that 'understanding something means understanding it as a *response*', that is, within the sway of an always already linguistically mediated reality.[191] Hence, Venard challenges the 'two-truth' view that maintains a clean, disjunctive break between the disciplines and which casts literature, as some theologians do, as ultimately a form of idolatry.[192] This manner of doing theology, for him, keeps far too narrow a conception of transcendence and results in a radical separation between words and Word.[193] Such a misunderstanding, for Venard, occurs because both disciplines see themselves in dispute over human consciousness, as 'the scene on which meaning appears in human life' as well as 'the very faculty of meaning' which, in turn, orients all response.[194] Modern literature, bewitched by 'the sublime', has built itself as a kind of non-religious religion, appropriating to itself the fields of meaning traditionally ascribed to the religious. In this way, a psychologised 'stream of consciousness' is postulated as the source of meaning instead of what was traditionally understood to be an instance of the 'inner word conveying in the soul the voice of God'. But these changes result from the most profound change of them all, that is, the change '*from logos to language*'.[195] Perceiving the universe as a realm radically divorced from transcendent expression is at the root of the project of modernity: it powers the metaphysics that divorce 'nature' from 'culture' and humans from God. I will explore this issue in more detail in the next chapter.

Hence, theologians concerned with 'theology and literature', for Venard, must challenge the metaphysical assumptions behind this move, which amount to an 'idolatry of language'.[196] In his own work, he seeks to resolve this by merging the profound attention to language that is peculiar to literary studies with the truth-seeking element of theological enquiry, to bear witness to the 'dazzling darkness' that modern poetry and medieval theology alike *both* evoke as 'ultimate concern'. Genuine literary study, for him, corresponds with a kind of sacred practice, since it is in fact permeated by a divine call: 'in the study of the literary expression the mystery of God invites us to religiously explore the mystery of language'.[197] Here, Venard quotes Hans Urs von Balthasar's own reflections on Gerald Manley Hopkins: 'what is unheard of in a poet's language is a theological phenomenon *that one cannot otherwise comprehend*'.[198] This loving patience towards the poetic also reconstitutes theological writing, which becomes an 'unveiling of the name of the unknown God... towards which literature gestures' and a mode of study in which 'human speech discovers itself *already spoken* in the creation that it is trying to figure: it gives voice to that which calls it'.[199] For Venard then, as in some sense for Hoff and Hampson, postmodernity and theology join one another in their striving for a mysterious transcendent, even though for the former it remains without a name, and for the latter, it is always already named.

In trying to discern Aquinas' poetic practice, Venard makes the audacious move of appealing to Rimbaud. But because of their arising within metaphysical assumption that assume a form of bond between word, world and Word, medieval writings also enable us to highlight other crossovers between the two disciplines that are helpful to this study. In a suggestive work (2006), Robert McMahon has exposed the literary underpinnings of the writings of Augustine, Boethius and Anselm, as well as the theological and philosophical aspects of Dante's literary practice, in the light of a 'grammar of ascent' whose narrator merges with the speaking voice of the reader ('speaking', of course, because composed for the medieval *praxis* of reading out loud) to become a pilgrim figure.[200] Anselm's *Proslogion*, for example, is written in a voice that should not be confused with semi-biographical theological musings, but rather as a prompt for a kind of *devotional reading practice,* articulating, reformulating and moving beyond key insights, as the speaking narrator gradually 'returns' towards her origin.[201] But McMahon does more than merely indicate the convenience of a Platonic scheme of origination-conversion and return to such literature. What he illuminates in such texts are the literary inflections of *credo ut intellegam*: that to 'believe' and to 'understand' are indissoluble from the voicings of *speech* understood fundamentally as intentional: an address to God that, moved by the force of desire, speaks its own understanding as it begins to understand its own speaking. Here again, language, moved by its donative roots, becomes a medium of revelation.

This figure of the ascending pilgrim crosses over literature and theology in numerous ways, with what is perhaps its most significant medieval iteration appearing in Dante's *Divine Comedy*. Here too, the importance of the doxological register is essential. For Montemaggi (2016), reading the *Commedia* as theology means to understand that, even though language will always fall short of a full articulation of the divine, Dante shows that insight into the divine is possible, 'if through (not despite) our failing statements, offered and received in and as love, our minds are able consciously to tend toward and achieve deiformity'.[202] This journey towards divinisation paradoxically allows one 'to recognise how all language, with all its limitations, is *already* a marker of our inherent divinity'.[203] Hence, on this view, language as gift to God coincides with the gift of our own being. Conversely, Dante's poet-narrator is a kenotic figure making himself, as Robin Kirkpatrick remarks, '*macro* [gaunt] in the service of heavenly and earthly truth', providing a paradigm of what a theological approach can offer literary studies, a movement beyond the safety of second-order academic language to 'the first-order discourses of creeds, prayers, hymns, and liturgies'.[204] As poet *and* theologian, Dante shows this fundamental truth about language: that praise lies at the very heart of poetics.[205]

It may of course be objected that Dante, like Anselm and Aquinas, are figures to be read squarely within a kind of medieval cosmological 'synthesis'. Surely, post-Reformation Shakespeare, writing long after the fracturing of this worldview, cannot be approached in the same terms? Yet, here, we return to the concerns explored at the beginning of this chapter: if a theological exploration of language is subsumed by an aspect of worldview, a mode of existential questioning, or made evanescent in the light of historicist tergiversations, we miss a central aspect of its phenomenon. For Montemaggi, language both attests to our human nature and to its divine potential, thus becoming the specific human locus for the manifestations of divine love as actualised in human encounter.[206] Anthony Baker (2019) makes a related point with regard to Shakespeare: it is specifically a providential aspect of language which offers 'an excess of agency or presence beyond what the plot would seem to warrant'.[207] For Baker, God in Shakespeare remains hidden, 'unstaged', precisely because of this category of 'excess' through which a divine that is almost too-much-present becomes signified. In a sense then, paradoxically, Shakespeare is at his most theological when least overtly so: 'when he is most insightful or creative in his display of the human form'.[208] To be alive to the theological dimensions of his words is to know that language is marked with just such a trace of the divine in a kind of 'non-competitive differentiation'.[209]

Hence, for Shakespeare, argues Baker, to tease out what the grace of words might be entails that we forego searching for 'the presence of God on stage or in character' and instead be attentive to 'the mediation, or even problematic repetition of divine grace through difficult human choices and ambiguous human language'.[210] To begin to approach language in Shakespeare from the point of view of doxology, we might add that, if human language is truly the locus for the expression of divine love as the unfinished, ongoing utterance that emanates from the Word made flesh, these linguistic ambiguities are counterpointed by a deeper music, at once elusive and intimately immanent. Indeed, no linguistic mean is too common nor resource too scarce for the ever-new expression of this salvific gift of love, at once human and more-than-human; as Kirkpatrick puts it in a Dantean context, 'even satire and scandal are enlisted in the service of praise'.[211] Hence, from bawdy language and curses to witticisms and irony, from rhetorical power-manoeuvrings to ecstatic poetry, Shakespeare's linguistic universe can be read as alive with a polyphony of creative responses all underwritten by the gift of words, all ensouled by the salvific potencies of words as gifts. Drawing at length on the relationship between Cusa and Shakespeare, the following chapter will further explore the theoretical underpinnings of such a vision.

Notes

1. In approaching Shakespeare in the context of 'theology of literature' (and not 'theology and drama'), I follow scholarship that interprets him as a 'literary dramatist', whose art unites and transcends both literature and theatre. See Lukas Erne, *Shakespeare as Literary Dramatist* (Cambridge: CUP, 2003). For recent studies of the relationship between theology and the performing arts, see Stephen Guthrie and Trevor Hart (eds.), *Faithful Performances: Enacting Christian Tradition* (Aldershot: Ashgate, 2007); Kevin Vanhoozer, *Faith Speaking Understanding: Performing the Drama of Doctrine* (Louisville, KY: John Know Press, 2014).
2. Austin Farrer, *The Glass of Vision: The Bampton Lectures of 1948* (London: Dacre Press, 1948), ix.
3. For recent overviews of these debates, see Nicholas Birns, *Theory after Theory: An Intellectual History of Literary Theory from 1950 to the Early 21st Century* (Peterborough: Broadview, 2010); Vincent B. Leitch, *Literary Criticism in the 21st Century: Theory Renaissance* (London: Bloomsbury, 2014).
4. George Wilson Knight, *Myth and Miracle* (London: J. Burrow, 1929), 22.
5. Knight, *Shakespearean Production* (Harmondsworth: Penguin, 1949), 231–232.
6. Knight, *The Sovereign Flower* (London: Methuen, 1958), 49.
7. Knight, *Shakespeare and Religion* (New York: Barnes & Noble, 1967), 27.
8. Michael Dobson, 'Wilson Knight's *Wheel of Fire*', *Essays in Criticism* 52.3 (2002), 242.
9. Alan Sinfield, Review of Ewan Fernie's *Spiritual Shakespeares* (2005), *Textual Practice* 20.1 (2006), 161. Sinfield draws a long list of 'culprits' including eminent Shakespeareans such as T. S. Eliot, C. L. Barber, Helen Gardner and F. R. Leavis.
10. See Roland Mushat Frye, *Shakespeare and Christian Doctrine* (Princeton, NJ: Princeton UP, 1963).

11 For a recent example of this approach, see Jonathan Bate, *How the Classics Made Shakespeare* (Princeton, NJ: Princeton UP, 2019).
12 On this, see R. A. Foakes, *Hamlet versus Lear: Cultural Politics and Shakespeare's Art* (Cambridge: CUP, 1993).
13 R. W. Chambers, *King Lear* (Glasgow: Jackson, Son and Co, 1940); John Lothian, *King Lear: A Tragic Reading of Life* (Folcroft, PA: Folcroft Library Edition, 1970).
14 Knight, *The Wheel of Fire* (Oxford: OUP, 1930), 220.
15 S. L. Bethell, *Shakespeare and the Popular Dramatic Tradition* (London: King and Staples, 1944), 59; John Danby, *Shakespeare and the Doctrine of Nature* (London: Faber, 1972), 128.
16 Maynard Mack, *King Lear in Our Time* (Berkeley, CA: UCAL, 1965); William Elton, *King Lear and the Gods* (Lexington: Kentucky UP, 2015 [1966]).
17 Jan Kott, *Shakespeare Our Contemporary*, trans. Boleslaw Taborski (London: Methuen, 1967), 297–298.
18 *Ibid.*, 298.
19 Foakes, *Hamlet versus Lear*, 74.
20 Malcolm Evans, *Signifying Nothing: Truth's True Content in Shakespeare's Text* (London: Harvester, 1989); Jonathan Goldberg, 'Perspectives: Dover Cliff and the Conditions of Representation', in *Shakespeare and Deconstruction*, ed. G. D. Atkins and D. M. Bergeron (New York: Lang, 1988), 245–265.
21 Jonathan Dollimore, *Radical Tragedy: Religion, Ideology and Power in the Drama of Shakespeare and His Contemporaries* (London: Harvester, 1984).
22 See Coppélia Kahn, 'The Absent Mother in *King Lear*', in *Rewriting the Renaissance: The Discourses of Sexual Difference in Early Modern Europe*, ed. Margaret W. Ferguson, Maureen Quilligan and Nancy J. Vickers (Chicago, IL: UCP, 1986), 33–49; Janet Adelman, *Suffocating Mothers: Fantasies of Maternal Origins in Shakespeare's Plays* (London: Routledge, 1992), 103–129.
23 See Gary Taylor and Michael Warren (eds.), *The Division of the Kingdoms: Shakespeare's Two Versions of King Lear* (Oxford: OUP, 1983).
24 For a perceptive reading of the rise—and fall—of these influences, see Neema Parvini, *Shakespeare and Contemporary Theory: New Historicism and Cultural Materialism* (London: Bloomsbury, 2012).
25 Kiernan Ryan, *Shakespeare* (Basingstoke: Palgrave, 2002). For a good overview of 'presentist' theory in Shakespeare studies, see Hugh Grady and Terence Hawkes (eds.), *Presentist Shakespeares* (London: Routledge, 2007).
26 David Scott Kastan, *Shakespeare after Theory* (New York: Routledge, 1999), 18.
27 John Cox, *Seeming Knowledge: Shakespeare and Skeptical Faith* (Waco, TX: Baylor UP, 2007).
28 *Ibid.*, 2. Stanley Cavell's work is further discussed below, and in Chapters 3 and 4.
29 *Ibid.*, 9–15 and *passim*.
30 *Ibid.*, 85.
31 *Ibid.*, 27.
32 For an overview of the confessional debate, see John Cox's comprehensive review essay, 'Was Shakespeare a Christian, and If So, What Kind of Christian Was He?', *CAL* 55.4 (2006); Beatrice Batson (ed.), *Shakespeare's Christianity: The Protestant and Catholic Poetics of Julius Caesar, Macbeth, and Hamlet* (Waco, TX: Baylor UP, 2006). Richard Wilson

Shakespeare, Language and Religion 39

is one among many authors who argue for an 'encoded' Catholicism in Shakespeare's plays: see his *Secret Shakespeare: Studies in Theatre, Religion and Resistance* (Manchester: Manchester UP, 2004); see also Clare Asquith, *Shadowplay: The Hidden Beliefs and Coded Politics of William Shakespeare* (London: Perseus Books, 2005). For other Catholic readings, see David Beauregard, *Catholic Theology in Shakespeare's Plays* (Newark, NJ: University of Delaware Press, 2008); John Waterfield, *The Heart of His Mystery: Shakespeare and the Catholic Faith in England under Elizabeth and James* (Bloomington, IN: iUniverse, 2009); Alfred Thomas, *Shakespeare, Catholicism and the Middle Ages: Maimed Rights* (New York: Palgrave, 2018). For a refutation of the Catholic position, see Robert Bearman, 'John Shakespeare: A Papist or Just Penniless?', *SQ* 56.4 (2005), 411–433. For few among the many voices appropriating Shakespeare to a Reformed poetics, see Claire McEachern, *Believing in Shakespeare: Studies in Longing* (Cambridge: CUP, 2018); David Daniell, 'Shakespeare and the Protestant Mind', *SUR* 54 (Cambridge: CUP, 2001), 1–12; Graham Holderness, *The Faith of William Shakespeare* (Oxford: Lion, 2016); Grace Tiffany, 'Paganism and Reform in Shakespeare's Plays', *Religions* 9.7 (2018), 214.

33 Daniel Swift, *Shakespeare's Common Prayers: The Book of Common Prayer and the Elizabethan Age* (Oxford: OUP, 2013). Hannibal Hamlin, *The Bible in Shakespeare* (Oxford: OUP, 2013); see also Thomas Fulton and Kristen Poole (eds.), *The Bible on the Shakespearean Stage: Cultures of Interpretation in Reformation England* (Cambridge: CUP, 2018).
34 Alison Shell, *Shakespeare and Religion* (London: Bloomsbury Arden, 2010), 117.
35 Richard McCoy, *Faith in Shakespeare* (Oxford: OUP, 2013), ix.
36 McEachern, *Believing*, 21.
37 *Ibid*.
38 McCoy, *Faith*, 9. See Stephen Greenblatt, *Shakespearean Negotiations: The Circulation of Social Energy in Renaissance England* (Berkeley, CA: UCAL, 1988), 109–113, and *Hamlet in Purgatory* (Princeton, NJ: Princeton UP, 2013); Louis Montrose, *The Purpose of Playing: Shakespeare and the Cultural Politics of the Elizabethan Theatre* (Chicago, IL: UCP, 1996).
39 For a 'manifesto' of Cultural Materialism, as well as an exploration of its coincidences and divergences with New Historicism, see Jonathan Dollimore and Alan Sinfield (eds.), *Political Shakespeare: New Essays in Cultural Materialism* (Manchester: Manchester UP, 1994). The two differ on a crucial point: whereas the former presents a narrative in which social selves are indivisible from subterranean power politics, and thus the primacy of political control over individual freedom, the latter espouses an agenda of social and political change.
40 For a history of the development, see Parvini, *Theory*, 82–95.
41 Not all of those who broadly subscribed to this theoretical 'movement' argued on the same lines: see for example Patricia Parker's more attentive exploration of language as a material practice: *Shakespeare from the Margins: Language, Culture, Context* (Chicago, IL: UCP, 1996).
42 Stephen Greenblatt, *Learning to Curse: Essays in Early Modern Culture* (London: Routledge, 1990), 3.
43 Greenblatt, *Negotiations*, 1–20.
44 Parvini, *Theory*, 87.
45 Richard Wilson, *Worldly Shakespeare: The Theatre of our Good Will* (Edinburgh: Edinburgh UP, 2016), 7.
46 Parvini, *Theory*, 85ff.
47 See for example, Wilson, *Secret*; Gary Taylor, 'The Cultural Politics of Maybe', in *Theatre and Religion: Lancastrian Shakespeare*, ed. Richard

Dutton, Alison Findlay and Richard Wilson (Manchester: Manchester UP, 2003), 242–258; Stephen Greenblatt, *Will in the World: How Shakespeare Became Shakespeare* (London: Jonathan Cape, 2004).
48 Stephen Greenblatt and Giles Guns (eds.), *Redrawing the Boundary: The Transformation of English and American Literary Studies* (New York: The Modern Language Association of America, 1992), 6.
49 David Aers and Sarah Beckwith, 'Introduction: Hermeneutics and Ideology', *JMEM* 33.2 (2003), 211.
50 Parvini, *Theory*, 86.
51 For an overview of these debates, see Anne Baynes Corio and Thomas Fulton (eds.), *Rethinking Historicism from Shakespeare to Milton* (Cambridge: CUP, 2012).
52 Ken Jackson and Arthur Marotti, 'The Turn to Religion in Early Modern English Studies', *Criticism* 46.1 (2004), 176.
53 See for example Huston Diehl, *Staging Reform, Reforming the Stage: Protestantism and Popular Theatre in Early Modern England* (Ithaca, NY: Cornell UP, 1997); Jeffrey Knapp, *Shakespeare's Tribe: Church, Nation, and Theatre in Renaissance England* (Chicago, IL: UCP, 2002); Regina Schwartz, *Sacramental Poetics at the Dawn of Secularism: When God Left the World* (Stanford, CA: Stanford UP, 2008); Debora Shuger, *Political Theologies in Shakespeare's England: The Sacred and the State in Measure for Measure* (Basingstoke: Palgrave, 2001).
54 For the secularisation narrative, see C. John Sommerville, *The Secularization of Early Modem England: From Religious Culture to Religious Faith* (New York: OUP, 1992).
55 Knapp, *Tribe, passim*.
56 See for example Brian Cummings, *The Literary Culture of the Reformation: Grammar and Grace* (Oxford: OUP, 2002).
57 Julia Reinhard Lupton, *Citizen Saints: Shakespeare and Political Theology* (Chicago, IL: UCP, 2005), 4.
58 Lupton, 'The Religious Turn (to theory) in Shakespeare Studies', *English Language Notes* 44.1 (2006), 145–146. For recent examples of 'political theology approaches', see Lupton and Graham Hammill (eds.), *Political Theology and Early Modernity* (Chicago, IL: UCP, 2012); Jennifer Waldron, *Reformations of the Body: Idolatry, Sacrifice and Early Modern Theater* (Basingstoke: Palgrave, 2013); Victoria Kahn, *The Future of an Illusion: Political Theology and Early Modern Texts* (Chicago, IL: UCP, 2014).
59 Graham Hammill and Julia Reinhard Lupton, 'Sovereigns, Citizens and Saints: Political Theology and Renaissance Literature', *RAL* 38.3 (2006), 1.
60 Lupton, 'Renaissance Profanations: Religion and Literature in the Age of Agamben', *RAL* 41.2 (2009).
61 Lupton, *Thinking with Shakespeare: Essays on Politics and Life* (Chicago, IL: UCP, 2011), 230.
62 Phebe Jensen, *Religion and Revelry in Shakespeare's Festive World* (Cambridge: CUP, 2008); see also Gillian Woods, *Shakespeare's Unreformed Fictions* (Oxford: OUP, 2013). For the *locus classicus* of this 'festive' approach, see C. L. Barber, *Shakespeare's Festive Comedy: A Study of Dramatic Form and Its Relation to Social Custom* (Princeton, NJ: Princeton UP, 1967).
63 See Diehl, *Reform*; Anthony Dawson and Paul Yachnin, *The Culture of Playgoing in Shakespeare's England: A Collaborative Debate* (Cambridge:

Shakespeare, Language and Religion 41

CUP, 2001); Adrian Streete, *Protestantism and Drama in Early Modern England* (Cambridge: CUP, 2009).
64 Beatrice Groves, *Texts and Traditions: Religion in Shakespeare, 1592–1604* (Oxford, Clarendon Press: 2007), 59. A similar argument, though with different readings, is made in Jean-Christophe Mayer, *Shakespeare's Hybrid Faith: History, Religion and the Stage* (New York: Palgrave, 2006), who argues that the plays 'self-consciously harbour the old and the new' and 'not only have the power to pose pressing questions but also to allow potential contradictions to remain', 155.
65 For similar approaches, see Maurice Hunt, *Shakespeare's Religious Allusiveness: Its Play and Tolerance* (Aldershot: Ashgate, 2004); Brian Walsh, *Unsettled Toleration: Religious Difference on the Shakespearean Stage* (Oxford: OUP, 2016).
66 Robert Whalen, *The Poetry of Immanence: Sacrament in Donne and Herbert* (Toronto: University of Toronto Press, 2002); Judith Anderson, *Translating Investments: Metaphor and the Dynamic of Cultural Change in Tudor-Stuart England* (New York: Fordham UP, 2005); Timothy Rosendale, *Liturgy and Literature in the Making of Protestant England* (Cambridge: CUP, 2007); Schwartz, *Sacramental*. See also Kimberly Johnson *Made Flesh: Sacrament and Poetics in Post-Reformation England* (Philadelphia: Pennsylvania UP, 2014). Beckwith's work is engaged with at greater length below.
67 Sophie Read, *Eucharist and the Poetic Imagination in Early Modern England* (Cambridge: CUP, 2013), 6.
68 *Ibid.*, 7.
69 Reported in Matthew Smith, 'The Disincarnate Text: Ritual Poetics in Herbert, Paul, Williams, and Levinas', *CAL* 66.3 (2017), 365.
70 See Sarah Beckwith, *Shakespeare and the Grammar of Forgiveness* (Ithaca, NY: Cornell UP, 2011); Patrick Gray, *Shakespeare and the Fall of the Roman Republic: Selfhood, Stoicism and Civil War* (Edinburgh: Edinburgh UP, 2019); Patrick Gray and John Cox (eds.), *Shakespeare and Renaissance Ethics* (Cambridge: CUP, 2014); Regina Schwartz, *Loving Justice, Living Shakespeare* (Oxford: OUP, 2016); Lupton, *Thinking*.
71 David Lowenstein and Michael Whitmore (eds.), *Shakespeare and Early Modern Religion* (Cambridge: CUP, 2015), 11.
72 *Ibid.*, 303.
73 Piero Boitani, *The Gospel According to Shakespeare* (Notre Dame, IN: Notre Dame UP, 2013), 132.
74 *Ibid.*, 1.
75 David Scott Kastan, *A Will to Believe: Shakespeare and Religion* (Oxford: OUP, 2014), 3, 76. Emphasis mine.
76 Rita Felski, *The Limits of Critique* (Chicago, IL: UCP, 2015), 174.
77 For a call to 'back-to-basics' Shakespeare criticism beyond postmodern theory and over-specialised historicism, see Neema Parvini, 'The Scholars and the Critics: Shakespeare Studies and Theory in the 2010s', *Shakespeare* 10.2 (2014), 212–223.
78 'Afterword' in *The Cambridge Companion to Shakespeare and Religion*, ed. Hannibal Hamlin (Cambridge: CUP, 2019), 291.
79 This will be further developed in Chapter 2.
80 Gadamer saw this as exemplified in the thought of Nicholas of Cusa, a key figure in this book. See Hans-Georg Gadamer, *Truth and Method*, trans. Joel Weinsheimer and Donald G. Marshall (London: Continuum, 2004), 431–435.

81 *Ibid.*, esp. 405–425. As he puts it, 'there is... an idea that is not Greek that does more justice to the being of language, and so prevented the forgetfulness of language in Western thought from being complete. This is the idea of Christian *incarnation*', 418.
82 *Ibid.*, 303.
83 *Ibid.*, 306.
84 *Ibid.*, 399.
85 *Ibid.*, 340.
86 *Ibid.*, 404–405.
87 *Ibid.*, 134–144. See also 'The Nature of Things and the Language of Things', in *Philosophical Hermeneutics*, trans. David E. Linge (Berkeley, CA: UCAL, 2004), 69–81.
88 Gadamer, *Truth*, 370. The phrase is taken from an unfinished poem by Hölderlin, 'Conciliator, You That No Longer Believed In...'.
89 *Ibid.*, 345.
90 *Ibid.*
91 *Ibid.*, 342.
92 *Ibid.*, 470.
93 For suggestive interplays between the two thinkers, see Nicholas Davey, 'Experiences, its Edges, and Beyond', *Open Philosophy* 2 (2019), 299–311.
94 Rowan Williams, *The Edge of Words: God and the Habits of Language* (London: Bloomsbury, 2014), 16.
95 *Ibid.*, 17.
96 *Ibid.*, 86.
97 *Ibid.*, 92.
98 *Ibid.*, 19.
99 *Ibid.*, 137.
100 This concern also chimes in some way with recent works of Shakespeare criticism, influenced by Jane Bennett and Bruno Latour, that have tried to contextualise his works through a pre-modern concept of the natural and material world. See for example Philip Armstrong, 'Preposterous Natures in Shakespeare's Tragedies', in *The Oxford Handbook to Shakespearean Tragedy*, ed. Michael Neill and David Schalkwyk (Oxford: OUP, 2016), 104–119; Jean Feerick, 'Economies of Nature in Shakespeare', *Shakespeare Studies* 39 (2011), 32–42; Gail Kern Paster, *Humoring the Body: Emotions and the Shakespearean Stage* (Chicago, IL: UCP, 2004); Laurie Shannon, *The Accommodated Animal: Cosmopolity in Shakespearean Locales* (Chicago, IL: UCP, 2013).
101 Williams, *Words*, 102.
102 *Ibid.*
103 *Ibid.*, 103.
104 Gadamer, *Truth*, 130–138.
105 *Ibid.*, 194.
106 *Ibid.*, 195.
107 Catherine Pickstock, 'Matter and Mattering: The Metaphysics of Rowan Williams', *MT* 31.4 (2015), 607–608.
108 Kastan, *Will to Believe*, 75.
109 John Milbank, *Theology and Social Theory: Beyond Secular Reason* (Oxford: Blackwell, 2006), 4.
110 *Ibid.*, 282.
111 *Ibid.*, xxii.
112 *Ibid.*, 279.
113 See John Milbank, *The Word Made Strange: Theology, Language and Culture* (Oxford: Blackwell, 1997).

114 John Milbank, *Being Reconciled: Ontology and Pardon* (London: Routledge, 2003), ix.
115 *Ibid.*
116 Milbank, *Reconciled*, x.
117 Patrick Gray echoes this analysis in a Shakespearean key, in writing of the tragic inadequacy of the former position in the Roman plays: see Gray, *Fall*, *passim*.
118 Milbank, *Reconciled*, 138–143.
119 *Ibid.*, 143–146; 154–161.
120 *Ibid.*, 146.
121 *Ibid.*
122 *Ibid.*, 147.
123 *Ibid.* These remarks of Milbank's reflect an ongoing debate regarding the significance of tragedy for theology. I accept Milbank's observation of a passage between *King Lear* and *The Winter's Tale* as significant (see Chapters 3 and 4) and take the categories 'tragic' and 'post-tragic' to be convenient markers within that scheme. I do not suggest, however, that the purpose of 'tragedy' is *merely* transitional, on the way to a 'post-tragic' imagination. It is furthermore not clear whether *Lear* fits comfortably under the classical rubric 'tragedy' since it also owes much to the tropes and motifs of medieval theatre and literature. See Helen Cooper, *Shakespeare and the Medieval World* (London: Bloomsbury Arden, 2010), 44ff; 131–138; 165–169. On the theology and tragedy debates, see Kevin Taylor and Giles Waller (eds.), *Christian Theology and Tragedy* (Farnham: Ashgate, 2011); Rowan Williams, *The Tragic Imagination* (Oxford: OUP, 2016), 108–136.
124 Milbank, *Reconciled*, 147.
125 *Ibid.*, 149.
126 *Ibid.*, 150.
127 *Ibid.*
128 *Ibid.*, 151.
129 *Ibid.*, 156.
130 *Ibid.* See also 'Can a Gift Be Given?' in *Rethinking Metaphysics*, ed. L. G. Jones and S. E. Fowl (Oxford: Blackwell, 1995), 119–161.
131 Milbank expands on this manner of reading in 'Fictioning Things: Gift and Narrative' in *Theology and Literature after Postmodernity*, ed. Zoë Lehmann Imfeld, Peter Hampson and Alison Milbank (London: Bloomsbury T&T Clark, 2015), 215–252.
132 Dollimore, *Radical Tragedy*, 4 and *passim*. John Hughes, 'The Politics of Forgiveness: A Theological Exploration of *King Lear*', MT 17.3 (2001), 267.
133 Hughes, 'Forgiveness', 264; 262.
134 *Ibid.*, 262.
135 *Ibid.*, 267.
136 *Ibid.*, 269.
137 *Ibid.*, 270.
138 *Ibid.*, 281.
139 *Ibid.*
140 *Ibid.*, 267.
141 *Ibid.*, 270.
142 On the theological framework behind these theatrical motifs, see R. G. Hunter, *Shakespeare's Comedy of Forgiveness* (New York: Columbia UP, 1965).
143 Beckwith, *Forgiveness*, 6.

144 *Ibid.*, 92.
145 *Ibid.*
146 *Ibid.*, 2.
147 For a critique of this historical narrative, see Brian Cummings, *Mortal Thoughts: Religion, Secularity and Identity in Early Modern Culture* (Oxford: OUP, 2013), 10ff.
148 *Ibid.*, 130.
149 For other approaches in a similar Austinian-Wittgenstinian vein, see Keir Elam, *Shakespeare's Universe of Discourse: Language Games in the Comedies* (Cambridge: CUP, 1984); Lynne Magnusson, *Shakespeare and Social Dialogue: Dramatic Language and Elizabethan Letters* (Cambridge: CUP, 1999); David Schalkwyk, *Speech and Performance in Shakespeare's Sonnets and Plays* (Cambridge: CUP, 2002).
150 Beckwith, *Forgiveness*, 2.
151 *Ibid.*, 92. Emphasis mine.
152 *Ibid.*
153 For a sympathetic yet cogent theological critique of Cavell's ordinary language philosophy, see Judith Wolfe, 'Acknowledging a Hidden God: A Theological Critique of Stanley Cavell on Skepticism', *Heythrop Journal* 48.3 (2007), 384–405.
154 Johannes Hoff and Peter Hampson, 'Cusa: A Pre-Modern Postmodern Reader of Shakespeare', in *Postmodernity*, ed. Imfeld *et al.* (London: Bloomsbury T&T Clark, 2015), 115–136.
155 There are now several such works: for examples of 'post-critique' see Felski, *Limits*; Caroline Levine, *Forms: Whole, Rhythm, Hierarchy, Network* (Princeton, NJ: Princeton UP, 2015).
156 'Introduction', in *Postmodernity*, ed. Imfeld *et al.*, 8.
157 This is a rich terrain of cultural history, explored most famously by Frances Yates, *The Occult Philosophy in the Elizabethan Age* (London: Routledge, 2001). See also Hilary Gatti, *The Renaissance Drama of Knowledge: Giordano Bruno in England* (London: Routledge, 1989); Akie Hayashi, *Shakespeare and the Sidney Circle: Giordano Bruno's Influence in Renaissance England* (Tokyo: Yushodo, 2008).
158 Interest in this tradition, though often ignored by literary scholars, is also not new: see John Vyvyan's readings of Shakespeare in the light of Ficino's Christian Platonism; *Shakespeare and Platonic Beauty* (London: Shepheard-Walwyn, 2013 [1965]); see also Jill Line, *Shakespeare and the Fire of Love* (London: Shepheard-Walwyn, 2004).
159 Hoff and Hampson, 'Cusa', 121.
160 Charles Taylor, 'The Politics of Recognition', quoted in *ibid.*, 117.
161 Cusa's metaphysics of participation will be further discussed in Chapter 2.
162 *Ibid.*
163 *Ibid.*
164 *Ibid.*
165 For the term *scientia laudis*, used here and throughout this book, see Peter Casarella, *Word as Bread: Language and Theology in Nicholas of Cusa* (Münster: Aschendorff Verlag, 2017), 70–87.
166 For a similar approach in an Augustinian key, see Jason Byassee, *Praise Seeking Understanding: Reading the Psalms with Augustine* (Grand Rapids, MI: Eerdmans, 2007).
167 *Ibid.*, 123.
168 *Ibid.*, 120.
169 Quoted in *ibid.*, 133–134.

170 Quoted in *ibid.*, 135.
171 *Ibid.*, 133.
172 *Ibid.*, 131.
173 *Ibid.*, 134.
174 David Jasper, 'The Study of Literature and Theology' in *The Oxford Handbook of English Literature and Theology*, ed. Andrew Hass, David Jasper and Elisabeth Jay (Oxford: OUP, 2009), 15.
175 Mark Burrows, 'Introduction', in *Poetic Revelations: The Power of the Word III*, ed. Mark Burrows, Jean Ward and Małgorzata Gregorgzewska (London: Routledge, 2017), 4–5. Emphasis mine.
176 William Dyrness, *Poetic Theology* (Grand Rapids, MI: Eerdmans, 2011), 115.
177 Paul Tillich, *Systematic Theology*, vol.1 (Chicago, IL: UCP, 1951), 42.
178 Graham Ward, 'Why Literature Can Never Be Entirely Secular', *RAL* 41.2 (2009), 21.
179 *Ibid.*, 23.
180 *Ibid.*, 26.
181 *Ibid.*, 25.
182 Steiner, *Real Presences* (London: Faber, 1989), 3.
183 Malcolm Guite, *Faith, Hope and Poetry: Theology and the Poetic Imagination* (Farnham: Ashgate, 2012), 2; 15.
184 *Ibid.*, 60.
185 Regina Schwartz and Vittorio Montemaggi, 'On Religion and Literature: Truth, Beauty, and The Good', *RAL* 46.2–3 (2014), 111.
186 *Ibid.*, 112.
187 Olivier-Thomas Venard, *Thomas d'Aquin, poète théologien*, vol. 1, *Littérature et Théologie: Une saison en enfer* (Geneva: Ad Solem, 2002); vol. 2, *La langue de l'ineffable: Essai sur le fondement théologique de la métaphysique* (2004); vol. 3, *Sacra Pagina: le passage de l'écriture sainte à l'écriture théologique* (2009).
188 Venard, *Littérature et Théologie*, 232. Here and below, my translations.
189 Venard, '"Theology and Literature": What Is It About?', *RAL* 41.2 (2009), 90.
190 *Ibid.*, 90–91.
191 Venard, *Littérature*, 38–39.
192 Venard, '"Theology and Literature"', 88.
193 Alain Michel, 'Preface' in Venard, *Littérature*, 14.
194 Venard, '"Theology and Literature"', 89.
195 *Ibid.*, 91; emphasis mine.
196 *Ibid.*
197 Venard, *Littérature*, 52.
198 *Ibid.*, 51–52.
199 *Ibid.*, 475–476.
200 Robert McMahon, *Understanding the Medieval Meditative Ascent: Augustine, Anselm, Boethius and Dante* (Washington, DC: Catholic University of America Press, 2006). See also Jacob Sherman, *Partakers in the Divine: Contemplation and the Practice of Theology* (Minneapolis, MN: Fortress Press, 2014).
201 *Ibid.*, 159–210 and *passim*. On this reading practice, see also Mary Carruthers, *The Craft of Thought: Meditation, Rhetoric, and the Making of Images, 400–1200* (Cambridge: CUP, 1998).
202 Vittorio Montemaggi, *Reading Dante's* Commedia *as Theology: Divinity Realised in Human Encounter* (Oxford: OUP, 2016), 38.

203 *Ibid.*, 39.
204 Robin Kirkpatrick, 'Polemics of Praise: Theology as Text, Narrative, and Rhetoric in Dante's *Commedia*' in *Dante's* Commedia: *Theology as Poetry*, ed. Vittorio Montemaggi and Matthew Traherne (Notre Dame, IN: Notre Dame UP, 2010), 24.
205 *Ibid.*, 28.
206 Montemaggi, *Reading*, 244.
207 Anthony Baker, *Shakespeare, Theology and the Unstaged God* (Abingdon: Routledge, 2020), 7. I came upon this work very late in my research and was thus unable fully to benefit from its many insights.
208 *Ibid.*
209 *Ibid.*, 15 and *passim*. Baker's conception of 'differing differently' is influenced by Kathryn Tanner. See *God and Creation in Christian Theology: Tyranny or Empowerment* (Oxford: Blackwell, 1988).
210 *Ibid.*, 12.
211 Kirkpatrick, 'Polemics', 32.

2 'A Wide and Universal Theatre'

Shakespeare, Cusa and Doxology

Introduction

In the previous chapter, I suggested that the interdisciplinary study of 'theology and literature' can be grounded in an understanding of language as doxological. This chapter takes at its starting point the suggestive reading of Shakespeare in the light of Nicholas of Cusa proposed by Peter Hampson and Johannes Hoff.[1] Cusa is relevant in several ways: first, like Shakespeare, he lived at a time when 'late medieval certainties were giving way to early modern pluralities',[2] in line with the cultural transition 'from *logos* to language' which will be further discussed below. Numerous scholars have been concerned with him for this reason: whether understood as the last of the medievals or the first of the moderns, Cusa is often seen as a liminal figure, the guardian of a threshold between two ages, a prophetic visionary deeply aware of seismic cultural shifts and concerned with providing adequate and creative responses to such changes.[3] Accordingly perhaps, his own interests were multiple and his output prodigious: as a philosopher and theologian, but also as a scientist, astronomer, antiquarian, mathematician, international diplomat, as a composer of 'mystical' works, a Cardinal of the church concerned with ecclesial and ecumenical unity and with 'peace between the faiths'.[4] Importantly, and despite the rich intellectual underpinnings of his work, he maintained a lifelong concern for the lived reality of genuine, practical devotion.

Indeed, in the wake of the epistemic and theological pessimism that were prevailing in his time, Nicholas sought to affirm and preserve the union of the affective and intellectual elements of the religious life. He understood that a philosophical approach that provides no spiritual insight is as impoverished as a devotional path which seeks no wisdom or understanding. It is this concern that gave rise to his famous notion of 'learned ignorance' (present already in Augustine but much developed by Nicholas) which, more than a neat but evasive solution to intellectual dilemmas, represented for him a genuine spiritual *praxis*, a 'way of life',[5] uniting faith and the intellect, practice and contemplation.[6] Yet, perhaps most importantly, his work is marked by a concern to show how *all*

DOI: 10.4324/9781003223276-3

these elements can be grounded in a participatory understanding of the cosmos as a theophanic reality that holds together word and world. My approach to Cusa will thus seek to understand his work as original and pertinent, rather than merely transitional. A brief contextual discussion below (see the next section), although framed in terms of a 'passage to modernity', will primarily serve to locate his unique response to the philosophical and theological trends of his time.

With regard to language, Nicholas showed sympathy for the nascent humanism of his day, sharing the concern of humanist scholars with the retrieval of speech from overly abstract, arid scholastic debates and back to its roots as a vehicle for the virtuous life, the sharing of wisdom and genuine insight.[7] In fact, his philosophy of language is varied and spread across his *opus*, but is impossible fully to discern without engagement in his theology of the Word.[8] Prompted by Hoff and Hampson, this chapter will draw on an original development in his work: his 'science of praise' (*scientia laudis*); a notion of language that unites the spiritual practice of learned ignorance, a Christocentric account of a theophanic reality, and a manner of revealing and affirming the dynamic unity word and world. Cusa's doxological approach is, as Hampson and Hoff suggest, a fundamentally aligned yet, in some sense, pre-reflexive and pre-critical participation in a reality that constantly but 'non-coercively' calls for our response to the true, the beautiful and the good—what Hoff refers to as 'doxological reduction'.[9] They also offer this Cusan approach to reading Shakespeare as an *alternative* to the *aporia* of postmodernity, with its affirmation of univocal difference, its suspension of value-judgement and its humbling of language's participatory power in the world. As I will argue in the next two chapters, the movement of Shakespearean tragedy chronicles a similar 'fall' of language; that is, a denial of the ultimate reach of words, and thus a slipping away from the participatory condition that makes words *gifts*. This denial coincides with a separation between characters, their reality and their transcendent ground; a tragic fracture which is only healed by retrieving the ultimate efficacy of words to express the gift of love and forgiveness. As a theologian who wrote at a cultural moment perhaps much like Shakespeare's, and whose theology offers a manner of reaffirming a meaningful connection between language and reality, he is doubly pertinent to this work.

Though I do not intend to conjecture a historical link between Cusa's theology and Shakespeare's work, the former can be encountered as an influence in Elizabethan and Jacobean circles through the dissemination of the thought of Giordano Bruno.[10] A more immediate influence on 17th-century literature and literacy in England, especially on John Donne, has also been noted.[11] A broader vein of literary research has moreover suggested an indirect link in Shakespeare's rich debt to Erasmus. Writing on the Erasmian origin of 'wise fools' and 'foolish wits' in Shakespeare, Walter Kaiser notes the pervasive influence of Cusa's own *docta ignorantia* on Erasmus.[12] '*Witty* and *wit*', he notes, 'are equivocal terms; they may refer either to laughter or to wisdom, to the fool or to the wise', and it is 'out of the paradoxical concepts of Kempis and Cusanus' that Erasmus, and Renaissance culture in general, 'capitalises' on such a rich paradoxical equivocation.[13] Indeed, Erasmus' *Morae Encomium*, for Kaiser, so worked out 'the implications of an ironic and paradoxical dramatization of Nicholas of Cusa's *docta ignorantia*... that one may doubt if Viola [in *Twelfth Night*] could have observed of Feste that "This fellow is wise enough to play the fool,/And to do that well craves a kind of wit," had she not... read her Erasmus'.[14] We will have occasion to return to the relationships between wit and wisdom in the next chapters.

Yet, these cultural and literary connections are themselves insufficient to suggest that Shakespeare was a reader of Nicholas, or knew anything of his metaphysics and theology.[15] To be sure, the absence of direct historical links need not prevent the teasing out of a broader intertextuality; as Greenblatt observes,

> history cannot simply be set against literary texts as either stable antithesis or stable background and the protective isolation of these texts gives way to a sense of their interaction with other texts and hence of the permeability of their boundaries.[16]

In attempting to do justice to such permeability, the resonances I draw out between Shakespeare and Cusa are rather more suggestive of a broad constellation of ideas that spreads across humanistic and Christian Platonic currents, views and habits of mind that become shapers of an intellectual heritage. Indeed, the artistic and poetic movements of the Renaissance and early modern times, for all their emphasis on the novelties of the age, were also, in many ways, an attempt to re-forge the bond between word and world that had begun to erode in late medieval culture.[17] This makes drawing out parallels between the thought of Nicholas of Cusa and the plays of Shakespeare at times a matter of ambitiously working out what may be implicit in one or the other. To do so, I will also draw on contemporary voices whose work sheds light on the implications of Cusa's 'science of praise' and its affinities with Shakespeare's art.

Focusing on the theme of speech, I draw out aspects of Cusa's theology of the Word in the light of his Christocentric and theophanic cosmology. This, in turn, will serve to illuminate how genuine speech originates and culminates in *praise*, a mode of speech that is participatory and heuristic and hence also a form of 'knowledge' (*scientia laudis*). Renaissance and early modern poetry make frequent uses of the explicit registers of praise: from love poetry stemming from the Petrarchan tradition to eulogistic and encomiastic verse, from history plays and royal pageants to numerous literary dedications to lovers, patrons and aristocrats.[18] My aim is not to highlight the theological extension of such literary tropes, but rather to uncover a doxological element to language *as such* and to show how praise coincides with true speech. To do this, I will be more concerned with teasing out the *implicit* dedications in Shakespeare's words, understanding those in terms of ultimate metaphysical and theological addresses that are expressed *through*, and as irreducible aspects *of* language.

Thus, the second part of this chapter will perform a transition from the theological back to the literary, drawing out implicit aspects of Cusa's thought by setting them in conversation with more recent philosophical, theological, and literary voices. As the dynamic of praise can only be apprehended in a universe saturated with speech, I will consider the responsorial structure of doxological language, explored through Jean-Louis Chrétien's phenomenological work and a reading of Shakespeare's use of soliloquy. A discussion of the nature of the doxological 'speaker', in dialogue with recent debates around the notion of Shakespearean 'selfhood', will be developed through the work of Catherine Pickstock on liturgy and the middle-voice. Finally, all of the above will be brought to bear on a consideration of the responsibility of the speaking, 'praising' voice to the creation as a whole.

Hence, this chapter will attempt to sketch out the doxological approach which will become more fully articulated through my primary readings in Chapters 3 and 4. In doing so, I hope to show that, for Cusa as well as for Shakespeare, the human person is constantly prompted by truth itself to speak truly and summoned by love itself to speak with words of love. To speak truly and with love becomes, in a theological context, *to give praise to God*, who is both truth and love. Genuine speech, in this way, can be seen as a fulfilment of human desire, a participatory mode of dwelling in the world, and ultimately a creative and donative mode of expression. In this and the following chapters, I hope to show how this participatory, 'doxological' universe, where the fount and the *telos* of speech is the Word itself, can be a theological key through which to hear Shakespeare's cosmic and symphonic drama, where the ultimate reaches of speech coincide with his 'wide and universal theatre' (*AYL* 2.7.137).

Cusa, Theology and Language: Context and Background

Before considering Cusa's theological and metaphysical approach, it is important to contextualise some of the ideas considered below. Such considerations are not merely relevant to situate Cusa's works, which arguably were composed at the onset of a transition towards modernity, but are also relevant to Shakespeare's, who wrote at the close of this process. For Louis Dupré, cultural historian and Cusa specialist, modernity is more than a moment in a linear historical narrative: it is a momentous and 'fateful' occurrence, 'an event that has transformed the relation between the cosmos, its transcendent source, and its human interpreter'.[19] The birth of modernity, as Dupré shows, corresponds to a gradual displacement of language's role as a symbolic mediator between the three terms of this relation. From belonging to a symbolic and meaningful cosmic order, as it had been in the middle-ages, *logos* becomes, in early modern times, increasingly identified with its descriptive mode. Like many others, Dupré reads these changes as emanating from theological, rather than merely cultural, changes: he sees the advent of modernity as coincident with the 'fateful separation' of nature and grace, with the former increasingly mechanised and objectified and the latter redrawn as a remote, 'supernatural' power, uninvolved with a radically 'fallen' material order. In his account, Cusa stands out as 'the last major alternative' to modernity, a figure who makes a distinctive and highly original attempt to keep the two terms united.[20]

Philosophy's age-old speculative confidence in the Socratic adage of 'following the *logos* wherever it leads' had long chimed with the distinct Christian revelation that such *logos,* having been made flesh, could be read as a cosmic principle with uniquely salvific dimensions.[21] This worldview became disrupted in the late middle-ages with a loss of confidence in the power of language to shed light on the cosmos and provide a way back to its creator. This change in outlook, for Dupré, coincided with the rise in influence of two specific theological currents: voluntarism, with its emphasis on God's inscrutable power and transcendence over against the radical contingency of the created order, and the account of the purely arbitrary character of language that resulted from the speculations of the nominalists.[22] For Dupré, it is the emphasis on God's radical transcendence of the former, as well as the epistemic and semantic pessimism of the latter, that eventually open the gateway for the transition to modern times, thus breaking the age-old contract between word and world.[23]

It is beyond the scope of this chapter to develop a genealogy of modernity in order to draw out Cusa's singular contribution. Yet it is important to consider that part of Cusa's project was a response to these theological trends, and that the influence of both outlooks had consequences both for a philosophy of language and for a theology of the Word. Indeed, by the 15th century, radical developments in voluntarist theology, stemming from the concern properly to emphasise God's *potentia absoluta,* made it possible to think of God's orientation of the human will towards the Good as being so directed only because of God's free decision, rather than as the natural outcome of an analogical continuity between created beings and divine Being itself.[24] If absolute freedom was understood as the primary qualification of the divine, it followed that the cosmos itself was left without 'inherent' order and goodness of its own, since it was seen to depend on a wholly other power.[25] In fact, the arguments of this voluntarist trend (singled out by Dupré in the thought of William of

Ockham) implied that 'no predictable order ruled the world and hence that only empirical observation could establish the nature of that order'.[26] The world became a purely contingent reality, entirely dependent on an inscrutable divine decision. To emphasise the unfathomable nature of the divine will inevitably coincided with the abasement of the cognitive and linguistic faculties of the human person.

This outlook also corresponded with developments in nominalist theology. Originally, 'nominalism' had referred to a doctrine which denied the reality of transcendentals, limiting them to concepts in the mind.[27] But in the late middle-ages, this trend in theology, together with the rising influence of voluntarism, precipitated an approach to language which saw words as restricted to indirect and purely conventional referents to an objective nature. A result of nominalism was its emphasis on the doctrine of 'univocity', which challenged the traditional account of the cosmos as analogically related and permitted instead a *speaking* of the finite and the infinite *in the same terms*, positing the infinite itself at the end of a long chain of created and uncreated beings.[28] Of course, philosophical arguments between nominalists and realists had been very ancient, but the nominalist position (the *via moderna*) gradually took hold in universities and theological faculties when, combined with the outlook of voluntarist theology, it could more readily explicate the inscrutable omnipotence of an otherworldly God.

Part of Dupré's wider point is that these debates were not matters of theoretical interest for theologians in ivory towers, but expressed, albeit in an intellectual fashion, cultural attitudes that were widespread and symptomatic of the period. English poetry, for example, offered its own witness to these concerns in the meditations of the anonymous author of *Pearl* and *Sir Gawain and the Green Knight*, and numerous other literary connections have been conjectured: with Chaucer, for example, or in the insistent gesturing to a radically inscrutable, omnipotent God in the Chester Play Cycle.[29] In fact, the subsequent humanist revival of eloquence, for Dupré, can be understood as an attempt to *reunite* word and world, albeit bypassing the terse debates of scholastic theology in favour of a return to classical ideals of rhetoric and oratory—an attempt which, for Dupré, was nonetheless doomed to fail, since in its hostility to Scholasticism and exclusively literary concerns, it was ultimately 'defenceless against its rationalist opponents' and could not oppose the widening influence of the descendants of those medieval schools.[30]

What is especially relevant to this study is Dupré's overall point that if theological reflection could no longer discern a sense of the intelligible order of things, it followed too that *the powers of language* had to be restricted to what a fundamentally deficient human reason could achieve. As Dupré writes, '[if] we can no longer take for granted that God's decrees follow an intelligible pattern, then we also cease to trust that the eternal Logos secures the basic veracity of human speech'. In the wake of such a semiotic and epistemological crisis, 'words were to be used at man's risk and discretion without carrying the traditional guarantee that, if properly used, they touch the real as it is in itself'.[31] For Dupré then, Cusa is 'the last major alternative' to the sway of nominalist and voluntarist theology and their eventual separation of 'nature' and 'grace', because he sought specifically to offer solutions to the problems raised while at the same time carefully avoiding the stale and controversial debates that had become associated with the various 'Aristotelian Sects'.[32] Here, Hoff adds to Dupré's account, showing how Cusa 'radicalised' the older, analogical ontology to make it at first seem like a radical variant of nominalism, 'though it can be simultaneously interpreted as an attempt to defeat the univocal rationality' of nominalist teaching 'by its own means'.[33] For Hoff, in fact, Cusa 'deconstructs the nihilistic features of modern rationality just at its point of emergence' by developing a way of thinking that remained rooted in a pre-modern, analogical vision of the world, synthesising immanence and transcendence, reason and revelation.[34] He thus carefully negotiated (and sometimes avoided) the quarrels between those who maintained that faith and reason could be harmonised (the *antiqui*) and those who, following the voluntarist/nominalist pathways, fundamentally questioned the reaches of language and human reason, stressing instead the value of affective piety at the expense of philosophical contemplation (the *moderni*). Nicholas was, in all likelihood, exposed to *via moderna* influences during his studies at the university of Heidelberg, which he briefly frequented in 1416. Though he never *explicitly* pronounced on these debates, his writings can be read in their wake, and some of their controversies affected him directly.[35] This broad cultural situation thus shows how Cusa can be read as an alternative metaphysical and theological way to encounter the difficulties peculiar to (post)modernity, especially with regard to the change 'from *logos* to language'.[36]

The Limits of Language and the Crafting of Names

Nicholas' own theological involvement with the question of language appears to have been lifelong: as his first sermon is a consideration of the prologue of John, his last writings put forward the argument for a 'science of praise'.[37] A cursory glance at his work might simply place Cusa in the 'apophatic' lineage of Dionysius the Areopagite, an approach which would certainly be supported by aspects of his writings.[38] Nevertheless, the richness, breadth and polyphonic nature of his work resists a systematic 'theory of language' and calls for a more complex involvement with the theological spirit of his *opus*.[39] Grasping these complexities also requires, as Jacob Sherman notes, an involvement with the

54 Approach

'dramaturgical' component of his writings, 'which stages certain artefacts, bodily movements, actions and reactions as an integral part of the text's performance and argument'.[40]

In line with this observation, I explore below a notion of language that arises performatively, amidst a semi-theatrical dialogue, *Idiota de Mente* (1450) held between three characters who also typify three ways of using words: a scholastic philosopher, a humanist orator, and a layman, 'master of learned ignorance'. Through the figure of the layman, this dialogue seeks to mediate and transcend both the rhetorical education of Renaissance humanism and the 'Aristotelian', scholastic approach of the universities.[41] This theme is introduced when the philosopher, perplexed by his unsuccessful investigations into the nature of 'mind', meets an orator who leads him to an uneducated layman, whose wisdom has deeply impressed him.[42] There is something embarrassing for them both in this opening scene: instead of the ancient and famed 'Temple of Mind' which they were looking for, they end up at this humble craftsman's workshop, a 'small underground dwelling', where they find him deeply absorbed in the carving of a simple wooden spoon.[43] The 'peripatetic' philosopher is particularly intrigued by the layman's playful and un-scholastic use of etymologies in which he conjoins mind (*mens*) with measurement (*mensurare*). 'I haven't read among the various derivations of the word "mind" that anyone has held this view', says the philosopher, expert in received opinions.[44]

In answer to this, the layman enjoins the scholastic to explore 'more carefully' the 'meaning' of a name. He proceeds to expound what might seem like a 'nominalist' view: since human understanding cannot grasp the 'quiddity' of created things, and words are attributed to things by the human understanding, it follows that no name can truly attain the 'thingness' of created being. The philosopher immediately approves of this discussion of 'profound issues': names, he believes, 'have been assigned *at will* according as it occurred to each imposer [thereof] as a result of his reason's operation'.[45] For the philosopher, names seem arbitrary and subject to the requirements of reason, having no relationship with the things to which they are merely the external referent.

Yet, such 'profundity' is not discerning enough for the layman: 'I want you to understand more deeply', he marks. 'Every name is united [to an object] by virtue of the fact that form has come to matter', so that the *true* names of things 'do not arise by imposition but rather are eternal'.[46] For the layman, the 'natural' name of a thing is not the common conceptual referent that different languages aim towards, but rather something that flows from the thing's essential *nature*, and towards which artificial names *tend*.[47] To make his meaning clearer, he asks the philosopher to turn to the carving of the wooden spoon. Here, Cusa orients the attention both to the wondrous uniqueness of a simple object *and* to the art that brings it about, in order to show that, through such skilful crafting, the wood receives the name 'spoon' only through a creative 'advent of the form'.[48] Though unknowable in its fullness, the form nevertheless comes to 'shine forth fittingly' in the wood through an artistic process.[49] Not only does the layman here suggest that art corresponds to a peculiar kind of *knowledge*, he also implies that 'naming' is alike to a craft, and is thus a *creative* (rather than merely imitative) human endeavour.[50] Somehow, then, the simple *art* of spoon-making can provide a way into the problem of naming that philosophy cannot: since naming, like spoon-carving, is a skilful practice, an art, and every human art derives from 'the infinite Divine art'.[51] Thus, something incomprehensible, that is, the *natural* or precise name, which belongs to God, becomes comprehensibly luminescent in the crafted bestowal of a contingent name.[52]

Of course, the 'natural name', the layman says, is only imperfectly encountered in the varieties of names that different cultures use.[53] The nature of contingent things is to appear as delineated, or 'defined', and only what is thus defined can become comprehensible. Yet, in its aiming for precision, such contingent naming chimes in some way with the unutterable yet natural, 'precise' name. 'Preciseness' here does not suggest a search for an adequate verbal label attached to a remote object, but rather an asymptotic aim towards a fullness of being which coincides in God's naming; for as the layman puts it,

> if the precise name of one thing were known, then the names of all things would be known, because there is no preciseness except with God. Hence, if anyone attained unto a single instance of precision, he would have attained unto God, who is the Truth of all knowable things.[54]

Here, naming is not merely an arbitrary practice, since every name that aims to the quiddity of things is made possible *by virtue of* the 'natural name' which belongs to (and is said by) God. Insofar as its creative aspects are properly oriented, human language approximates this natural name, seeking to become a vehicle in which the natural name can 'shine forth fittingly'; but it is this initial Divine 'shining forth' that is in all 'natural' names that gives to contingency its felicitous participation in ineffability.[55] Hence, it turns out to be the learned-ignorant layman, rather than the sophisticated philosopher or the skilful orator, who knows this, having learnt it through the wondrous attention and genuine devotion that comes with authentic crafting.

As the layman shows, speaking, like making, can be seen as the art of orienting the soul *towards* a natural name, or form. Names become 'fitting' when they participate in this form, just as the art of speech becomes fitting when it participates in the 'infinite Divine art'; indeed,

> every finite art derives from the Infinite Art. And so, the Infinite Art will have to be the Exemplar of all arts and the Beginning, the

Middle, the End, the Measure, the Truth, the Precision, and the Perfection of all arts.[56]

Thus, the speaking art becomes the means by which that which is present in nature as the 'natural name' becomes luminous. It is through the art of learned ignorance, rather than through philosophical cogitation or rhetorical fluency, that language becomes truly creative, insofar as it occasions the wonder that brings to light something that is at once natural and an artifice.[57] Robert Miner artfully sums up this point: 'Cusanus thinks of artifice as the medium in which the natural shines forth. What from one standpoint seems extraneous to nature appears from another perspective as the medium for its expression'.[58]

Hence, the layman shows that the complete arbitrariness of names does not presuppose a split between mind and reality agonised over by philosophers and deplored by orators; rather, it embraces the contingency of language as a part of a *coincidentia oppositorum*, the coincidence between nature and artifice, which bears witness to the inexpressible expressible-ness of things. 'Therefore', the layman concludes,

> there is one Ineffable Word, which is the Precise Name of all things insofar as these things are captured by a name through the operation of reason. In its own manner this Ineffable Name shines forth in all [imposed] names. For it is the infinite nameability of all names and is the infinite vocalizability of everything expressible by means of voice, so that in this way every [imposed] name is an image of the Precise Name.[59]

In the infinite and ineffable God, contingency coincides with necessity, because God hallows the inexpressible plenitude that orients every name. As Dupré puts it,

> it is only through the *intentionality* of the naming act that the mind transcends the particularity of the [divine] names. The names themselves refer only to the intrinsic dependence of all finite reality on the infinite... Through them the mind expresses a presence that exceeds all expression.[60]

Because ineffability is also what guarantees the *very aim* at precision of a name, ineffability is not for Cusa the boundary of language, but on the contrary that which gives language the very glow of its showing forth: *it is in fact by virtue of what is un-sayable in them that words can become meaningful*.[61] The otherness beyond which they cannot reach has become, without being collapsed, a manner of orienting names given by the first Name which has already oriented all name-speakers. The unnameable divine transcendence does not stand aloof from language as the harrowingly unsurmountable terminus of every word, but rather *gives* every act of expression in language the propensity to reach beyond itself. The very asymmetry between what can and cannot be expressed is not the end of language; it is a propitious coincidence of opposites and thus the ground of genuine speech.

Thus, Cusa modifies the voluntarist sense of God's radical transcendence by amplifying it to its logical conclusion—clearly, an insurmountable semiotic and epistemic fault-line would simply be *too small* for the creator and redeemer of the universe; instead, God's inscrutability and ineffability is precisely what safeguards and guarantees the power and fecundity of speech. As Nicholas succinctly remarks in an early sermon: 'God's name is the name through which every [other] name is a name, and His name is the essence of all names'.[62] The business of words, in other words, is not primarily a conceptual mapping out of the world, but a journey towards harmonisation with its first utterance, which is the Word itself. 'Our names', writes Hoff,

> are suitable to refer to a unique and universal truth only to the extent that they are *guiding* us to this truth, or, better to say, only to the extent that they allow us to be guided to the truth by the truth itself, which is the divine Word.[63]

The same layman expresses this clearly:

> if I am to disclose to you the concept that I have of God, then if my language is to be of help to you, it must be such that its words are significative—so that in this way I can lead you (through the meaning-of-the-word which is known to us both) unto what is sought. Now, it is God who is being sought. Hence, this is a theology of language [*theologia sermocinalis*] by which I am endeavouring to lead you unto God—in the easiest and truest way I can—through the meaning of a word...[64]

Mysteriously and intimately slipping into language, God has bestowed words their 'theosemiotic' quality, and the meaning of a word can extend beyond itself into a search to speak the truth, a search always already granted by truth itself.

Thus, for Cusa, as Hoff notes, 'the event of incarnation reveals a unique liturgical procedure to solve the aporia of naming:' it is the ineffable yet intimate co-mingling of Word and flesh, encountered not merely in reflection but through the simple act of praise, that enables human language to flourish.[65] The language of the Gospel of John gives Nicholas occasion to explore this carefully:

> those words are the light of our understanding—those words of the Gospel where Jesus says "[I am] the Beginning, I who, indeed, am speaking unto you." For the Word made flesh speaks; i.e., that

Word—who is also God, who is the Beginning—speaks perceptibly. And the following is not difficult to grasp: viz., that the eternal Form-of-being speaks perceptibly in the things that, through it, exist in a perceptible way. To speak is to reveal or to manifest. Therefore, since everything existent exists, it exists from That which exists per se and which is the Form of its substance; [this Form's] speaking is its revelation, or manifestation, of itself.[66]

As the God-man, Christ the Word can be seen as a unique mode of reconciliation between the contingent signs and narratives specific to a tradition and the intellectual requirement for a universal truth.[67] Indeed, for Nicholas, Christ is nothing less than an anthropological and cosmological principle: Christ's being enacts both the eschatological promise of what humanity will be and the essence of what humanity *is* since the creation: a partaker in the divine Logos.[68] As David Albertson puts it,

> [t]he world reflects what the incarnate Christ manifests singularly: the paradoxical double origin from both eternity and time. Creation itself is Christomorphic, such that the mystery of the world's origin in God incurs all the paradoxes that mark the classic Christological formulations.[69]

Christ is thus the Cusan *coincidentia oppositorium,* the very figuration of learned ignorance and the incarnation of the very meaningfulness of speech, being both its beginning and its end. Because 'Christ placed himself in the order of signs', to borrow Maurice de la Taille's famous phrase, signs place themselves under the creative aegis of Christ.[70] The Christomorphic nature of creation leads Cusa to assert a cosmic anthropology (quoting the Hermetic writings):

> For man is god, but not unqualifiedly, since he is man; therefore he is a human god. Man is also world, but he is not contractedly all things, since he is man; therefore man is a microcosm, or a human world.[71]

This cosmic anthropology, bringing together the human speaker with her world, is the vantage point from which to glimpse Nicholas' holistic and Christocentric vision of language. As Nicholas himself puts it,

> [Christ] is, as the goal of every utterance, *there* heard incomprehensibly. For every utterance has come forth from Him and terminates in Him. Whatever truth is in an utterance is from Him. Every utterance has as its goal instruction; therefore, [every utterance] has as its goal Him who is Wisdom itself. "Whatever things were written were

written for our instruction." Utterances are befigured in written characters. "By the Word of the Lord the heavens were established." Therefore, all created things are signs of the Word of God. Every corporeal utterance is a sign of a mental word. The cause of every corruptible mental word is an incorruptible word, viz., a concept. Christ is the incarnated Concept of all concepts, for He is the Word made flesh. Therefore, Jesus is the goal of all things.[72]

From this point of view then, speech is not an epistemic instrument for securing reality but an artful manner of living in alignment with its mystery, which partakes of this mystery and is thus also *redeeming*. Though 'every utterance has as its goal instruction', the paradoxical nature of wisdom-language makes it irreducible to an underlying 'doctrine' or a set of propositions that corresponds to a clearly defined objective reality. As the learned-ignorant figure of the layman teaches us, genuine speech retains its creative, poetic figuration as an essential aspect: like Christ, language is, in its essence, creative and redemptive.

Praise, *Possest* and Poetics

We have seen that for Cusa, names are blessed by the performative qualities of wisdom in language, that of 'shining forth fittingly' with the glow of the incomprehensible divine name which gives to comprehensible names their very savour. Insofar as they are begotten 'through the Beginning', that is through the Word itself, words in their turn can orient the speaker, overcoming epistemic anxieties through speech oriented to the true, good and beautiful. The primary role of language is not to secure an adequate schema of reality, but to guide the speaker toward the mystery that is at its very heart. 'The aporia of naming' is then 'solved' by a 'unique liturgical procedure' insofar as Cusa does not distinguish between theoretical or scientific aims to knowledge and the spiritual aims of contemplative practice to educate our attention to respond to the lure of the divine. This holistic project defines what stands behind his 'science of praise'.

Nicholas articulates this project explicitly in his late compendium of metaphysics and theology, *De Venatione Sapientiae* (1462), a work intended as a guideline for the education of the soul, a treasure-map for those who seek wisdom. Indeed, wisdom is understood as the soul's most precious nourishment, since '[b]y an appetite innate to our nature we are stimulated toward obtaining not only knowledge but also wisdom, or delicious knowledge'.[73] The proceeding chapters take the wisdom-seeker through ten 'fields' in which true wisdom may be found, and many Cusan themes are here reprised: among others, 'learned ignorance', *possest* and God as Not-Other. If the first describes a spiritual attitude of soul adequate to its thirst for wisdom, the latter two are, in some sense, divine 'names'—names in which something comes to 'shine forth fittingly', thus orienting the soul to God.

'*Possest*' is a neologism, one that gestures to Cusa's own linguistic performative and creative tendencies. Yet in some way, this term, linking together *posse* (possibility) and *est* (being), already suggests the solution he seeks to demonstrate, that is, the overcoming of the ontological priority of power that had been the voluntarist position. Here, Nicholas reprises the argument of his earlier treatise *De Possest* (1460) in which he suggests, as Dupré puts it, that 'the divine principle [is] a unity of possibility and actuality which precedes their differentiation in the created order'.[74] Such a coincidence allowing both interlacing and distinction, it follows that '[n]o Leibnizian choice between possible worlds precedes the act of creation'.[75] Since being and power, possibility and act coincide in God, the principle of *coincidentia oppositorum* represents in Nicholas' view a much more fruitful manner of contemplating the divine mystery through the intelligibility of the universe. Indeed, it becomes possible to consider God not merely as an ontologically prior pure Being of which all possibility is a lack, but rather as *signified in the very depth of possibility itself*. In some sense then, one might say that God both *is* and *is underway*, being the very ground that transcends both modalities.[76]

To contemplate such mystery, for Cusa, is to go beyond the traditional limits of reason ultimately validated by the principle of noncontradiction.[77] The name *possest* is not a fudge to mediate disputes between competing schools of theology but a manner of reasoning symbolically unto the divine: this Nicholas suggests—again, playfully yet seriously—in 'seeing' that the 'e' in *possest* symbolically expresses something of the triune nature of God:

> I see that the 'e' is a simple triune vowel. For it is a vowel of 'posse,' of 'esse,' and of the union of both. Assuredly, the very simple vocalization of 'e' is triune: insofar as 'e' relates to 'posse,' it does not relate to 'esse'; insofar as it relates to 'esse,' it does not relate to 'posse'; and insofar as it relates to the union of both, it does not relate [solely] to 'posse' or [solely] to 'esse' but to their union. Therefore, with 'e,' I see that these unconfused relations—each of which is true and perfect by itself—are not three vowels, or vocalizations, but are one most simple and indivisible vocalization.[78]

Thus, one can explore how, in some way, God is in the world like the vowel 'e' is in the word *possest*, for through it 'the world has (1) what it is able to be, (2) what it is, and (3) the union of these two'.[79] A further playful homonymic echo is suggestive, that of *possest* with poetics, for if participation in God is essential to the generative potential of creation, then the creative process of naming is also involved in the co-creative shaping of the world. To name things is also, in some way, to participate in God's unfolding art. As Milbank notes, one can see in this way that 'the Creation in sharing in act shares also in *dynamis*', and thus 'the real is more fundamental than being, since it is both being and the power to be'.[80] Thus, 'participation in reality as both actual and dynamic—as the self-generative power that is at once life and art—is more fundamental than participation in being'.[81]

This is why *possest* becomes more than an elegant concept, but a *name* to meditate on, the name of the Creator with whom creation shares the *creative* power of speech *and* the font and ultimate point of coincidence of art and being. As Nicholas puts it:

> [t]his name leads the one-who-is-contemplating beyond all sense, reason and intellect into a mystical vision, where there is the end to the ascent of all cognitive power and the beginning of the revelation of the unknown God.[82]

Here, the 'name' is, as Lawrence Bond notes, a *guiding* principle which orients the mind, calling the soul to its own plenitude: thus, in a sense, 'Divine name has become icon'.[83] As *possest,* the very name of God becomes an artwork, an image which guides those who contemplate towards the guarantor and referent of the mystic marriage between art and nature. Under the aegis of this name, our very speech partakes of this iconic gesture.

Having reflected on *possest* in his 'hunt for wisdom', Nicholas eventually enters the peculiar field of 'praise'. In previous fields, Nicholas had uncovered ten properties which belong primarily to God because their naming coincides with the naming of God.[84] As he enters, he *exclaims* that the ten properties he had previously glimpsed, having beautifully 'defined' that which is beyond definition, are indeed first and foremost *praises*:

> *And I said:* "Since this beautiful and gladdening field yields only those [properties] and their likes, those... are praises directed toward God."[85]

This half-playful 'and I said' represents the only time in the treatise when the Cardinal takes on a speaking part. It already suggests in other words that praise is *irreducibly* a mode of *saying*. The genuine affirmation of God's greatness, *doxological* speech in other words, is only genuine as and through speaking, and not as a pre-established, planned utterance. Recalling the layman, such speech, like the pursuit of wisdom itself, is occasioned not by self-controlled reflection but by genuine wonder.[86]

But Cusa goes further: because the properties mentioned above are also *sayings*; that is, 'names', they are manners of *speaking-to* God, because their very being cannot but elicit admiration and adoration: 'from the fact that all things are praisings and blessings directed toward God, they are that which they are'.[87] Accordingly, 'in the field of praise', Cusa grasps that the delightful and nourishing knowledge of wisdom is in fact also a word of love to God. Indeed, it seems to him that prophets, philosophers and saints alike have conducted 'their devout pursuits' primarily as manners of praise.[88] There is therefore a mode of seeking for wisdom which is intertwined in love and exaltation, from which mode things are understood in their very being. Far more than a rhetorical addendum to express approval or confer prestige, the commerce of praise is with the essence of things—inevitably so, because as 'Definition that defines all other names' God primarily participates in defining that being.[89]

These considerations lead the Cardinal to a specific anthropology: as a name-giver, a speaker and in some sense a definition-giver, the human being is first and foremost 'a certain living and intelligent and very excellently composed hymn of praisings of God' and receives from God, who is at once the fount and object of praise, the task 'to praise God unceasingly and above all other things'.[90] Thus, to be human means to give to God that which we have received in order to exist, the very music of our being. Once again, ontology is displaced into a more primordial and aboriginal *donology*, or more precisely *doxology*, since here genuine existence is not pure being but a more primordially giving of praise and expression of one's authentic love—thus coming to know, in one sense, what one already loves.

Yet Cusa is referring here to more than the explicit 'act' of praising. Just as what passes our lips is not necessarily praise, what we vocalise *as* praise is not necessarily a genuine expression of our soul's adoratory *élan*. In fact, outward praise can be inward idolatry, which is a going against one's nature, and our own nature, for Nicholas, will inevitably reproach us for it.[91] If it is in our nature to speak and love the Good, to invert this natural relation results in a situation in which nature, as well as our own nature, *calls and recalls us* to return to our primordial and genuine orientation. This is because praising coincides with the affirmation of one's very nature and, at the same time, the recognition of the mystery that underlies one's nature. It is thus a double affirmation: of ourselves as well as of the ground of our being as gift. Those whose lives are in accordance with their nature are, for Nicholas, the 'saintly spirits', whose very being is an outpouring of praise:

> The more they love, the more praise they voice; and the more they praise, the more praise they themselves obtain and the more closely they draw near unto Him who is infinitely praiseworthy, even though they will never arrive at equality with Him.[92]

Since our being flows from God's praise, our praise returns our being to Being itself. A true life in this way is a *vita laudis*, a virtuous life in which the overflow that radiates from our being becomes *expressive*—whose very being is a song. Nicholas exemplifies this by drawing on the archetypal figure of David, the singer-of-praises *par excellence*, enlarging this example to encompass an anthropology of praise:

> Three things are required if there is to be the singing of psalms: a harp composed of two things—viz., of a sound-board and of strings—and a harp-player: in other words, intelligence, nature, and an object. The harp-player is the intelligence, the strings are the nature, which is moved by the intelligence, and the sound-board is [the object], which befits the nature.[93]

To praise is thus a creative playing of the music of our nature, which paradoxically also *is* our nature: we are, as it were, Psalmic beings. But the linguistic economy of praise is here not only that of a signifier to a signified but also, more importantly, that of a lover to a beloved: language itself, then, is underwritten by its potentiality to become a purely loving gift. In other words, Cusa's science of praise implicitly locates language as something which, in equating being, gift and speech, presents the essential orientation of one's being to reality as an act of utterance. This authentic speech results in an everlasting movement of closeness, an asymptotic 'never arriving at equality' but always 'drawing near' as that of a lover who desires an intimacy that *exceeds* the simple flatness of self-identical union.

Again, this 'drawing near' to the divine through praise is paradoxically also a mode of knowledge. As he puts it, 'in this field of praise I have grasped the fact that very delicious knowledge consists in praise for God, who fashioned all things from out of His praises and for the purpose of their praising Him'.[94] Language can be donated because we were first given, along with language, in a great twofold act of creation and laudation. 'To give' and 'to speak' are so proximal because God-the-infinitely-praiseworthy is, paradoxically, the first to *give* praise. If God's act of creation and God's act of praise belong together, to speak authentically is somehow to speak in the sway of God's own acknowledgement of the goodness of creation in Genesis—it is in some sense, to be caught in the interplay between two affirmations, 'God said' and 'God saw', the verbs that ensoul the dynamic of the seven days of creation. Hence, to know something of God's nature entails a knowledge of the nature of things since, as God shows in Genesis, *to affirm the goodness in things is to know them for what they are*. Praise is truly a kind knowledge, then, and its expression is not the aesthetic judgement of a sovereign rationality or a Kantian transcendental subject, but is first of all a relational, creative affirmation that participates in both *posse* and *est*. As Nicholas puts it, it is a drawing near to God, who is 'not [someone] who partakes of praise but is Absolute Praise itself'.[95]

It is in this sense, too, that praise 'belongs' to God: not merely that God is due praise, but because this mode of speech is God's vision 'in the beginning'. As I have suggested, in the beginning, the sight of God— 'And God saw that it was good'—touches the creation with a laudatory affirmation of its very being. In his spiritual treatise *De Visione Dei* (1453), written as a meditation on the all-seeing 'Icon of God' for the Benedictine monks at Tegernsee, Cusa declares this very truth:

> I stand before the image of Your Face, my God—an image which I behold with sensible eyes. And I attempt to view with inner eyes the truth which is pointed to by the painting. And it occurs to me, O Lord, that Your gaze speaks; for Your speaking is none other than Your seeing.[96]

Visually, the painting 'points to' God, but it does so by *speaking to* Nicholas. To be seen by God is to be seen in all our goodness, and such speaking gaze coincides in some sense with the human speech that can laud the good. In affirming and articulating the Good, we speak *to* God, and thus are seen *by* God. This 'occurrence' reveals itself to the Cardinal not as a result of an abstract philosophical cogitation, but moved by the spiritual *praxis* of ascent, the contemplation of a mystery: a contemplation that *speaks* and so moves the speaker to speak.

As I suggested above, *Scientia laudis* is also not merely the fruit of a mystical ascent to the vision of God, but an explicit attempt to join together word and world, since it is speech that, in speaking, somehow participates in the First Praise. As was argued above, Nicholas' neologism *possest* came into being to hold together possibility and actuality and thus join what voluntarist and nominalist theologies had begun to sunder apart. Yet again, that name itself was not a solution to an abstract intellectual difficulty, but an embedded response to a profoundly disorienting theological situation, an attempt to reunite the life of genuine faith with that of noetic contemplation. Ultimately, *possest* evokes the divine coincidence of nature and artifice, poetics and being, in the light of a source that transcends both. As Nicholas himself notes at the close of *De Venatione Sapientiae*:

> Therefore, since I see that *possest* is the Cause of all praiseworthy things and that all ten praiseworthy [properties] are praiseworthy because of their partaking of praise, I call *possest* Praise which is that which it can be, because it is the Fount and Cause of praiseworthy things. And so, not inappropriately, I praise *possest* as Praise, since the great prophet Moses says in his song: "The Lord is my Praise."[97]

Thus, for Cusa, the doxological *élan*, so fundamental to our being, coincides with the mysterious nature of God, at once dynamic and actual, being and underway. As the name of God, *possest* intimates the plenitude of all that can be praised, and shows how the 'Psalmic', laudatory and 'poetic' orientation of our being begins to voice into song what it can come to know, a glimmer of the mysteries of God's own life.

Calling and Responding: The Voices of the Soliloquy

So far, I have argued that for Cusa, authentic speech is grounded in an orientation of being whose art creates the 'fitting' coincidence of opposites of natural and arbitrary names. Since the original speech is that creative and laudatory mode of praise, all other modes of language are somehow derivations of the primary utterance, God's creative speech, the 'speaking gaze' which sees all things as Good and thus affirms their being. Yet we have also seen that God is also dynamically unfolded in creation, entangled in human creative endeavours: one could say God is both First Praise and praise-yet-underway. This implies a generous reading of the various inflections of human language as somehow already implicitly involved in the call to praise: a call which can be responded to, but also ignored, shirked or refuted.

With this approach to language in mind, the next three sections begin a gradual transition from Cusa to Shakespeare. Bringing together Cusan insights with Shakespearean themes in dialogue with contemporary voices, I will seek to show how the lure of praise always already underscores human speech, in its relations with things and with beings, with humans and with the world. It is this approach to language that will ground my primary readings of the plays in Chapters 3 and 4.

This section explores the phenomenon of praise as *a response* to the call of the First Praise, through an engagement with this theme in Jean-Louis Chrétien's work. Chrétien's own treatment of the soliloquy as a form of response provides a bridge to begin teasing out some of these themes in Shakespeare's language, and this section concludes with a brief reading from *King Lear*.

As I have already argued, God's praise always already *precedes* our own in that it coincides with God's act of creative seeing. Thus, in genuine speech our voice is—literally—first given to us by God, as the Psalmist sings: '[f]or there is not a word in my tongue, but lo, thou knowest it wholly, O Lord. Thou holdest me strait behind and before, and layest thine hand upon me' (139:4–6).[98] Hence, words are not spoken in an unresponsive vacuum but are always already a response to an encounter, in a world predisposed to such encounters. Praise arises insofar as we ourselves encounter the primeval act of praise in which we ourselves were fashioned. The First Praise, out of which all things were created, thus somehow underwrites our praises; we speak because we have first been called, addressed and apprehended by that First Speech. The famous opening of Augustine's *Confessions* powerfully illustrates the draw on our being that emanates from this original address: 'You arouse us so that praising you may bring us joy, because you have made us toward yourself [*ad te*], and our heart is unquiet until it rests in you'.[99] From this point of view, our speech glows with the radiance of this desire because it is already oriented 'toward' the object of this desire. Such desire, expressing itself in speech, is in some sense a response to that aboriginal call which, for Cusa as for Augustine, transforms the entirety of created being into a world of signs.[100] Human speech is thus framed by a relationship that spans creatures and creator, time and eternity, beginning and end: it is no longer merely speaking but always speaking *to*; and not merely speaking *to*; but replying, *responding*. 'To speak of response', writes Rowan Williams, 'is to gesture towards the primary reality of *address*, an address to which we are always subsequent, even a gift which we are seeking to receive appropriately'.[101] How we respond to this call and receive this gift bears witness to this 'address', made not only in speech but even with the language of what Martin Buber calls 'primary words', that is, the relational expression of our being.[102] This latter point makes the word 'response' particularly pertinent, as its semantic field evokes an ethical bearing: response is also a commitment, a 'pledge' (intimated by the Latin word *spondere*); it is *responsibility*. Again, the aim here is not to collapse all language into *explicit* response to God, but to discern the response to the primary address as a dimension interlaced into all language.

Jean-Louis Chrétien's writings are deeply grounded in an exploration of the interweaving between speech, voice and language in the light of the primacy of response, so much so that one recent commentator has proposed the term 'responsorial thought' as an adequate rubric for his work.[103] But Chrétien's idiosyncratic writings do not easily fit classification. Since his first work *Lueur du Secret* (1985), Chrétien has sought to move beyond traditional philosophical requirements for univocal transparency and the hegemony of a concept of 'language', and towards that of the human *voice* as a phenomenological reality.[104] This is perhaps because, as Camille Riquier points out, Chrétien's work modulates his descriptive-phenomenological exploration to stay rigorously true to a lived, fragile experience: in his work, 'it is no longer a matter of text and discourse, but of voice, no longer interpretation and reception, but hospitality, no prediction or rules, but promise, neither transparency, but nakedness, neither indeed of language, but of speech'.[105]

For Chrétien, then, the primacy of the *call* permeates the phenomenon of the human speech. As with Augustine (his theological reference point) and Cusa, speech is for Chrétien understood at the level of the response of our whole being to a call that precedes and orients it—a response, for him, voiced not merely in our words, but also in our silences, in our gestures and in the manifold sensorial life of our bodies. Yet, he also seeks to show that the primacy of the call does not simply postulate a 'calling power' in the sense of a definable something or someone calling us. The phenomenon of the call, more subtle and more immediate, becomes rather fully manifest *only* in the response, such as the response to beauty, which shows that 'it is only when I respond to [the call of beauty] with wounded joy, with enthrallment, with desire, with my exclamations that [the call] *ensues as call*'.[106] The human voice becomes the prime corporeal locus of our response; it is in fact first and foremost a home, a dwelling place for the call, a place where it can become 'worded', and so comes to dwell among us.[107]

It is thus the call that precedes human dialogue and human speech, embracing and bearing witness to the manifold ways in which we communicate. As Chrétien points out,

> to make interhuman dialogue subordinate to the response to a call is not to restraint or lessen the importance of this dialogue, neither is it to place the ineffable before and beyond speech. Whatever the call, indeed, whether silent, or arising from that which is not human, it remains the case that I hear it, and that I respond to it only by hearing it. I hear it only in language and according to language, every call reaches me according to the *Logos*, and even the *verbum mentis* is a kind of language.[108]

Speech is thus not a venturing of words into nothingness, nor is it a frail communicative bridge across the chasm of irreducible alterity, but is always already interwoven with the attentiveness of our being to other voices. Listening is in some sense, the *first* response, the first speech: it is 'what founds any possible community' because 'between our ears and our voice, other voices and other kinds of listening are equally active'[109]; it is a 'dispossession', a self-effacement, not a knowing posture; a genuine 'learned ignorance'.[110] The foundation stone of speech is *attention*—that is, a careful aliveness to the realities of speech. The call heard in this attentive receptivity calls forth speech as response with a sharp, lived urgency, that gives our words a timbre vibrating in subtler frequencies than the dull sound of frivolous argumentation.[111]

But the call is a genuine call only if it calls for both response (*répondre à*) and responsibility (*répondre de*).[112] This responsive/responsible aspect in fact becomes the arbiter of the *binding* nature of speech and guarantees the primacy of the call-response. On the other hand, speaking with no relationship to the urgency of the call makes language 'profuse and labyrinthine', open to the dissimulations of sophistry. Indeed, to shirk the call, to elide it, to ignore it, are *also* manifold forms of responses: 'flight before God, hatred of beauty, misology, evasion before the other' are modes of responding, a response that evades its responsible aspect and thus becomes a form of dissembling speech, divided against itself.[113]

68 Approach

This is equally the case in the word that calls attention away from genuine response, the 'seductive word' that speaks only to be heard and thus, as such, does not listen, does not heed.[114] Speech that fails to listen is speech *without responsibility*, an attempt to shun or sidestep the inescapably primal nature of speech as binding, as 'pledge' (*respondere*).

Paradoxically, the responsive structure of speech is developed in Chrétien's descriptions of soliloquies and solitary responses, and their relationship with the register of prayer. Solitary speech once again illustrates the aboriginal primacy of the call as the founding event of the response: the possibility to respond to oneself, to address oneself is also what makes possible one's responsibility towards others. This self-address and self-response, however, does not inaugurate speech. It is not the act of an already-constituted, sovereign *cogito* transparent to itself, but is precisely that through which the self constitutes itself: we are, in other words, as our responses are.[115] Drawing on ancient Greek tragedies, as well as the words of the Psalmist and the ubiquitous influence of Augustine, Chrétien explores the reaches and inflections of responsive solitary language, of which the language of prayer becomes the phenomenon *par excellence*. Prayerful language, addressed to—because *called by*—the divine *Thou,* also illuminates the interlacing and belonging to one another of speech to oneself and speech to God.[116] For the Psalmist, it is because of the original response of God to humans in the covenant that one can address oneself: remembering, chiding, encouraging oneself in the light of God's first response.[117] The language of prayer is then the language that is first given to us by God in the beginning, as a gift, and that underwrites the spectrum of prayer in all its articulation, from the doubtful and despairing to the joyful and the exultant. Prayer is thus not a kind of speech; rather, *speech as such always shimmers with a kind of prayer.*

This reading of prayer as a mode of speech that is somehow involved with all speech suggests how Chrétien's responsorial approach might relate to Shakespeare. There are, of course, many prayers in Shakespeare's works; some offered by the poet of the Sonnets, some in the plays, given by characters to one another, some half-formed, ambiguous, distractedly muttered in an aside or spoken in a soliloquy. John Cox has rightly noted that the 'multiform and ubiquitous' character of prayer-language in Shakespeare makes it hard to fully distinguish from the multitude of speech-acts Shakespeare uses.[118] As Cox shows, the language of prayer in Shakespeare inherits not merely its petitionary register, but the early modern understanding of prayer as a 'means of self-formation', a speaking of the self before God.[119] Yet, this self-forming is possible because, following Chrétien, we express through its response what is at stake for us, what calls us. This is a vital part of what we give, or return, to God. The language of prayer, because it is first of all susceptible to be 'wounded' by the Divine *Thou*, reveals the orientation of our responses.[120] In such speech, writes Chrétien,

> another has silently introduced himself in my dialogue with myself, and has radically transformed and broken it... it is precisely because I am not talking to myself, I am not talking for myself, that my own speech, altered at its very origins, and perhaps before that, turns back on me with singular force.[121]

Thus, the prayerful dimension forms the speaking self by revealing its responses.

Yet, as Chrétien shows, even my singular response is polyphonic: it articulates the music of a dialogue in which, by means of *responses*—appeals, apostrophes, allocution—I discover myself as speaker among other speaking beings. Here, the responsorial element suggested by the ubiquitous and half-defined register of prayer in Shakespeare is more clearly evidenced in the theatrical soliloquy. Soliloquies in Shakespeare often function in creative interplay with classical rhetorical conventions of dramatic rhetoric, dancing between forensic, deliberative and epideictic modes.[122] Yet, these speeches do not occur as standalone rhetorical displays, but amidst the multivocal complexities of the dramatic action.[123] In speaking them, the characters do not abstract themselves from the linguistic world of the play in order to express a kind of emerging inwardness that is too easily assumed to be an effect of early modern culture. As Brian Cummings observes, 'the Shakespearian soliloquy does not arrive out of nowhere as the expression of a newly minted secular interiority'.[124] Instead of a 'transparent revelation of the self', Cummings notes, soliloquizing is a 'rhetorical and experimental' exercise; less the exposure of an already-organised inner truth waiting only to be voiced, and more of a dialogical search, 'a literary form which gets at truth through its own process of enquiry'.[125] Seeing the root of the soliloquy in this form of spiritual exercise, Cummings quotes Augustine's own paradoxical adage: *et cum ipso me solo coram te*—'with myself all alone in front of you'.[126] The Shakespearean soliloquy then, is as 'hybridized mode of speech' in which characters debate, dialogue, admit, affirm and hide their own thoughts and their own being in response to the manners in which they are addressed: the quality of being *in front of* the divine *Thou* permeates their speech while not reducing it to self-transparent thinking.[127]

Soliloquies are thereby primary instances in which to glean this oriented, responsorial element in Shakespearean language. In fact, even while sophisticated rhetorical manoeuvring in soliloquies ambiguates and dissimulates, in some sense expressing an *avoidance* of the call, they nevertheless all the more *reveal* the responsive orientation of characters.

One can read, for example, Edmund's famous address to a 'Goddess Nature' in *King Lear* (1.2.1–22) as a speech which, masquerading as a rational, self-possessed, deliberative *oratio*, is nonetheless full of numerous half-spoken contradictions which eventually *collapse* its rhetorical logic.

> Thou, Nature, art my goddess; to thy law
> My services are bound. Wherefore should I
> Stand in the plague of custom, and permit
> The curiosity of nations to deprive me,
> For that I am some twelve or fourteen moon-shines
> Lag of a brother? Why bastard? wherefore base?
> When my dimensions are as well compact,
> My mind as generous, and my shape as true,
> As honest madam's issue? Why brand they us
> With base? with baseness, bastardy? Base, base?
>
> (*KL* 1.2.1–10)

This is a speech which is a cry for liberty, yet is also tortuously imprisoned by its very language. As A. D. Cousins and Daniel Derrin remark, '[r]epudiating the concept of illegitimacy, [Edmund] cannot free himself from its lexicon'.[128] His obsessive repetitions of the various terms associated with its socio-cultural semantic field—'legitimate', 'base', 'baseness', 'bastard' and 'bastardly'—show his dependence on the very conventions he seems intent to break, just as his argument against 'custom' is in fact a customary thesis against humanist orthodoxy often voiced in the Renaissance. Though seemingly addressed to 'Nature', the speech is in fact directed to himself and his preoccupation with derivation and deprivation. The rhetorical *Thou* is here in fact an *It*, denoting an absence of genuine relation both to 'Nature' and, ultimately—as the play shows—to himself.[129] His response to the unjust and arbitrary customs that suffocate the world of *King Lear* is merely to affirm the same self-possession and malcontent at divestiture that the 'opposing' party, the King and his own father, will both come to decry.

Hence, this speech is at once a kind of response *and* an inability to *truly* respond: language initially spoken in an apostrophic mode of praise to a transcendent other—'Thou, Nature'—becomes caught in a lexical labyrinth that, while gesturing at an imagined self-sovereignty, a freedom from 'the plague of custom', is nevertheless warped, limited by the very convention he seeks so desperately to shake off. Though called to affirm, articulate and praise the Good, Edmund's speech cannot move beyond the metaphysics of self-sovereignty he is attempting to vindicate. In place of the divine as the locus and goal of authentic address, Edmund has posited a truncated image of himself as the begetter and motivator of language. Though his argument may motivate the audience's sympathy, Edmund's triumphant speech exposes its deeper fault-lines; it is an address which is in fact 'self-directed, deliberative but also self-disordered and self-defeating', a response which cannot *truly* respond to the situation in which he finds himself, because too implicated in the rhetorical manoeuvres that have helped bring it about.[130] Chapter 3 will further develop these themes with regard to the whole play.

The Liturgical and the 'Middle-Voice'

If the soliloquizing self is not a self-possessed Cartesian *cogito* speaking in the metaphysical vacuum of the subject-object duplex, as Chrétien suggests, but is the 'wounded' bearer of a response to a call, the question of the self as responding speaker is brought into play. How does the voice that is responsive to a call which is also a gift truly speak in the mode of gift? And, how could such a theological notion bring new light to a conception of Shakespearean language? The following suggests, through a dialogue with the work of Catherine Pickstock, an appropriate construal of this doxological 'speaker', one that suggests the 'liturgical' as its primary category. The following argument, positing the realm of the liturgical as both the roots and *telos* of language, further suggests the viability and relevance of a doxological approach to Shakespeare by means of a brief survey of recent debates on characterisation.

As was discussed in Chapter 1, the 20th century saw the emergence of a kind of Shakespeare criticism which argued for the pre-eminence of power-driven 'social energy' as against the idea of an autonomous, self-transparent *cogito*. For the New Historicists, as we saw, the human self was only ever a cultural artefact, an epiphenomenon, made 'tongue-tied by authority', determined and terminally haunted by Edmund's 'plague of custom'.[131] Yet, the movement beyond this anti-humanist mode of scholarship and its theoretical hegemony has lead recent Shakespeare scholars to a reconsideration of a concept of selfhood increasingly freed from the postmodern embarrassment associated with this notion.[132] Strange as it might have seemed 20 years ago, it is now once again possible to assume that Shakespearean drama might have an ethical dimension, that characters face *genuinely responsible* moral decisions and that their responses, in language and in action, bear freedom and authenticity. Summarising the debates between the notions of moral autonomy (inherited from the Kantian tradition) and postmodern 'determinism' that so captured the imagination of 20th-century Shakespeare scholarship, Patrick Gray and John Cox suggest a useful early modern analogy. This doublet, they argue, is not the creation of contemporary scholarship, but arose along with the renewed interest in the classics in the Renaissance, which mandated authors and thinkers to cast their net further than the traditional Aristotelian and Neoplatonic sources, and ensured the significant cultural revivals of Skepticism, Stoicism and Epicureanism. In *Julius Caesar*, for example, Shakespeare searchingly theatricalises the philosophical positions of Stoicism, particularly in a longing for the detached autonomy and self-control associated with self-poise, or *ataraxia*.[133] Yet, conversely, currents emanating from the Reformation severely challenged this sense of moral autonomy and self-determination, stressing instead fallen humanity's complete dependence on a wholly transcendent divine grace for redemption. For Cox and Gray, just as the neoclassical concept of detached moral agency prefigures Enlightenment rational autonomy, radical (predestinarian) brands of Protestantism provides an early modern analogue of postmodern deterministic and anti-humanist pessimism.[134] It is in his engagement with these lively debates over the notions of the self that, for Cox and Gray, the reach of Shakespeare's ethical thought can be teased out.[135] While neither neoclassical autonomy nor radical self-dislocation constitute genuine selfhood, Gray has suggested a dialogically open, Shakespearean 'vulnerable self' as a middle point between the two.[136]

My suggestion here is to supplement the dialogical with the doxological. Shakespeare, I contend, does not hesitate between, but rather *resolves* these apparently contradictory positions, in understanding genuine speech as an act of love that responds to the call of the divine *Thou*. In line with moral agency, such speech arises and expresses the orientation of our being. Yet, this manner of speech is *also* a gift that is begotten from love itself, and is thus also to some extent a displacing of stable selfhood and an awaiting of a bestowal from beyond. Hence, doxological speech expresses a Cusan, paradoxical 'coincidence of opposites': neither fully in command nor radically disempowered, it is intrinsically *middle-voiced*. Seen from this point of view, the speech of praise transcends both a mimetic figuration of the interiority of an autonomous self and the sense of a determined product of subterranean *or* supernatural workings.

Appealing to the doxological register as a truly self-forming, middle-voiced practice suggests the metaphysical and theological inflections of 'the ritual' and 'the liturgical'.[137] Combining metaphysics, poetics and theology, Catherine Pickstock's singular work on these categories attempts to reflect on liturgical practice as both the ground and consummation of language, religious life and human reflection. For Pickstock, the pre-eminence of the liturgical touches on the mysterious primacy of a symbolic theurgic *praxis* that unites art and life, suggesting, in turn, that it is the gift-like nature of such performance that in some way precedes and grounds an instrumental stance to language, rather than the other way around.[138] If language is grounded in donative ritual, its roots are entwined in a particular kind of complex performance and sacramental play. The mysteriously primordial quality of liturgy and ritual are at once what grants theological reflection and yet, as its foundational impulse, remains beyond its grasp.[139] To think of a liturgical 'self' gestures towards the paradoxicality of an identity constituted amidst other identities, who in their turn *enact* a manner of being, as they re-present and reproduce a cosmic dance with divinity, where copying, sign-making or what she calls 'non-identical repetition' are primary.[140] All this entails that the language of praise is to be understood in terms of a gratuitous and irreducibly polysemous mode of speech that at once grounds and eludes cognition.

For Pickstock, liturgical speech is middle-voiced: charged with the porous energies of ritual, it surpasses the aporia of the two kinds of selves mentioned above, for as she puts it, 'liturgical language is neither autonomously in command of itself, nor an instrument controlled invisibly by a lurking and manipulative power'.[141] Instead, since it is at once a gift from God and a sacrifice to God, liturgical language reformulates relationality, since it is 'a reciprocal exchange which shatters all ordinary positions of agency and reception'.[142] Yet, these positions are 'shattered' only to become strangely reconstituted, for praise involves a decentring giving away of oneself that results in the return of one's true nature in the manner of a gift. By offering to God, the doxological speaking subject enters the perpetual self-giving of the Trinity and thus at the same time, we 'enter into ourselves as genuine subjects—defined as that which offers gifts'.[143] For this to be genuine, however, it needs to coincide with a genuine expression of desire, a desire for 'partnership' or 'relationship' with the divine, a relationship which paradoxically 'already includes us' and thus redefines our relationship to one another, to things and to beings.[144] If *verbum* is a kind of *donum,* it is a *donum* in which I also find myself: as that which offers gift, the *I* here is not a self but a doxologue, a speaker of praise to the Good. Hence, the sense in which the term 'middle-voice' is used, not to single out a grammatical mode and to transcend reciprocal and self-reflexive speech, but instead serving 'to express the mediation of divine by human action'.[145] Of course, in one sense, its ecstatic mode gives voice to an 'impossible' return, since there can be no 'return' for the gift which God gives that can be subject to a simple law of exchange. But rather than signifying an otherworldly terminus that words can never reach, God's distance is *itself* a gift, awakening true desire in the soul: and '[i]t is in and through this gift of distance that we receive God into our bodies, in such a way that we are given to comprehend transcendent "distance" as coinciding with the moment of optimum and penetrative relationality'.[146]

For Pickstock, liturgical speech gives the possibility for both a 'redemptive restoration of genuine subjectivity', and a new relationship with the world, a 'dismantling of the "object" as that which does not exceed its physical extension'.[147] This turn to the liturgical thus speaks to my concern for the embodied and material elements of speech already alluded to in my discussion of Williams in Chapter 1. Indeed, by involving sensual intelligence, embodiment and play, the moment of 'liturgy' or 'ritual' also intimates that there is infinitely more to *logos* than verbalised language, infinitely more to speech than voiced words. Here, the middle-voice also constitutes the summoning of a certain orientation of the soul, which is conjured up by the mingling of performed text and embodied ritual. Indeed, the emphasis on embodied performance in liturgy, Pickstock shows, articulates the mystery of the incarnation, reaching into the depth of the human person and permitting a participatory kinship with animality and organic being—with the whole of the physical cosmos, in some sense—that abstract, disembodied cognition cannot reach. Such practices constitute a particular mode of drawing near to the divine, for even

> [t]he dumb simplicity and lack of reflexivity in physical things, or the spontaneity of animals, show to us aspects of the divine simplicity and spontaneity itself, which cannot be evident to the somewhat reflective, discursive, and abstracting operation of limited human or angelic minds.[148]

Sacramental signs are thus more than symbolic or metaphorical: they have 'a *heuristic* function... they prompt us to new thought and guide us into deeper modes of meditation because they contain a surplus that thought never fully fathoms'.[149] Such heuristic aspects also reconcile the lure of the divine with the lure of things and beings, since liturgy enacts the divine closeness to things and to beings, and in doing so also enacts the closeness of things and beings to the divine.

Echoing in a different context, the Renaissance tradition of *serioludere*,[150] liturgy is itself a serious kind of play: a play that is also a pledge (*spondere*), performed for its own sake rather than as an item in a kind of spiritual utility calculus: in such a play, the senses can be 'deployed, liturgically, to restore the mind'.[151] Yet, liturgy is also the most serious event, because it embodies and re-enacts the cosmic drama of fall and redemption, and unites the frailties and hardships of life with the truth-bearing faculty of *mimesis*. Thus, paradoxically, the human person becomes most herself when she is most a work of art: when 'we are transformed into a wholly signifying—because worshipping—body, we are at that moment closest to our fulfilment as human beings'.[152] Voicing the speech of praise and worship in this dramatic manner, liturgical speech is a mode of participation in the creation as sanctified and redeemed by the incarnation, which is 'the first liturgy and the continuing inner reality of our own liturgies'.[153] This creative, open-ended surplus, the speech of the middle-voice, is the heuristic function of praise, and brings us again to Cusa's *scientia laudis* and its curious commerce between knowing and praising. Here, liturgy is the instance in which language, middle-voiced, becomes superabundantly charged with its doxological roots.

Uniting *mimesis* and authenticity, seriousness and play, art and life, such speech has an *irreducibly* performative dimension: it must be embodied and enacted. In its heuristic function, it is also open-ended, oriented eschatologically towards a fulfilment beyond time. Yet, it is also an acknowledgement of incompleteness *in* time which hallows this self as responsorial, open to love, acknowledge and forgive *and* to be loved, acknowledged and forgiven, thus redeeming and restoring relationships.[154] Hence, in some sense, both the desire for controlled autonomy and the sense of radical dispossession are superseded, or rather, transmuted into gifts offered to God's love and mercy. It is such a wondrous acknowledgement of incompleteness that brings about a surprising completeness, according with the communal nature of the liturgy, for the gift offered back by doxological language is 'the relational reception and bestowal of peace', ultimately the 'vision of sacral community as consummating space and time'.[155] This vision of a transfigured community is, as I will show in Chapter 4, also at the heart of post-tragic Shakespearean drama. As we will see, there is in *The Winter's Tale* a tending towards this mode of participatory 'serioludic' dimension, and a final, yet elliptical, suggestion that an authentic human community coincides with this ritual participation—as though the cosmos, throughout the play, has been felicitously prepared to perform one great theurgic rite.

Response as Responsibility: The Hospitality of Words

We have seen that this middle-voiced approach, as exemplified in the liturgy, suggests a modulated return to the notion of 'responsibility', since now it appears no longer as the response of a morally autonomous self, nor is it 'impossible' in either a radical-Protestant nor a postmodern sense, haunted by irreducible alterity. Its particular 'embodied' mode suggests a further participatory correlation. As we have also seen, the liturgical body participates in the body of Christ—the body of the Word—and so also, mimetically, touches all other bodies, from inorganic being to animality. Returning to Chrétien and to Cusa, this final section suggests how the doxological approach, in its responding to the call, also must affirm and articulate the material world.

Chrétien considers human response and responsibility in precisely this embodied sense: he sees the human voice a being able to extend *hospitality* to all things in giving, as Theseus might put it, 'a local habitation and a name'.[156] His notion of hospitality begins in silence; but for him, even silence already speaks, wording in attention and listening the first hospitality of speech.[157] Here, as Cusa would say, 'to be silent is to speak'.[158] As speech arises into dialogue, voices become formed

76 Approach

and words exchanged, hospitality becomes synonymous with dialogue, 'and yet this conversation cannot take in a vacuum: it is in the world, this world we never cease to share—among ourselves but also with other forms of presence, the presence of animals, of vegetal being, of things'.[159] Our dialogue with one another thus takes place in a dialogue both *in* and *with* the world: the speech of the creation makes itself felt in our creative voices.[160] In the first human speech, figured in the Bible through the naming of the creatures by Adam, names become praises: 'the first guardians' of animals, their first 'safeguard' *against* seizing and controlling instrumentality.[161] Humanity is thus defined both by its relationship to God in whose image it is created, and in its relation to all other things and beings, with whom it is constantly speaking.[162] *With* whom, rather than merely *to* whom: for the earth too speaks, and its voice enters our responses to constitute together a gift of offering.[163]

For Chrétien, this manner of offering calls for both a sense of moral responsibility and the poetic and creative extensions of our expression: again, 'speech is antiphonal, responds by listening, listens by responding, by translating the silence' into word.[164] The poetic voice, along with the human, has ultimate 'priestly' qualities: 'The poet wants the world to concelebrate its praise with him, and he with the world. In this multiple *yes*, which the world bears in it and which we bring to song', human beings 'make it inhabitable. For a world without poetry is uninhabitable'.[165] Hence, the human voice has a cosmic-liturgical function: 'It is by being sung that the world is properly a world'—and yet also a responsive and responsible function since 'we cannot sing the world unless the world itself sings already'.[166] Here, the praising, poetic voice implies a dialogue with things that heeds their own call, felt at the edges of speech.

This offering to God is also an offering back to the world, since 'it returns from it clarified and enriched, and not destroyed'.[167] What is being returned has been enriched with the laudatory brightness peculiar to poetry, to hymn.[168] It is in this mode of relationship, implying listening, creative responding and safeguarding, that our speech can become a 'welcome place' from the world, an 'Ark of Speech' proper, in which the world is nurtured and safeguarded from destruction and death. It is an Ark which, by enabling us to be hospitable and thus safeguard the creation, 'first safeguards us'.[169] The human voice, then, becomes a temple, a place of worship and gift, where the language of praise can articulate its cosmic dimension and become 'a place in which the world can return to God'.[170]

Cusa too draws the cosmic implications of God's word as both creative *and* redemptive, thus *summoning* the material world to arise and inhabit the real. The continuum that gathers together earthly and human voices is thus continuous with God's creative speech:

> By Your Word You speak to all existing things, and You summon into being non-existing things. Therefore, You summon them in

order that they may hear You; and when they hear You, they exist. Therefore, when You speak, You speak to all; and all the things to which You speak hear You. You speak to the earth, and You summon it to [become] human nature; and the earth hears You, and its hearing is its becoming human. You speak to nothing as if it were something, and You summon nothing to [become] something; and nothing hears You, because that which was nothing becomes something. O Infinite Power, Your conceiving is Your speaking.[171]

If we interpret 'its hearing is its becoming human' in the light of the above, we encounter again the human voice as the sanctuary of creation, the place which heeds the call and can offer back the material world to God, in a way that also re-affirms it.

This suggestive image also recalls a theme in Nicholas' mystical contemplation alluded to above: God's speaking gaze. For in his meditative contemplation of the Icon in *De Visione Dei*, Cusa discovers the coincidence between God and the things God has spoken into being: 'O God, You have led me to the place where I see Your Absolute Face to be the natural Face of all nature, the Face which is the Absolute Being of all being'.[172] This is what Jacob Sherman refers to as Cusa's 'paniconism'[173]; all things are icons of God and take their being in the light of God's speaking gaze: 'You appeared to me as visible by all [creatures] because a thing exists insofar as You see it, and it would not exist actually unless it saw You. For Your Seeing gives being, because [Your seeing] is Your essence'.[174] To know God is therefore not to leave the world behind but to see the creation as speaking forth, however mysteriously, the speech of God, in and through which they have their own being. Responding to what is calling out to him, Nicholas sees that his response already actualises the gift present in the call itself:

> How will my prayer reach You who are altogether unreachable? How will I entreat You? For what is more absurd than to ask that You, who are all in all, give Yourself to me? How will You give Yourself to me unless You likewise give me the sky and the earth and everything in them? Indeed, how will You give Yourself to me unless You also give me myself? And while I am quietly reflecting in this manner, You, O Lord, answer me in my heart with the words: "Be yours and I will be yours!".[175]

Here, Nicholas voices how the voice becomes a dwelling place for creation: by receiving the creation as gift, he receives himself as gift, and thereby returns both, in his 'entreaty', as *gifts*. In this sense, the 'Ark of Speech' belongs to the continuum of vision that is God's speaking gaze: doxology is not merely praise of the transcendent Good, but a praise of all that is good and bears the imprint of the Good itself. The voice that loves the creation is the voice that articulates the donated nature of the

78 *Approach*

world. It is in this sense that human beings, situated 'on the horizon of time and perpetuity' can participate in the continuum that is wisdom, which unite those two dimensions—so that we may become, as he puts it, 'the ligature of the universe'.[176] Approached doxologically, language is therefore a mode of care or, to say again what has been said above, a response that 'pledges' care, a response that is also responsible.

How does Shakespeare reveal this aspect of human speech, its deep calling to be hospitable to the world? And how does this notion of the 'Ark of Speech' as the safeguard of creation take place amidst the density of the drama? The next two chapters will explore how the redemption of speech also entails the redemption of the world—showing how the affirmation of the material world is intertwined with praise of its transcendent ground. It will be important then, to explore how *King Lear* and *The Winter's Tale* both portray the creation, which will entail a discussion of the polysemic concept 'nature', teasing out in what ways such a word might articulate a connection to things and to beings and, conversely, in what way the appeal to such a concept conceals a manner of isolation and alienation *from* such things and beings—a shirking of the call to praise.

Conclusion

In this chapter, I have given a broad framework for a doxological account of language. For Nicholas of Cusa, as we saw, praise is an affirmatory mode of love *and* a heuristic mode of knowledge, and a way to draw close to God, who is the 'First Praise'. Because all speech arises from the first praise, all speech is potentially praise. And as praise, words ring with inexhaustible love and affirmation for what is good, and for the Good from which all good springs. As such, praise is in some sense the ground *and* end of speech, its *arché* and *telos*. We have seen, too, that language is inhabited by a call to establish authentic relation, and that such relation is established in and through a laudatory affirmation of things, of beings and thus of God. This call also resounds in the creation, illuminated by its creator, and redemptive speech embraces the cosmos because the cosmos inhabits speech. The doxological speech is thus also an 'Ark', a mode of care which affirms and preserves the binding contract between word and world. The registers of liturgical expression, offering a participatory, middle-voiced mode of speech, affirm the primacy of donative speech over the instrumental or necessary.

To begin a transition towards the literary, I have supported my argument with considerations of some Shakespearean themes. As my next two chapters consist in primary readings of Shakespeare, it is important to stress that this doxological approach should not amount to a reduction to Shakespeare's seemingly boundless linguistic creativity to any 'pure' religious address—as though religious language can only be understood as opposite to or a subcategory of 'profane' speech. Instead, my readings will be concerned with discerning this doxological quality as an unalienable aspect of *all* speech. Reading in this key is inevitably ambitious, for it is an endeavour concerned with the whole spectrum of language and not merely its ecstatic reaches. Nevertheless, I hope to show in the next chapters that it is possible to read Shakespeare doxologically: maintaining an account of speech as praise that *also* attends to its numerous contradictions, irresolvable ambiguities and multiple, overlapping registers—from the bawdy to the poetic, the despairing to the exultant, the vituperative to the conciliatory—along a doxological continuity. The next two chapters, then, will be offering this account of speech as a key to the extraordinary cosmic dimensions of Shakespearean drama—this 'wide and universal theatre'.

Notes

1 An early version of the argument in this chapter appeared in V. Gerlier, 'Wonder, Adoration and the Ground of Language in Nicholas of Cusa', *Journal of Medieval Mystical Theology* 27.2 (2018), 89–102. I thank the Eckhart society for allowing me to reproduce its gist.
2 Hoff and Hampson, 'Cusa', 121.
3 For the former view, see Hans Blumemberg, *The Legitimacy of the Modern Age*, trans. Robert M. Wallace (Cambridge, MA: MIT Press, 1983); For the latter, Ernst Cassirer, *The Individual and the Cosmos in Renaissance Philosophy*, trans. Mario Domandi (Oxford: Blackwell, 1963). Numerous other scholars see Cusa as embracing either one or the other position: see Catalina M. Cubillos, 'Nicholas of Cusa between the Middle Ages and Modernity: The Historiographical Positions Behind the Discussion', *American Catholic Philosophical Quarterly* 86. 2 (2012), 237–249.
4 On this, see his *De Pace Fidei* (1453); a much more ambivalent treatment of Islam is given in his *Cribatio Alkorani* (1460).
5 In the sense suggested by Pierre Hadot in his *Philosophy as a Way of Life: Spiritual Exercises from Socrates to Foucault*, trans. Michael Chase (Oxford: Blackwell, 1995).
6 See Sherman, *Partakers*, 131–204.
7 On Cusa's use of humanist rhetoric, see Mauro Donnini, 'Niccolò Cusano e la Retorica', in *Niccolò Cusano: L'uomo, i Libri, L'Opera: Atti del 52° convegno storico internazionale* (Spoleto: Centro Italiano di Studi sul Basso Medioevo, 2016), 301–323. Donnini shows how Cusa dismisses rhetorical sophistry in his sermons, yet actively uses rhetorical ornament in his more speculative and mystical work.
8 This is the central argument of Peter Casarella's *Word as Bread*.
9 Hampson and Hoff, *The Brill Companion to Nicholas of Cusa*, 122. For 'doxological reduction', see Johannes Hoff, 'Mystagogy Beyond Onto-theology: Looking Back to Post-modernity with Nicholas of Cusa' (forthcoming).
10 See Chapter 1, 157n.
11 On this, see Thomas Wilson Hayes, 'Nicholas of Cusa and Popular Literacy in 17th Century England', *Studies in Philology* 84.1 (1987), 80–94. On John Donne specifically, see Catherine Gimelli Martin, 'The Erotology of Donne's "Extasie" and the Secret History of Voluptuous Rationalism',

Studies in English Literature, 1500–1900 44.1 (2004), 121–147; Kirsten Stirling, '"As a Picture That Looks Upon Him, That Looks Upon It": Cusanus in Donne's Sermons', *American Cusanus Society Newsletter* 35 (2018), 7–14.

12 Walter Kaiser, *Praisers of Folly: Erasmus, Rabelais, Shakespeare* (Cambridge, MA: Harvard UP, 1963), 9. See also Chris Hassel, *Faith and Folly in Shakespeare's Romantic Comedies* (Athens, GA: Georgia UP, 1980). On Shakespeare and the Erasmian tradition, see for example Indira Ghose, *Shakespeare and Laughter: A Cultural History* (Manchester: Manchester UP, 2008).

13 Kaiser, *Praisers*, 12.

14 *Ibid.*, 22.

15 For a New Historicist study linking Cusa and Shakespeare, see Ronald Levao, *Renaissance Minds and Their Fictions: Cusanus, Sidney, Shakespeare* (Berkeley, CA: UCAL, 1985). Levao sees Cusa as engaged in skilful yet unstable poetic negotiations with the tensions and ambiguities of their world, deploying 'the release of extraordinary ingenuity in a problematic universe', xxii.

16 Greenblatt, *Negotiations*, 95.

17 Louis Dupré, *Passage to Modernity: An Essay in the Hermeneutics of Nature and Culture* (New Haven, CT: YUP, 1993), 102–112.

18 For an introduction to the classical tradition and decline in the modern age of laudatory poetry, see J. A. Burrow, *The Poetry of Praise* (Cambridge: CUP, 2008).

19 Dupré, *Modernity*, 249.

20 *Ibid.*, 57–61; 167–189. See also 'Nature and Grace in Nicholas of Cusa's Mystical Philosophy', *American Catholic Philosophical Quarterly* 64.1 (1990), 153–170; Louis Dupré and Nancy Hudson, 'Nicholas of Cusa', in *A Companion to Philosophy in the Middle Ages*, ed. Jorge Gracia and Timothy Noone (Oxford: Blackwell, 2002), 466–474. Scholars who have advanced arguments for theological roots to modernity are too many to mention: for a few whose work is broadly pertinent to this study, see Amos Funkenstein, *Theology and the Scientific Imagination from the Middle Ages to the Seventeenth Century* (Princeton, NJ: Princeton UP, 1986); Michael Gillespie, *The Theological Origins of Modernity* (Chicago, IL: UCP, 2008); Brad Gregory, *The Unintended Reformation* (Cambridge, MA: Belknap Press, 2012); Milbank, *Social Theory*; Thomas Pfau, *Minding the Modern: Human Agency, Intellectual Traditions, and Responsible Knowledge* (Notre Dame, IN: Notre Dame UP, 2013).

21 Plato, *Phaedo*, 107b.

22 Dupré, *Modernity*, 39–40; 80–88; 105–112. For voluntarism on divine power, see 123–128; 176.

23 *Ibid.*, 87–88 and *passim*.

24 I use the capitalised 'Good' with reference to the 'goodness of being', as outlined in the Preface, and also with God's seeing of all things as good in Genesis – the latter is discussed in more detail below.

25 *Ibid.*, 176.

26 *Ibid.*, 124.

27 See Alain de Libera, *La querelle des universaux: de Platon à la fin du Moyen Age* (Paris: Seuil, 1996).

28 See Dupré, *Modernity*, 38–39. Dupré does not use the term 'univocity', though his analysis of nominalism greatly suggests it. For a critique of univocity and its relationship to modernity, see Catherine Pickstock, 'Duns Scotus: His Historical and Contemporary Significance', *MT* 21.4 (2005),

543–574; For a defence of univocity, see Richard Cross, 'Idolatry and Religious Language', *Faith and Philosophy* 25.2 (2008), 190–196.
29 On Chaucer, see Helen Ruth Andretta, *Chaucer's* Troilus and Criseyde: *A Poet's Response to Ockhamism* (New York: Lang, 1997); Richard Utz (ed.), *Literary Nominalism and the Rereading of Late Medieval Texts* (Lewiston, NJ: Edwin Mellen Press, 1995). On the Chester plays, see Kathleen Ashley, 'Divine Power in Chester Cycle and Late Medieval Thought', *Journal of the History of Ideas* 39 (1978), 387–404; Peter Travis, *Dramatic Design in the Chester Cycle* (Chicago, IL: UCP, 1982), 42–173. For Dupré, this metaphysical vacuum also had the unintended effect of creating 'a wider space for metaphorical creativity'. *Modernity*, 105.
30 Dupré, *Modernity*, 102–112; 119.
31 *Ibid.*, 104.
32 The term is Cusa's: see *Apologia Doctae Ignorantiae* 1–9. For a comprehensive review of Cusa's relationship to nominalism and voluntarism in qualified agreement with the views expressed in this chapter, see Meredith Ziebart, 'Cusanus and Nominalism', in *Nicholas of Cusa and Times of Transition: Essays in Honour of Gerald Christianson*, ed. Thomas M. Izbicki, Jason Aleksander and Donald F. Duclow (Boston, MA: Brill, 2019), 219–241; Casarella, *Word*, 266–274 and *passim*.
33 Hoff, 'Mystagogy'.
34 Hoff, *Analogical*, 25.
35 See Ziebart, *Nicholas of Cusa on Faith and the Intellect: A Case Study in 15th Century Fides-Ratio Controversy* (Boston, MA: Brill, 2013), 12ff.
36 For readings similar to Hoff's, see for example Michael E. Moore, *Nicholas of Cusa and the Kairos of Modernity: Cassirer, Gadamer, Blumemberg* (New York: Punctum, 2013); Kazuhiko Yamaki (ed.), *Nicholas of Cusa: A Medieval Thinker for the Modern Age* (Surrey: Curzon, 2002).
37 Cusa, *Sermo 1: In Principio Erat Verbum* (25 December 1430) and *VEN* (1462), 18–20.
38 For example, in *DDI*, 1.16.86–89. See also Peter Casarella, 'Cusanus on Dionysius: The Turn to Speculative Theology', *MT* 24.4 (2008), 667–678.
39 See Donald Duclow, *Masters of Learned Ignorance: Eriugena, Eckhart, Cusanus* (Aldershot: Ashgate, 2006).
40 Sherman, *Partakers*, 173.
41 Donald Duclow, 'Life and Works' in *Introducing Nicholas of Cusa: A Guide to a Renaissance Man*, ed. Christopher Bellitto, Thomas Izbicki and Gerald Christianson (New York: Paulist Press, 2002), 38.
42 The encounter with the layman and the orator is the subject of the first part of this two-volume dialogue, *Idiota de Sapientia*.
43 *DM*, 1.54.
44 *DM*, 2.58. Unless otherwise indicated, all references to Cusa's works are to *Complete Philosophical and Theological Treaties of Nicholas of Cusa*, trans. Jasper Hopkins, 2 vols. (Minneapolis, MN: Banning Press, 1998–2001) and *Nicholas Of Cusa's Early Sermons: 1430–1441*, trans. Jasper Hopkins (Minneapolis, MN: Banning Press, 2003).
45 *DM*, 2.59. Emphasis mine.
46 *Ibid.*
47 Jasper Hopkins, *Nicholas of Cusa on Wisdom and Knowledge* (Minneapolis, MN: Banning Press, 1996), 44.
48 Casarella, *Word*, 53.
49 *DM*, 2.63.
50 *Ibid.*, 2.62.
51 *Ibid.*, 2.59.

82 Approach

52 Hopkins, *Wisdom*, 44.
53 *DM*, 2.64.
54 *DM*, 2.69.
55 See *VEN*, 33.97.
56 *DM*, 2.61.
57 See *DM*, 13.147.
58 Robert Miner, *Truth in the Making: Creative Knowledge in Theology and Philosophy* (London: Routledge, 2004), 23.
59 *DM*, 2.68.
60 Louis Dupré, 'The Question of Pantheism from Eckhart to Cusanus' in *The Legacy of Learned Ignorance*, ed. Peter Casarella (Washington, DC: Catholic University of America Press, 2006), 74.
61 Cusa here is continuous with the late Neoplatonic tradition of Iamblichus and Proclus with regard to the presence of the transcendent within the immanent aspects of reality. See Gregory Shaw, *Theurgy and the Soul* (Kettering, OH: Angelico Press, 2014).
62 *Sermo* 20, 1.6.
63 Hoff, 'Mystagogy'.
64 *De Sapientia*, 2.33.
65 Hoff, 'Mystagogy'.
66 *De Principio*, 5.
67 Hoff, 'Mystagogy'.
68 *DDI*, 3.4.
69 David Albertson, 'That He Might Fill All Things: Creation and Christology in Two Treatises by Nicholas of Cusa', *International Journal of Systematic Theology* 8.2 (2006), 198.
70 Maurice de la Taille, *The Mystery of Faith and Human Opinion Contrasted and Defined*, trans. J. Schimpf (London: Sheed and Ward, 1930), 212. This is the phrase that so famously inspired David Jones. See his 'Art and Sacrament', in *Epoch and Artist: Selected Writings*, passim (London: Faber, 2017).
71 *De Coniecturis*, 14.143.
72 *DDI*, 3.11.247.
73 *VEN*, Prologue. Translation slightly altered.
74 Louis Dupré, 'Nature and Grace', 155–156. As Dupré notes, Cusa distinguishes possibility from creation in *VEN*, 3 precisely to overturn nominalists metaphysics, 'to reunite possibility with actual reality as two constitutive elements of one creative act'. *Ibid*.
75 *Ibid.*, 156.
76 *DP*, 27–29.
77 For John Milbank, Cusa maintained the analogical world view in full knowledge that to do so is to violate the principle of non-contradiction. 'Stanton Lecture 5: Participated Transcendence Reconceived': http://theologyphilosophycentre.co.uk/2011/03/12/john-milbanks-stanton-lectures-2011 (April 2020). See also Graham Priest, *Beyond the Limits of Thought* (Oxford: OUP, 2002), 24–25.
78 *DP*, 57.
79 *Ibid*.
80 Milbank, 'Stanton Lecture 8: The Surprise of the Imagined': http://theologyphilosophycentre.co.uk/2011/03/12/john-milbanks-stanton-lectures-2011 (April 2020).
81 *Ibid*.
82 *DP*, 15. Translation slightly altered. *Possest* later becomes *posse* in his *Compedium* (1464) and finally *posse ipsum* in *De Apice Theoriae* (1465)

but a speculative engagement with 'possibility' as a mystagogical name continued in his late work.
83 H. Lawrence Bond, 'Mystical Theology' in *Introducing*, Bellitto *et al.*, 220.
84 These properties are the good, the great, the true, the beautiful, the wise-making, the delightful, the perfect, the clear, the equal and the sufficient; *VEN*, 15.42.
85 *Ibid.*, 18.51.
86 See Gerlier, 'Incomprehensible Praise'.
87 *VEN*, 18.52.
88 *Ibid.*, 18.53.
89 *Ibid.*, 14.39.
90 *Ibid.*
91 *Ibid.*, 19.54.
92 *Ibid.*, 19.55.
93 *Ibid.*, 20.56.
94 *Ibid.*, 18.53.
95 *Ibid.*, 35.105.
96 *DVD*, 10.4.
97 *VEN*, 35.105.
98 Bible quotations are from the *The Geneva Bible* (1560) with spelling modernised to harmonise with quotes from Shakespeare used in this study.
99 Augustine, *Confessions* 1.1.1. The awkward translation here shows the point: as Robert McMahon points out, the Vulgate that would have been familiar to Augustine's contemporary readers renders 'in his image' of Genesis 1:26–27 as *ad imaginem*: that is, literally, 'toward [his] image'. *Meditative Ascent*, 67.
100 See, for example, *Compendium* 7 21. On this aspect of Augustine, see Rowan Williams, 'Language, Reality and Desire in Augustine's *De Doctrina*', in *Postmodernity*, Imfeld *et al.*, 253–268.
101 Williams, *Edge of Words*, 33.
102 Martin Buber, *I and Thou*, trans. Ronald Gregor Smith (Edinburgh: T&T Clark, 1959), 1–11 and *passim*.
103 Andrew Prevot, 'Responsorial Thought: Jean-Louis Chrétien's Distinctive Approach to Theology and Phenomenology', *Heythrop Journal* 56.6 (2015), 975–987.
104 On his own methodological commitments, see 'Essayer de penser au-delà de la subjectivité', Interview with Camille Riquier, *Critique* 790.3 (2013), 241–253.
105 Riquier, 'Jean-Louis Chrétien ou la parole cordiale', in *ibid.*, 196.
106 Chrétien, *Répondre: figures de la réponse et de la responsabilité* (Paris: P.U.F, 2007), 8. Here and below, my translations.
107 See Chrétien, *La voix nue: phénoménologie de la promesse* (Paris: Editions de minuit, 1990).
108 *Répondre*, 13–14. For Cusa's modification of the Thomistic-Augustinian sense of *verbum mentis*, see Casarella, *Word*, 34ff.
109 Chrétien, *The Ark of Speech*, trans. Andrew Brown (London: Routledge, 2004), 9.
110 *Répondre*, 12.
111 *Ibid.*, 22–23.
112 *Ibid.*, 14.
113 *Ibid.*, 16.
114 *Ark*, 12.
115 *Répondre*, 38.
116 *Ibid.*, 44.

117 *Ibid.*, 53.
118 John Cox, 'Shakespeare's Prayers', in *Renaissance Ethics*, ed. Cox and Gray, 123.
119 *Ibid.*, 124.
120 Chrétien, *Ark*, 37–38.
121 *Ibid.*, 21.
122 See, for example, Joseph Smith, 'Roman Soliloquy', in *Shakespeare and the Soliloquy in Early Modern English Drama*, ed. A. D. Cousins and Daniel Derrin (Cambridge: CUP, 2018), 15–28.
123 As Nancy Selleck argues, 'Renaissance language makes the other not merely the self's context but its source and locus'. *The Interpersonal Idiom in Shakespeare, Donne and Early Modern Culture* (Basingstoke: Palgrave, 2008), 2; On Shakespeare, see 89–122.
124 Cummings, *Mortal Thoughts*, 195.
125 *Ibid.*, 179.
126 *Ibid.*
127 Cousins and Derrin, 'Introduction', in *Soliloquy*, 11.
128 *Ibid.*
129 This speech will be more extensively discussed in Chapter 3.
130 *Ibid.*
131 For a recent 'defence' of an individualist and proto-libertarian Shakespeare and thus a reaction to postmodern criticism, see Peter Holbrook, *Shakespeare's Individualism* (Cambridge: CUP, 2010).
132 For a critical summary of the theoretical assumptions fuelling anti-humanist Shakespeare criticism, see Robin Headlam Wells, *Shakespeare's Humanism* (Cambridge: CUP, 2005), 177–203.
133 See Gray, *Fall*.
134 Cox and Gray, 'Introduction', in *Renaissance Ethics*, 9ff.
135 This tensional approach mirrors the argument of William Bouwsma's famous essay, 'The Two Faces of Humanism: Stoicism and Augustinianism in Renaissance Thought', in *A Usable Past: Essays in European Cultural History* (Berkeley, CA: UCAL, 1990), 19–64.
136 Gray, *Fall*, 1–46.
137 I am here using, as Pickstock does, 'ritual' and 'liturgical' interchangeably.
138 Catherine Pickstock, 'Sense and Sacrament', in *The Oxford Handbook of Sacramental Theology*, ed. Hans Boersma and Matthew Levering (Oxford: OUP, 2015), 659.
139 *Ibid.*, 661–663.
140 Pickstock, *Repetition and Identity* (Oxford: OUP, 2013), *passim*.
141 Pickstock, *After Writing: On the Liturgical Consummation of Philosophy* (Oxford: Blackwell, 1998), 176–177.
142 *Ibid.*
143 *Ibid.*, 242.
144 *Ibid.*
145 *Ibid.*, 35.
146 *Ibid.*, 246.
147 *Ibid.*, 221. Emphasis mine.
148 Catherine Pickstock, 'Liturgy and the Senses', *South Atlantic Quarterly* 109.4 (2010), 721.
149 *Ibid.*
150 For the Renaissance tradition of *serioludere*, see Edgar Wind, *Pagan Mysteries in the Renaissance* (New York: Norton, 1968), 222–235.
151 Pickstock 'Liturgy', 723.

152 *Ibid.*, 725.
153 *Ibid.*, 724.
154 For an example of the theatrical resonances of this theological open-endedness in Shakespeare, see Judith Wolfe (Tonning), '"Like this Insubstantial Pageant, Faded": Eschatology and Theatricality in *The Tempest*', *LAT* 18.4 (2004), 371–382.
155 Pickstock, *After Writing*, 237.
156 Guite, *Poetry*, 54–66.
157 Chrétien, *Ark*, 39.
158 *De Dato Patris Luminum*, 3.107.
159 Chrétien, *Ark*, 1. Translation slightly altered.
160 For an exploration of this theme in Chrétien, see Christina M. Gschwandtner, 'Creativity as Call to Care for Creation? John Zizioulas and Jean-Louis Chrétien', in *Being-In-Creation: Human Responsibility in an Endangered World*, ed. Brian Treanor, Bruce Benson, and Norman Wirzba (New York: Fordham UP, 2015), 100–112.
161 Chrétien, *Ark*, 3.
162 *Ibid.*
163 See Daniel Hardy and David Ford, *Praising and Knowing God* (Philadelphia, PA: Westminster Press, 1985), 47.
164 Chrétien, *Ark*, 131.
165 *Ibid.*
166 *Ibid.*, 132.
167 *Ibid.*
168 *Ibid.*, 134.
169 *Ibid.*, 7.
170 *Ibid.*, 37.
171 *DVD*, 10.42. Translation slightly altered.
172 *DVD*, 7.26.
173 Sherman, *Partakers*, 179.
174 *DVD*, 12.48.
175 *DVD*, 7.26. Translation slightly altered.
176 *VEN*, 32.95. Translation slightly altered.

Part II
Readings

3 The Unsaying of the World
King Lear

Introduction

In the previous chapter, I outlined a doxological approach to a theological study of Shakespeare's plays. I argued that words are irreducibly antiphonal, always already responding to the primacy of a call. In a Christological key, this call is the voice of the divine *logos*, the Word whose presence shimmers amidst words being, as Nicholas of Cusa has helped us to see, their non-coercive and infinitely yet 'incomprehensibly' expressible ground. Such speech cannot be collapsed into autonomous self-transparency or passive despair, and embraces instead the paradoxicalities of seriousness and play, art and life, theatricality and authenticity as instances of a grammar of gift. In the following, I will seek to extend this kind of liturgical sensibility to my reading of the plays, attempting to sense in the irreducible ambiguities of human speech, particularly palpable in Shakespeare, various modes of response to love's call, which always and everywhere calls us, refusing to be reduced to any privileged speech-form. In this sense, a reading of *King Lear*, a play in which words are portrayed as suspect, duplicitous and ultimately seemingly powerless, provides an especially apposite case in point.

As the next two chapters will show, a doxological hermeneutic takes *speech itself* as its central key. With this in mind, it is perhaps obvious to say that *King Lear* stages a situation in which the ground of true speech is abandoned; a dramatic arc in which words said without love result in a world in which love is without words. As Sarah Beckwith puts it, 'the play will show relentlessly, remorselessly, what a culture comes to look like when the paths to truthful expression are lost'.[1] In what follows, I will seek to show that the abandonment of a 'truthful expression' that arises from the ground of words, 'Praise itself', results in *every other mode of speech* attempting to compensate for this loss by creatively drawing deep on its own resources. Striving to re-articulate the Good, language turns to its poetic, paratactic and polysemous excesses in order to respond to love's call.

Language in *Lear* is subjected to a hostile take-over, affecting private relations, social bonds and relationships to the world. As we will

DOI: 10.4324/9781003223276-5

see, the banishment of love from words results in speech becoming increasingly overwhelmed by a cosmic *curse*: thus, words of *bond* become progressively saturated with curses and blasphemes which turn to the invocation of the annihilating powers of 'Nature'[2]; its Goddess, its material presence and its innate creative intelligence. A similar fate to 'Nature', however, extends to human 'arts'. The play chronicles the rise of certain characters (Edmund, Goneril, Cornwall, Regan, etc.) who depend on the sway of power over words and are therefore aggressively suspicious of the ambiguities of creative and symbolic speech. Human 'art' becoming sterile and unresponsive, the call of love must inhabit the edge of words: its silences and its screams, but also its reaches and excesses; love must reach beyond and beneath rhetoric to speak itself into the world. Whether through words of love (Cordelia), words of service (Kent), words of 'serioludic' wit (the Fool) and even an ambiguous, semi-demonic performance where words turn into pain (Edgar/Tom), human language endlessly strives to re-articulate its own ground.

One key image, that of the 'weight' of genuine language, will be touched upon throughout. For Simone Weil, *Lear* is 'a tragedy of gravity': it stages the inevitable consequences of a world dominated by the downward pull of pure force.[3] Though the movement of 'grace' is for her the vital exception countering the weight of necessity, it corresponds to a counter-pull which '[comes] down by a movement in which gravity plays no part', paradoxically '[making] us fall towards the heights'.[4] Beginning in a situation where Cordelia cannot 'heave her heart into her mouth' because love is too 'ponderous' for words, and ending with Edgar's heedful obeisance to 'the weight of this sad time', *King Lear*, I hope to show, gestures towards such a paradoxical movement in language. Genuine words, words of love, are at once pulled towards the material world and towards God by a kind of *counter-gravity*, which is love. The play's final scenes tentatively gesture at a kind of 'weighting' that is in fact a *waiting*, a new-found, attentive patience towards the truth-bearing quality of human speech re-emerging after the disaster of love's fracture from words.

As this study negotiates literature through a theological approach, an introductory word is needed about the question of 'the gods' in *King Lear*. Does the play argue for a providential universe ruled by divinities, or perhaps a *deus absconditus*, or are the rising tides of 'secularisation' beginning to make themselves felt? William Elton's magisterial study, *King Lear and the Gods*, sought to characterise the play as becoming 'progressively skeptical and Epicurean with regards to the gods', thus implicitly reflecting the epistemic and metaphysical instabilities articulated in the intellectual currents of its day.[5] Other critics have been more generous, arguing that Elizabethan and Jacobean audiences would have expected the gods invoked in *King Lear* to still function as stewards within a Christian universe.[6] But as John Cox rightly points out, the play continuously resists such clear-cut readings, whether theological, secularist or nihilistic.[7] In *King Lear,* then, the gods have clearly 'fallen silent', *only* if one expects a univocal cosmology on which to append a simplistic reading of 'providence' as a metaphysical machinery that, tragically, fails to work properly.[8]

It may be more useful, then, to explore the play's appeals to divinities neither in terms of allegiances to nor skepticism towards simplified metaphysical ideas, but rather in terms of the play's own densely articulated and irreducible poetic theophanies.[9] As Anthony Baker suggests, the gods in *Lear* can be distinguished through a framework of providence in which God's gift of temporal governance to the creatures becomes 'a creature's active acceptance of this gift of agency'.[10] For Baker, such agency is distinctly 'theopoetic' in the sense that it exhibits a complex relationship to providence through speech; in particular, in the language of 'exchange, gratitude and relation'.[11] In this sense, *King Lear's* gods are not conjectured ontic presences, but manifest as aspects of the divine gift that glimmers *in and through human words*, a speech which recalls a sense of its divine origin, as already alluded to in Chapter 2. Thus, as Baker paradoxically notes, 'we are the makers of the gods whose excessive presence shows up in our finite language'.[12] The gods' presence in words bears witness to the excessive, poetic nature of speech as a tending towards praise which creatively discerns *and* figures a universe saturated with agents of goodness. In this way, the gods sustain and preserve the very creativity of language, a dwelling of infinite potencies in finite words which symbolically marks human-divine encounters. In *King Lear,* conversely, the sense of a lack of divine presence is coterminous with the hostile take-over of language itself. The setting of *Lear* within a pagan universe is not meant to mark a theological lack, in the sense of a human history as-yet-unredeemed by a God-man not yet arrived. Instead, the pagan cosmos becomes an especially fortuitous setting for the sensing of the divine counter-force of love that constantly seeks to be born in the cosmos and actualise itself through human expression.

The turn to literary aspects of the play effected in the following pages is also an attempt to preserve this genuine theopoetic dimension rather than collapse it in a reductive theological narrative of 'suffering-and-redemption' as discussed in Chapter 1. The literary tradition, especially in recent times, has worked to resist the totalising impulses of systematic approaches. The following interpretation attempts to honour this tradition's manifold insights and thus perform a fruitful and respectful crossing of the porous boundaries between theology and literature.

Spatialisation versus Symbolic Speech

In a famous and hugely influential essay on *King Lear,* 'The Avoidance of Love', Stanley Cavell explores how the play hinges on the dramatic loss of the possibility in speech to bring about reciprocal acknowledgement. 'Acknowledgement' as Cavell understands it, corresponds to a 'letting oneself matter... equally to acknowledge that your expressions in fact express you, that they are yours, that you are in them. This means allowing yourself to be comprehended'.[13] To be comprehended is, correspondingly, to acknowledge your embodied utterance; it is both to matter and to be made of matter: 'to acknowledge your body, and the body of your expressions, to be yours, you on earth, all there will ever be of you'.[14] Such an acknowledgement occurs not simply through transparent linguistic self-disclosure but rather, even despite our very opacity to one another, by allowing language to bring about such fragile mutual revelations. The tragic move begins when such vulnerabilities are refused: here, one attempts to slip out of acknowledgement, implying an unreachable 'surplus' to our words: a kind of apophatic rhetoric of the self, liberated from the density and fragility of speech.[15] Cavell reads this avoidance as synonymous with much of the action in *Lear*. Veiling the soul and silencing the speech that most can speak our being, 'avoidance' is nothing less than 'the attempt to avoid recognition, the shame of exposure, the threat of self-revelation'.[16]

It is thus decisive that the play opens amidst an atmosphere of inarticulacy.[17] The King's first act of 'avoidance', in fact, is to evade the counsel of those who know and love him and in whom he trusts.[18] Indeed Kent and Gloucester, Lear's most faithful counsellors, begin the play by expressing their confusion with regard to the King's actions and decisions. The division of the kingdom in 'moieties' leaves unclear something they feel they once knew: exactly whom or what the King 'values most' (1.1.1–10).[19]

Avoiding the weight of words of acknowledgement, the King enters to confer his 'darker purpose': to divide the kingdom between his three daughters (35). As he explains, this action will allow him to 'divest' himself of cares and be free to live out his old age, and thus 'unburdened crawl toward death' (40). Wishing to hold to stately decorum while 'unburdening' himself from the challenges of truthful speech, Lear stages a ceremony, a playful love-trial, where the weight of words is itself theatricalised: 'which of you', he asks playfully, '*shall we say* doth love us most?' (51).[20] However, despite this playful stratagem, he warns that the words they choose will nonetheless articulate a kind of 'merit' which will lay claim on the King's generosity (53). This opening gambit, as Stephen Booth has noted, contributes to the allure of a 'theatrical pageant, a ceremonial enactment of events already concluded': as its master of the ceremonies, the King has scripted every outcome, attempting to secure a complete hold on speech.[21] Such transformation of ceremony into a dumb show justifies his daughters' subsequent utterances: they merely perform easily discernible parts in a predetermined performance.[22] The passing on of political power is here synonymous with a flourish of seemly yet tactical words.

It may be that this is a 'translegal' political manoeuvre—perhaps Lear is attempting to bypass the laws of succession by ensuring his favourite child receives the best prize.[23] However, as Paul Khan remarks, Lear's 'division of the kingdom' is also synonymous with a giving away of the King's powers of speech, 'a power to name' in order to '[make] real within the political order that which he names', calling things 'not as they are in themselves, but as they will be seen within the state'.[24] Kingdom and speech are, in this sense, symbolic of one another: the words of the King must affirm and articulate what is of value, what the Kingdom will hold to be 'good'. By asking for a dumb show of genuine love, the King attempts to marry inner truth with outer form, binding together private and public expression, familial and political speech.[25] Naming here becomes synonymous with political naming. Yet because, as we saw, it is love that has brought all speech into being—the unsayable by virtue of which all things are sayable—love itself cannot in this way be named. What cannot be named because it is the Name itself cannot be controlled by the King's political power of name.[26] Paradoxically, as we will see, this attempt to secure a hold on speech results in a situation in which words, in fact, can name 'nothing' and reveal 'nothing'.

Goneril quickly grasps that love has been excluded from the order of words. She obeys the rules of the rhetorical game but subtly changes its course. 'I do love you more than word can wield the matter' (54–55) she begins, playing on the connotations of rhetorical artistry and political control that *to wield* suggests: 'to rule, to reign over, to command' and 'to express, to utter'.[27] 'Wielding the matter', then, already implies a manoeuvre of domination on utterance; but as she explains, this is because love, in her view, exerts a tyrannical pressure on words: it makes 'breath poor and speech unable' (60). Her apophatic tactic is not the kind that 'shades into a poetics of the unsayable',[28] reverently gesturing to that which is beyond all speech. Instead, she quickly modulates to qualities that are, to her, hyperbolically precious: 'eyesight', 'space' and 'liberty' ('56'). Taken together, these words suggest a representational preference in the service of an eagerness for autonomy: 'eyesight' as the gaze which surveys and commands 'space', and 'liberty', which needs 'space' in order to freely express its self-mastery and emancipation from constraints and obstacles.

This is the first of numerous explicit references to eyes, vision and sight in the play, and many critics have seen in this 'pattern' a synecdoche for understanding and moral insight.[29] But Goneril's words do not suggest a lack of moral vision so much as a 'politics of the gaze', fixed on the kingdom which she wishes to acquire, and which the King has already represented and apportioned on his map (35–37). Lear's cartographic move presents, as Valerie Traub has argued in an influential article, a 'style of reasoning' in which 'land and body, kingdom and family' are 'part and parcel of a spatial epistemology': a unidimensional, equalised and predictable landscape.[30] As the trope of cartography eventually transmutes in the logic of anatomy, Traub notes, the play's tragic action will parallel the fault-lines inherent in this early modern construal of the new 'graphic idiom' of spatialising logic through its symbolic images: 'body, kingdom, crown, eyes, and brain (and with them life, power, authority, sight and rationality)—are continually spatialized, dissected and partitioned'.[31] Word and land become subjected to statistical measurement, prey to the calculative selections of the mind. Hence, what her father surrenders to her as 'shadowy forests... with champaigns riched... plenteous rivers and wide-skirted meads' (64–65) transforms, for Goneril, into *mere* 'space'. Importantly, her rhetorical move also modifies the King's ensuing words: as he hands Regan her part of the kingdom, he no longer refers to it by means of idyllic imagery, but simply as 'an ample third', 'no less in space, validity and pleasure' than Goneril's (80–81). Beyond this topographic construal, the 'spatialising' logic of early modernity also dismantles, as Catherine Pickstock has argued, the symbolic reach of *words* in favour of a system of logical signs susceptible to the restrictions of a mathematical grid. This engenders a language which transforms physical space into a 'purely rational, homogenous substrate which houses not "things", but idealised figures or signs which, as interior appear to "get outside" language itself'.[32] As Pickstock notes, this extra-linguistic element of early modern metaphysics was obtained through both the instrumentalisation and the 'humiliation' of language.[33] With his land and power to name, then, the King hands over the sway of symbolic words. The consequences of such moves upon the material world will be explored in more detail in the next section.

The rise of Goneril and Regan's political control, then, is coextensive with the restriction of speech from its symbolic and poetic reaches and the exclusion of love from words. Indeed, Goneril and Regan share the nominalist tendency already glimpsed with Edmund in the previous chapter: words for them are tied not to things but to the 'plague of custom'. Since custom anchors power and speech together in the King's person, it is imperative for them to acquire the King's power of speech. Once his symbolic nature as name-giver has been transferred, Goneril can, in the next scene, re-describe Lear in a chillingly literalising fashion: no longer a King or a father, he has become an anonymous 'Idle old man, / That still would manage those authorities/That he has given away' (1.3.16–18). His questioning of her change of behaviour is to her neither royal prerogative nor fatherly words, but 'new pranks' (1.4.228) that are unseemly for one who should play a part that 'befits [his] age' (242). In a similar spirit Regan, putting on exasperation at Lear's behaviour, will demand: 'I pray you, father, being weak, seem so' (2.2.390). Since the world of 'seeming' custom he once sanctioned is now no longer in his power, Goneril and Regan expect Lear to play a role simply dictated by physical appearance. Hence, Regan commands that Lear ask Goneril for forgiveness in a prescribed manner: 'Say you have wrong'd her' (2.2.341).[34]

Likewise, because their urge to power over words makes the uncontrollable reaches of symbolic speech especially dangerous, Goneril and Regan's aggressive spatialising campaign will seek to ensure that all symbolic associations that surround kingship gradually become 'nothing'.[35] This attack is a prominent part of their disputes: though the King had originally reserved for himself a symbolic following of knights (1.1.133–137), the daughters coolly reason away this 'unnecessary' entourage, and Lear's 'addition' of a hundred is steadily calculated down to zero ('what need one'? [2.2.453]).[36] This diminution is justified by the Knights' supposed bad behaviour; yet nowhere in the play-text is this contention substantiated, and Lear himself vehemently argues the opposite (1.4.255–258). It is rather the case that, no longer legitimated either by political sanction or familial duty, such retinue is the last remaining symbol of Lear's former status, and must be noughted by the power of spatialising reason (2.2.316–452). Lear's outburst—'Reason not the need!'—is thus also a furious protest against his power of speech being drained by such calculations: 'Our basest beggars/Are in the poorest things superfluous' he retorts, pointing out to Regan that 'nature needs not what thou gorgeous wear'st' (2.2.454–458). His kingship, he realises, is a symbolic vestment, itself intelligible only within an analogical apprehension of the order of the world, which the cold application of instrumental reason fundamentally threatens.[37] Yet, by attempting to protect what is superfluous, the King unknowingly alludes to what is at stake: the lustre of gift in the order of words. The attack on symbolism, indeed, is also as ploy on the uncontrollable aspect of grace in language.

Hence, Goneril and Regan's rise to power, as well as their eventual demise, is linked to their appropriating the power of speech by restricting speech to power, a state of affairs that the rhetorical manoeuvres in the first scene helps to bring about. The sisters' anti-symbolic conception of speech is perpetuated throughout the play and still echoes in Goneril's last words: 'the laws are mine, not thine/Who can arraign me for it?' (5.3.156–157). Since power and law are equivalent or her, there is none to whom she needs to answer. She dies seeing herself as not responsible for her words.

'Nothing in the Middle': Weightless Words, Ponderous Silences

Cordelia's first words, resolutely affirming that she must 'love and be silent' (1.1.62) are metatheatrical, alluding to what escapes the densely controlled rhetoric of the play. In fact, she soon understands that her silence will be a kind of eloquence, grounded in the surety that 'my love is more ponderous than my tongue' (78).[38] To be sure, this refers to a preference for action over words, as she herself later points out (226–228). But the word 'ponderous' also suggests a certain feel for the *weight* of love, not an angelic dream-like quality of innocence often associated with Cordelia, but a kind of *counter-gravity*. This 'ponderous' aspect recalls Augustine's exploration of gravity in the *Confessions*: 'our rest is where we belong', he writes,

> Love sublimates us to that place... Under its own weight a body gravitates to its proper place; that gravitation is not always downward, but rather to that proper place... What is out of its proper place is restless; once in its proper place it finds rest. My love is my weight [*pondus*]; wherever I am carried, it is love that carries me.[39]

Love is more 'ponderous', then, because only love carries speech where it belongs, that is, to itself: *love* is the gravity that draws words to their natural dwelling.[40] Cordelia's unease with speech is not Goneril and Regan's tactical apophaticism, neither is it Lear's desire to be made weightless, 'unburdened' from acknowledgement. Love's call, as she sees it, does not arrest but grounds the tongue.

Yet for such language to resonate, as we have seen in Chapter 2, there must be for it a resting place *in the world*, a manner in which it can dwell and be *received* as such. Such reception, as Chrétien suggests, coincides with a receptive mode of attention, a silence that is also an eloquent mode of hospitality, where listening coincides with speaking—perhaps something like what Augustine himself calls *aures cordis*: 'the ears of the heart'.[41] Indeed, in a Shakespearean key, the poet of the Sonnets asks the beloved to read his 'speaking breast' since 'to hear with eyes belongs to love's fine wit' (23.14). Far from making 'breath poor and speech unable', then, love's language re-aligns the senses to its own 'wit', sensing its expression with all the senses—becoming as it were their *sensus communis*.[42] It is in this material, embodied sense that 'ponderous' love can reside in speech: because it can be sensed by others. As John Hughes rightly argues, the play's gesture to a 'politics of forgiveness' is not a demand to practice an otherworldly logic of self-mortification but an attempt to *respond* to love's request to be affirmed and articulated *in* the world. It is in this sense that love-speech, its being embodied in 'a local habitation and a name', depends, as Hughes shows, on a genuine community of gift—it is such hospitality which contributes to make words 'ponderous'.[43] Conversely, the inhospitable rhetorical ambience created in the first scene have made the unfolding of a language 'ponderous' with love *inaudible* and therefore weightless. This situation, presenting words as the 'unburdened' apparatus of power versus words with a gravitational pull too deep to be spoken, foreshadows the fate of language in the play.

To be sure, Coleridge's famous reading of Cordelia's 'nothing' with its 'little faulty admixture of pride and sullenness' helps bear in mind the ingenuous and impolitic nature of her words.[44] Is she not, in some way, liable in not offering the excess of praise and gratitude due to her father? Is her 'fault' in saying too little whereas her other sisters have said too much? But we have seen that the initial ceremony is theatrical pageant and not a genuine ritual which, as we suggested in Chapter 2, articulates itself through the interweaving of life and art. Here, there is *only* a kind of lifeless art; one that has, as Beckwith puts it, disabled 'ritual from its work as participation'.[45] Without such participation and attentive hospitality, rhetorical excess cannot be distinguished from the excess suggested by the economy of gift.

Thus, Cordelia's silence does neither signify a prideful triumph over a language-game of public competition nor a wise gesturing beyond the limits of words. Ted Hughes' idiosyncratic mythopoetic readings of Shakespeare, drawing from all his works a rich and suggestive constellation of archetypal characters, figures Cordelia as the *very opposite* to a silent, loving daughter. For Hughes, Cordelia corresponds to the paradigm of a priestess-poet, one who is both 'the vessel containing the magical alphabet of poetry' as well as 'the living pyx of Shakespeare's poetic word'.[46] Her function within Shakespeare's universe is, or *should be*, one of uniting the world-shaping powers of an enchanted *wordhord* to the divinely ordained sacramentality of language itself. But here the vessel has been cracked, and the pyx remains closed. For Hughes, her speech-filled wordlessness suggests instead that 'the whole titanic drama turns on this "Nothing" and the bizarre fact that Cordelia's true love cannot find words to declare itself. And it is whirled on this axis by the fact that the treacherous, loveless ones possess an inexhaustible wealth of plausible language'.[47] Thus, Cordelia's mystic inarticulacy is the echo of a 'Divine Love' that, in turn, becomes Shakespeare's dramaturgic wager, since it 'cannot be dramatized and demonstrated at all, except as a creature suffering in a world where the egomaniac voices of the tragic error reject it, violate it, exploit it'.[48] Yet, as Hughes himself notes, this need not result in a fractured, Manichean cosmos: instead, the withdrawal of such truth coincides with a paradoxically creative situation in which words are given a 'Saturnalian freedom' to obey what gravity they might: thus, they can express the worst of excesses and abuses of language *or,* as we will see below, celebrate 'their inability to declare the truth directly' with the license to 'sing about it obliquely, and to glance towards it crookedly'.[49] One might say, following Hughes, that *King Lear* is a special tragedy for the poet: the tragedy of the creative word's hidden resources and of its superabundant counter-tactic deployed once language has been usurped by power.

It is in this way that her saying 'nothing' offers a theological parallel with the birth of the *logos* made flesh in the world. Such birth does not coincide with a transparent, fully unfolded linguistic communication; it is rather, as Lancelot Andrewes famously describes it, '*Verbum Infans*, the Word without a word; the eternal Word not able to speak a word'.[50] This speechlessness linked to infancy by means of a pun (*infans* also means 'speechless') is for Andrewes 'a sign to wonder at'.[51] If the fragile birth of the *logos* is a wondrous riddle of inarticulate articulacy that signs its divinity, it may suggest that in Cordelia's artless 'nothing' one should hear, in some sense, a word pregnant with the as-yet-unspoken language of love.[52]

Yet, in Lear's court, *neither* the silent nor the vociferous can communicate love; neither Cordelia's speechlessness nor Kent's subsequent boisterous denunciation—'whilst I can vent clamour from my throat/I'll tell thee thou dost evil' (166–167)—will be heard for what they are attempting to say. Chrétien poignantly describes the modesty that guards the word that, as most fitting response, nevertheless must remain unsaid:

> the word that would be most proper is not uttered… because I risk staining it with a feebleness in my voice that would desecrate it, or because I would risk screaming to the deaf that which can only be uttered in hushed tones—thus wounding the word itself.[53]

Here, Cordelia's 'nothing' is Kent's everything: what Cordelia will not stain, Kent screams to the deaf. Love-speech spills out of the non-listening Lear-world, either too quiet or too loud.

Banishing the prophetess of poetry and her clamouring minister, Lear, in turn, fashions his own word-magic, his own ritual. Calling on the cosmic gods to witness, on Jupiter and Apollo, on 'the sacred radiance of the sun,/The mysteries of Hecate and the night' (110–111), he attempts what Linda Woodbridge calls a 'magical expulsion of evil' resembling a scapegoat ritual which, as she points out, paradoxically desacralises his own symbolic position as King.[54] The seizure of words culminates in a seizure of ritual: because the conditions for the 'liturgical' are absent in this play, the rite must be a sacrifice, and the sacrifice turns out to be the sacrifice of words. What is prefigured in Hughes' mythopoetic reading of Cordelia as a priestess-poet suggests that what is at stake is more than the banishment of a loving daughter: such action coincides with a disenchantment of words and world, in which ritual turns against itself.

Inevitably, in the light of our doxological approach, there is a *social* consequence to this withdrawal. When Cordelia is asked to explain the meaning of 'nothing', she replies 'I love your majesty/*according* to my bond, no more, no less' (1.1.93). Rather than for its sullen inadequacy, this response can be read in the light of what, in this situation, cannot be said or more precisely, is being *unsaid*. With its connotation of *cor* (heart) the name 'Cordelia' recalls, as John Kerrigan notes, the natural bonds or 'holy cords' which Kent bemoans are gnawed by 'smiling rogues' such as the courtier Oswald (2.2.71–72), and also 'accord', a word which signifies 'harmonious, concordant, reconciled' as well as a particular sense of will ('of one's own accord').[55] Such words, as Kerrigan shows, continuously evoke the importance of social bonds and their being hallowed by the binding power of language.[56] Thus, Cordelia's *cor* is her accord; her heart is her bond—the binding nature of words is infolded in her response. Kent's condemnation of the 'slave' Oswald who wears a sword but 'no honesty' (70–71) resonates with Cordelia's doubts at her sisters' 'glib and oily art' (1.1.226): both indicate that the bonds that establish community are profoundly endangered by the arts of sophistry which fundamentally invert the powers of language to affirm and articulate relation in the light of the Good.

But the language that binds one to another also strikes roots into the land. The jointure of social bonds articulates, as Philippa Berry notes, a primal connection between the Kingdom and the soil on which it springs. Noting the suggestive parallel with the French *cordelier* ('tier of knots', from *lier*, 'to bind'),[57] she argues that Lear's rejection of Cordelia coincides with the untying of such a 'middle', which joins the 'animating spirit or soul of royal power' with its native land.[58] For Berry, this animating 'middle' parallels the 'interstitial, uncanny and implicitly feminine site that joins opposites (culture and nature, man and god)... and has the capacity to confer a supernatural blessing or curse upon the land'.[59] After Cordelia's departure, Berry suggests (like Ted Hughes) that this in-between realm can only be alluded to through 'obscure and riddling language', such as that of the Fool, who explicitly points out to the King: 'Thou has pared thy wit o' both sides and left nothing in the middle' (1.4.178–179).[60] The Fool's astute wit picks up how this leaving 'nothing in the middle' is also a situation where opposites cannot coincide, and thus where neither truth nor lie, speech nor silence can be tolerated: 'I marvel what kin thou and thy daughters are. They'll have me whipped for speaking true, thou wilt have me whipped for lying, and sometime I am whipped for holding my peace' (1.4.173–175). Lear and his 'kin', having banished love-words, usurp this 'middle' where all possibilities of speech will dissolve in the same 'whipping', the same primal violence. The tragedy of Cordelia's 'nothing' is thus also synonymous with the hushing of social words, the unknotting of a communal language of love and forgiveness. Needled and piqued by the Fool, even the King will eventually echo Cordelia's fateful word, only to tragically misunderstand her purpose: 'I will be the pattern of all patience, I will say *nothing*' (3.2.36–37) he promises in the storm: yet his aim, rather than to say 'nothing', is to be the 'pattern', the *pater* of patience which, as Kent will later point out, escapes him despite his boasts to the contrary (3.6.56–57).

King Lear's banishment of love and language can also be glimpsed through a comparison with his mirror image, the King of France. Perhaps with some awareness of the middling, 'interstitial' mystic springs that are the 'animating spirit' of his royalty, France is moved to wonder at the paradoxical nature of Cordelia's non-speaking speech: he praises her as 'most rich being poor,/Most choice forsaken and most loved despised'

(252–253). His prayer to the gods also echoes this paradoxical wisdom: 'Gods, gods! 'Tis strange that from their cold'st neglect/My love should kindle to inflamed respect' (256–257). France's words, which stoke the fire of Lear's anger (1.1.256–268) show how the ecstatic, paradoxical language of *admiratio* is out of tune with a rhetorical atmosphere that has permitted the reach of calculative reason over against the fragility and symbolic proclivities of the language of love.[61] His encomium only serves to show up Goneril and Regan's: his is true praise, theirs mere stratagem.

Shakespeare thus shows how the symbolic power of poetic speech and the sacramentality of words are that which can give words genuine weight; politically, they can somehow underwrite social bonds and even royal power.[62] Yet, the invocation of Cordelia as 'middle' suggests, beyond the political, a distinctly salvific dimension. The language of the Psalms, already invoked in Chapter 2, here offers a suggestive theological extension: there, the middle is not merely the soul of the land and the *anima* of royal power but also a space of praise, a jointure that unites temple, city and world: for just as the Psalmist sings of God 'working salvation in the midst of the earth' (74:12), he tarries for divine lovingkindness 'in the midst of [his] temple' (48.9), and calls for praise to be spoken 'even in the midst of thee, O Jerusalem. Praise ye the Lord' (116.19). Here, the middle is the place where praise is sung and where God's love is received. It is also the place where the *logos* dwells, as Cusa notes: 'I see, then, my God, that Your Son is the uniting Medium of all things, so that all things may find rest in You by the medium of Your Son…'.[63] For Cusa, the middle unites things precisely by confounding the logic of the univocal 'either-or'.[64] It is the interstitial 'God-man', who embodies the middle-ligature of the cosmos and towards which all true words are drawn by love's gravity.

I have dwelt at length on these passages to show that the 'division of the kingdom' is the result of a much more primal division between speech and the middle-ground by which all words are called and towards which they gravitate, seeking the rest that is also their full expression. Such division denies the life-giving jointure that binds together humans, words and world and creates the condition for the univocal dominion of 'eyesight, space and liberty'. It reconfigures the world as hostile to the fragile space of love-words; a world in which love is called to speak despite being 'unable to speak a word'. In this situation—*Pace* Gloucester—it seems that 'the quality of nothing' has every 'need to hide itself' (1.2.34–35). In the following, I try to trace the play's deployment of the kinds of speech that radiate from the 'middle' and, as Ted Hughes suggests, attempt to compensate for its loss: oaths and vows, wit, demonic speech and moral *sententiae*. The following section tracks the consequences of this inversion of speech on the material world, the land of *Lear*.

'Nature', or Creativity versus Curses

As has often been noted, one result of the fateful events of *King Lear* is that of the downfall of the world: the storm on the heath is but an instance of the gradual transformation of Lear's initially unified Britain into a 'gor'd state'. Originally alluded to with pastoral reference, 'with shadowy forests and with champaigns riched,/With plenteous rivers and with wide skirted meads', the world of *King Lear* transforms, as Leah Marcus notes, into

> a teeming world of shrubs, trees, barren heath, rats, dogs, pond-slime, thunder, whirlwinds and other elemental forces swirling about the humans—a presence that is so palpable to its characters that it almost deserves the status of an additional member of the cast.[65]

Yet, this tormented condition seems to render human and non-human things and beings porous to one another.[66] In fact, as Laurie Shannon has argued, the play consciously resists any sense of human 'exceptionalism'.[67] Within a few scenes, kings and nobles become 'unaccommodated men', 'naked fellows', beggars and madmen living in the straw amidst storms and tempests, and social norms decline to a level far 'below' that of the animal and the elemental. Britain gradually transmutes, by way of diluvial storms, unspeakable cruelties, wretches and blind men on murder-ridden heaths, into a blood-soaked battlefield.

This elemental 'additional member of the cast' is in fact suggested by the First Folio, which capitalises the word 'Nature': the word itself (including cognates) appears 42 times in the play, more so than in any other work of Shakespeare. This concern with nature and naturality has been a constant feature of literary approaches to the play, from the historicism of the early 20th century to the more recent interest in ecocriticism and ecofeminism.[68] Yet, the natural world in this play is not treated simply as a 'viciously unpredictable and dangerous' hostile other, as some ecocritics have argued.[69] The concept of 'nature', as C. S. Lewis has shown, bears witness to an almost unimaginably complex semantic reach.[70] As he notes, its Latin etymon *natura* 'shares a common base with *nasci* (to be born); with the noun *natus* (birth); with *natio* (not only a race or nation but the name of the birth-goddess)' and with female sexual organs.[71] Our overriding concern with speech also points to the ancestry of the literary figure of *Natura* as not merely an abstract principle of fertility but as a *teacher* and *voice* of wisdom in the cosmos, evidenced both in its usages in 12th-century literature as well as its ancestry in Boethius' figure of Lady Philosophy.[72] The world of *King Lear*, ultimately, presents 'nature' not as a definite abstract notion, but as a voice to be *responded to*, to be welcomed in our speech, even amidst this dense network of relationships. Though ubiquitous, 'nature' remains elusive: and it is such mysterious yet palpable presence that evokes a profound dimension of being incomprehensibly continuous with, and surging up in, human existence and meaning-making as distinct moments of expression.[73]

To be sure, the banishment of love-speech, leaving 'nothing in the middle', already suggests that such a network of relations is threatened by world-consuming conflict and chaos. Below, I will show that characters' appropriation of the word 'Nature' is in fact an attempt to *usurp* this middle with a sealed, immanent cosmology or what John Hughes has described as a 'foreclosed, materialist account of the world'.[74] As Hughes shows, this adoption of an immanent cosmology, uniting characters who are to one another opposed, has several effects: by reconfiguring nature along the continuum of 'eyesight, space and liberty', it confines it to a field of war of all against all, of primal violence.[75] Consequently, the doxological sway of speech is usurped by a sterile cosmology suspicious of creativity and fertility, by rhetorical sophistry and ultimately by the language of the death-curse. As the bond of words with world loosens, binding language becomes gradually saturated with a grammar of curse, alluding to the double sense that Kenneth Gross notes in the play: 'curse as a contingent utterance and curse as an inescapable truth'.[76]

Ironically, this sense of the world as carrier of a primordial blaspheme runs counter to the stable, harmonic notion of 'nature' that the 'old' characters attempt to hold.[77] Yet, it is precisely those characters' language that contributes to voice this curse into existence, in their condemnations of the creative powers both of nature and of words—a curse that touches on the divine origin of whom those creative powers are counterparts. Torn from its doxological roots then, language inundates the play with sterile and destructive curses, invading and eventually silencing doxological speech.[78] No longer received, preserved or celebrated in human words, 'nature', as we will see below, will be made mute. Thus, inevitably, the flood of curses and the denial of creativity in words will bring about chaotic consequences for the natural world.[79]

This resentment towards nature emerges from the play's very first lines, which stress both the interdependence and instability of sexual, familial love and political unity.[80] Accordingly, the language switches intermittently and confusingly between these three registers. Immediately upon discussing the ambiguity of Britain's political situation, Gloucester introduces Edmund to Kent with a form of social acknowledgement that is uneasily mixed with off-hand humour: 'I have so often blushed to acknowledge him', says Gloucester, 'that now I am brazed to't' (1.1.10).[81] When Kent unwittingly turns the language of the exchange to connotations of procreation ('I cannot conceive you'), Gloucester binds together the public and the private through awkward witticisms.

> But I have, sir, a son by order of law, some year elder than this, who yet is no dearer in my account. Though this knave came something

saucily into the world before he was sent for, yet was his mother fair, there was good sport at his making, and the whoreson must be acknowledged.

(1.1.17–24)

Here, Gloucester attempts to subject his private misconduct to public satire performing, though the same word is used, the ironic *opposite* to a Cavellian 'acknowledgement'.[82] Acknowledging Edmund as 'the whoreson', Gloucester reveals how, for him, sexual pleasure has resulted in an 'illegitimate' creation, feminine beauty being somehow implicated in a 'saucy' coming into the world. Barred from family inheritance, Edmund's birth is, in the Gloucester household, 'unnecessary', and therefore unseemly at court ('he hath been out nine years, and away he shall again' [31–32]). Gloucester glosses over this embarrassment with a reference to his 'natural' son, legitimated 'by order of law' (17). As Janet Adelman notes, this remark associates Edmund with inconvenient motherhood while tying Edgar to a paternalistic socio-political order: Edmund's mother and her womb are thereby 'present only as a site of illegitimacy'.[83]

This conspicuous absence of motherhood from the sphere of legitimacy paradoxically suggests a cosmology that fathers and children seem to share, and which, inevitably, soon begins to permeate how *divinities* are addressed in the play. The sting of Gloucester's off-hand jokes infiltrates Edmund's first soliloquy, where he ironically declares service to a new lawful mother, 'Goddess Nature'. Branded with 'bastardy' and 'baseness' by 'the curiosity of nations' and haunted by the term 'legitimate', Edmund offers his allegiance not so much to a deity as to an argument which holds 'nature' to be a fanciful cultural creation superimposed on a ruthless world in which only the lustful and ambitious thrive.[84] For him, then, it is in fact human society that is 'illegitimate', for it does injustice to the power of nature:

> Who in the lusty stealth of nature take
> More composition and fierce quality
> Than doth within a dull stale tired bed
> Go to the creating a whole tribe of fops
> Got 'tween asleep and wake. Well, then,
> Legitimate Edgar, I must have your land.
> Our father's love is to the bastard Edmund
> As to the legitimate. Fine word, legitimate!
> … Edmund the base
> Shall top the legitimate. I grow, I prosper:
> Now, gods, stand up for bastards!

(1.2.11–22)

Here, 'lusty' nature's gifts are 'composition' and 'fierce quality': no other powers are required to make life a fair fight. It is only to affirm such powers that Edmund calls on 'gods': he does not ask them to chastise, redeem or even forgive a world which looks unfavourably on bastards, but simply to 'stand up' for them. Edmund's gods are thus the gods of force, the archetypes of nature's war of all against all. His speech is circular, self-referential and bound by its own logic: sophistry has usurped doxology.

Despite their subsequent conflict, Edmund's contrasting of 'lusty stealth' with 'the plague of custom' is the reverse side of Gloucester's view of nature. In fact, Shakespeare artfully juxtaposes father and son's positions. Shocked at Lear's banishment of Kent and Cordelia, and convinced that his 'natural' son Edgar is out to betray him, Gloucester bemoans the cracking apart of his tightly knit cosmology:

> These late eclipses in the sun and moon portend no good to us. Though the wisdom of nature can reason it thus and thus, yet Nature finds itself scourged by the sequent effects. Love cools, friendship falls off, brothers divide: in cities, mutinies; in countries, discord; in palaces, treason; and the bond cracked 'twixt son and father.
> (1.2.104–112)

In an aside which again echoes his initial 'whoreson' remark, Gloucester's cosmology is ridiculed by Edmund:

> ...an admirable evasion of whoremaster man, to lay his goatish disposition to the charge of a star. My father compounded with my mother under the dragon's tail and my nativity was under Ursa Major, so that it follows, I am rough and lecherous. Fut! I should have been that I am had the maidenliest star in the firmament twinkled on my bastardizing.
> (1.2.126–133)

The belief in cosmic sympathies and the reasoning of the 'wisdom of nature' are here portrayed as a clever conceit of 'whoremaster man'—his father becoming the archetypal figure for an entire anthropology. Scholars have been quick to enlist Edmund's critique as yet another sign of the decline of medieval culture and the birth of secularisation. But as we have seen, Edmund critiques his father's cosmology without liberating himself from it: in trying to ridicule the 'fine word, legitimate' he nonetheless curses his own birth, since he reduces it to a mere by-product of a universal 'goatish disposition'.[85] He thus ends up both repudiating the invective with which his birth is plagued *and* accepting it, generalising it into a cosmological anthropology where 'whoremaster man' is in his turn governed by the 'whoremaster gods' of nature.

The Unsaying of the World 105

As another consequence of the 'lost middle', this shared cosmology unbinds father and children, making either one unwanted by the other: the inconvenience of bearing children, resulting in the sending away of Edmund, the betrayal of Edgar and the banishing of Cordelia, parallels the inconvenience of having parents, producing the humiliation and torture of Lear and Gloucester by their own children. Likewise, 'natural' ties of kinship are transformed into easily transferrable values: the initially undesired 'Edmund the base', soon becomes Gloucester's 'natural boy' (2.1.84) just as Edgar, whose father 'so tenderly and entirely loves him' (1.2.96–97) becomes a 'villain' whose birth can easily be blamed on an absent mother ('I never [be]got him'; [2.1.78]). Cordelia, once closest to Lear's heart, becomes an illegitimate 'sometime daughter' and Regan and Goneril 'unnatural hags' (2.2.466).

Like Gloucester, Lear implicates birth in the opening scene, collapsing its familial, political and metaphysical senses. While dividing the kingdom, he swears three times in the name of birth: twice to establish dynastic legitimacy, so that 'future strife may be prevented now' (1.1.66–67; 79–80). Yet, after Cordelia's withdrawal from the asphyxiating rhetoric of the scene, Lear turns to the language of sentencing: the third vow in the sequence, though legally an oath,[86] spills into a curse.

> Here I disclaim all my paternal care,
> Propinquity and property of blood,
> And as a stranger to my heart and me
> Hold thee from this for ever. The barbarous Scythian,
> Or he that makes his generation messes
> To gorge his appetite, shall to my bosom
> Be as well neighbour'd, pitied and relieved,
> As thou my sometime daughter.
>
> (1.1.115–121)

The fierceness of this sentence suggests what Gloucester and Edmund have implied: that outside the bonds of 'paternal care', 'nature' is a wasteland of barbarous cruelty. Yet, much like Edmund's radical critique of 'custom', this barbarous sentence amounts to a birth-curse, as Andreas Höfele suggests:

> expelling Cordelia into the wilderness, it is really Lear who ends up there. In vowing to treat his own child no better than he would the most brutish savage, he commits himself to acting—and thus becoming—just like such a savage.[87]

This circular curse also proceeds to reveal another intersection between the silencing of love-words and the flattening down of symbolic speech:

106 *Readings*

with Cordelia 'disclaimed', and Kent vociferously challenging his words, Lear expresses his new-found savagery by means of an inverted mythological image: 'Peace, Kent,/Come not between the dragon and his wrath!' (122). There is here, as Höfele notes, a subversive reference to the iconography of St George:

> the King, Kent and Cordelia re-enact the familiar triangle of knight-in-armour, dragon and virgin—except that the King is playing the wrong role. His self-bestialization puts the axe to the very base of that ladder of analogy which ensures the mutually reinforcing authorization of father and King.[88]

This inversion mutes the symbolic possibilities of the 'ladder of analogy', recalling what William Lynch sees as the effect of the 'univocal imagination': in reducing everything to a 'flat community of sameness', it seeks to 'eliminate the unlike, the different, the pluralistic as a kind of intractable and even hostile material'.[89] By taking the part of dragon, the King unleashes a univocal imaginary of single-minded and oppressive bestiality, which foreshadows the sub-natural semantic of the monstrous that gradually engulfs the human and non-human planes of being in the play, as Bradley recognised long ago.[90] Indeed, the sequence concludes with the semi-ironic command to Cornwall and Albany to 'digest this third' daughter's dower (128–129).[91] As part of their political investiture, the King requires a symbolic performance of the bestial feasting fit for 'barbarous Scythians'. As the King's speech transforms speaking into eating, it stops the mouth of those who love him. Their silencing coincides with the King's usage of binding words precisely to disclaim the ground of speech as gift: hence Cordelia is 'dowered with our curse and strangered with our oath' (205).

This usage of the binding power of speech to unbind, at once other-'strangering' and self-cursing, soon becomes generalised to all his daughters. To him, the great cosmic sin is 'filial ingratitude' (3.4.14), and thus the birth-Goddess herself must be appealed to condemn those who perpetuate it, as in this example to Goneril:

> Hear, Nature, hear, dear goddess, hear:
> Suspend thy purpose if thou didst intend
> To make this creature fruitful.
> Into her womb convey sterility,
> Dry up in her the organs of increase,
> And from her derogate body never spring
> A babe to honour her. If she must teem,
> Create her child of spleen, that it may live
> And be a thwart disnatured torment to her.
> Let it stamp wrinkles in her brow of youth,

With cadent tears fret channels in her cheeks,
Turn all her mother's pains and benefits
To laughter and contempt, that she may feel,
How sharper than a serpent's tooth it is
To have a thankless child.

(1.4.267–281)

To be sure, this outburst has the paradoxical effect of indicating to the audience the mounting impotency of Lear's word-power.[92] As Kerrigan notes, Lear does this by making *both* the Goddess and his child into his own image: in the case of the latter, it is 'a version of himself, wrinkled, afflicted and tearful, the parent of a child who will not repay benefits'.[93] Having conflated the transcendent order to his own torment, Lear can thus ask the Goddess to 'suspend her purpose' because gifts given will not be returned, commanding an inversion of nature's very principles of life in the name of revenge. Yet by doing so, Lear also reneges on a kind of familial duty, since his own symbolic heavenly descent, the king's mystic *corpus*, is given and guaranteed 'by all the operations of the orbs/ From whom we do exist and cease to be' (1.1.113). But here, his prayer to the Goddess makes *him* a 'thankless child', the command to raze Goneril's womb amounting to genuine 'filial ingratitude'. Lear curses himself by enacting the very sin he so repudiates.

'The cause of [Shakespearean] tragedy', writes Cavell, 'is that we would rather murder the world than permit it to expose us to change'.[94] Indeed, eventually, Lear's curse on birth degenerates into a curse on life as such. Outraged by Cornwall's mistreatment of his servant Caius (Kent in disguise) and of his daughters' collusion against him, Lear calls on the gods in the name of what he feels *must* be a divine complicity with human old age: 'If you do love old men, if your sweet sway/Allow obedience, if you yourselves are old,/ Make it your cause. Send down, and take my part!' (2.2.379–380). Yet through this petition, he forgets his *own* part as a mortal being. Just as he had earlier inverted the symbolic logic of St George and the Dragon, he now inverts the figures of the divinities: the image of the Goddess as an elderly Goneril-Lear is extended to the entire pantheon, and the gods themselves are figured as caught in permanent old age, endlessly crawling toward their own graves. Bereft of their place in the symbolic order of things, birth and old age, mortals and gods are now moveable terms, swallowed up in the sway of monologic vengeful speech.

Lear's univocity now demands that immanent and transcendent realms alike become birth-less as well as death-less; and he therefore gradually modulates his curse-words to request absolute annihilation. Raging in the storm, he calls for 'cataracts and hurricanoes' to 'spout' a diluvial destruction of biblical connotation but without the promise of rebirth, nor the safeguard of a covenantal temple-ark (3.2.1–38). Eventually, even the elements are seen to be ungrateful beings: 'I call you servile ministers/That will with two pernicious daughters join/Your high-engendered battles 'gainst a head/So old and white as this' (16–24). Because they will not be old men crawling towards death, the heavens here are now guilty of sustaining fertility only to oppose him. 'Lear at once adopts and disowns the storm that is the sign of his exile', Kenneth Gross glosses, 'as a god within a cosmos, he strives to make himself at home within the tempest, to make it something that he knows and that knows him'.[95]

Yet, Lear cannot re-found kinship, neither with daughters, gods nor elements: in each case, the speech of curse, having fashioned him as unique god-maker in a drowning world, overwhelms his relationship to things. The spatialised world has become an echo-chamber resonating with his own voice, deadened to the strange eloquence of thunder just as it is numb to the subtle overtones of love-speech. Hence, Lear appeals to thunder only to undo the Goddess' fertile work: 'strike flat the thick rotundity of the world,/Crack nature's moulds, all germens spill at once/That make ingrateful man!' (3.2.7–9). For Lear, the womb of the world must be razed to the ground, its archetypes destroyed, and all inseminating possibilities wasted in a moment of primeval climax. The curse on the world becomes the prime instance of a language completely inverted against its roots, twisted in a kind radical double-ness. Rather than a gift given, it becomes a form of radical dissimulation; an attempt, to use Paul Griffiths' words, 'to own speech as if it had been created from nothing by and for the speaker'.[96] This uprooting speech from its ground produces the final result of directing speech *against* the material world, and thus also against itself.

Hence, Lear, Gloucester and Edmund all show how a cosmology of 'spatialisation', bereft of the language of praise, reduces the orders of reality to a single, univocal plane. In this sense, the language that touches on 'nature' is ironic; rather than intelligible within the context of an 'immanent religion', it represents a world in which genuine religious speech has become impossible.[97] We saw in Chapter 2 how the sway of doxological speech is offered to a God who is the ground of both *est* and *posse*, extending *posse* into *est* and *vice versa*. But here, the take-over of language entails a diminution of the potencies of language and of life: for Lear, Gloucester and Edmund all appeal to Nature as a static and uncreative *est*, attempting to keep 'potency' in their control. The abasement of the symbolic and transcendent reaches of speech comes together with a mistrust of *both* matter *and* word. Bereft of the lure of praise, speech increasingly turns against itself, caught in a world-denying self-curse. Rather than an 'Ark of Speech', the human voice has become the diluvial drowning of creaturely being. The misogynistic sentiments so detectable in the play point to more than a simple re-affirmation of the patriarchal order: through it ring a deeper rejection of the creativity of words, a wrenching of speech away from its own womb, 'Praise itself'.[98]

Lear's curse, however, is ultimately unsuccessful: rather than a primeval flood which drowns the world, the cleansing rain will in fact unite with the drenched earth to provide a landscape of renewal: 'the storm-watered wasteland of the play's middle', observes Berry, 'provides the uncanny matrix, or breeding ground, in which elements that have been ejected and refused both by the old and the new political order' can acquire 'new insights through their exploration of this "rank" geography'.[99] Words have dissolved social bonds just as rain threatens to wash over territorial boundaries, yet for the world to continue, the play's 'middle' must provide new words of fertility and regeneration— the 'Saturnalian freedom' that words enjoy will ensure that the resources of speech come to the aid of a praise-less world. It is how these efforts to re-articulate a salvific bond between word and world that we now turn.

Swearing and Jesting in Vain

As Lear calls on the gods to banish the language of love, his court shakes with a thunder of words. If the King's action has caused Cordelia's speech to flicker on the edge of silence, Kent's words threaten to explode the court with anger. Speech for him is a visceral, bodily gesture: speaking 'plainness', he 'vents clamour from the throat' demanding that the King 'revoke [his] gift' (1.1.165–167). For Kent, courtly speech *only* serves to express his absolute dedication to Lear—'Royal Lear,/Whom I have ever honoured as my king,/Loved as my father, as my master followed,/As my great patron thought on in my prayers' (1.1.140–143)— otherwise, the niceties of such rhetoric are for him subjected to satire, even at the cost of his well-being, as when he is rebuked by Cornwall for affecting 'plain' speech (2.2.103–106). In accord with Cordelia's silence, Kent initially strives to protect the 'middle', for he attempts to come 'betwixt' the power of speech of the King and his unjust sentence (1.1.172), '*between* the dragon and his wrath' (1.1.22), and between Lear's vow to the gods and its destination, interrupting 'Now, by Apollo—' with 'Now by Apollo, King/Thou swear'st thy gods in vain'.[100] Even the name of the gods, be they Apollo, Jupiter or Juno, only serve to swear to the King that the order of things has been violated, and hence that the divinely given power of speech to swear oaths has been made powerless (1.1.162–163; 2.2.210–212).

Disguised as Caius, Kent discloses to the audience that his heart labours for his master (1.4.1–7) even despite having been termed a 'recreant' and no longer being in the King's service.[101] Service is for him a transcendent principle, ontologically prior to other socio-political

110 Readings

obligations, and placing an absolute ethical demand on humanity.[102] Bound to his mission, he nonetheless expresses the necessary condition for its success: '*If but as well* I other accents borrow/That can my speech diffuse' (1.4.1–2). Unlike for Edgar later, the play is not specific about Kent's 'accents' but, in fact, the unsettling paradoxical power of his 'plainness', adopting a performance of plain language in order to condemn the performance of language, is never 'diffused'.[103] Just as Cordelia cannot speak beyond returning her duties 'as are right fit', Kent cannot go beyond his clamorous denunciation of perverted service. As he encounters his archetypal opposite, Goneril's steward Oswald, Kent flares up into a passionate tirade of unprovoked insults, naming him

> A knave, a rascal, an eater of broken meats; a base, proud, shallow, beggarly, three-suited, hundred-pound, filthy, worsted-stocking knave; a lily-livered, action-taking knave, a whoreson, glass-gazing, super-serviceable finical rogue; one-trunk-inheriting slave, one that wouldst be a bawd in way of good service, and art nothing but the composition of a knave, beggar, coward, pandar, and the son and heir of a mongrel bitch: one whom I will beat into clamorous whining, if thou deniest the least syllable of thy addition.
> (2.2.14–23)

Recalling Edmund's entanglement in the lexicon of 'bastardy', these formidable invectives are built around the refrain of 'knave', a semantic centre which yokes together images of sycophantic service, a foppish concern for appearances and a nebulous place in the order of things underwritten by cowardice. For Kent, the reason for such vehemence is simple: 'no contraries hold more antipathy/Than I and such a knave' (2.2.85–86). Cornwall and Gloucester, unable to understand this, quickly conclude that this amounts to needlessly rash behaviour; yet, Kent points out to them that it is Oswald who is in fact 'unnecessary': the 'whoreson zed', an illegitimate letter in the alphabet of honour (2.2.62). For Kent, 'anger has a privilege' (2.2.67), which is to protect the bonds of speech: what one says, for him, shows what one serves. To speak otherwise is blasphemy.

As Giorgio Agamben has shown, the blasphemous impulse is one which threatens the power of the oath as the bond between God and words and thus the very 'sacrament of language'.[104] The power of the oath is sustained by the very name of God, a power synonymous with language itself: 'to speak is, above all, to swear to believe in the name'.[105] For Kent then, the *middle* of language is an oath of loving service. For one whose life is but a 'pawn' in the King's hand, Oswald thus commits the ultimate blasphemy: he usurps the sacred power of the oath. Hence for Kent, Oswald's very existence is a blaspheme, since this 'knave' is one who purposefully gnaws at the bond of words: a 'rat' who 'bite[s] the holy cords atwain/Which are too intrince to unloose' (63–72). Thus,

Kent's language, which performs his very duty, must turn to pure invective. 'Knave' is more than a term of affront: it is the blasphemous curse-word that has usurped the divine name under which all oaths are guaranteed.

Yet, this fruitless and sterile repetition of one curse-word never generates new understanding, but only succeeds in providing the inverted image of the non-identical repetition that is genuinely creative speech.[106] Hence, paradoxically, it is the name 'knave' which lands Kent in the stocks. Without the mediating power of the 'middle', Kent simply cannot 'go out of his dialect' (2.2.107) and cannot create a language of regeneration. Because his words *are* his allegiance to Lear, Kent cannot move beyond the logic of 'antipathies' and equivocal opposites or what Roland Barthes calls 'that semantic solidarity which unites simple contraries'.[107] Thus united to his own 'contrary' Oswald, Kent's absolute ontological allegiance imprisons him. Powerless, he must turn to other words of hope: Cordelia's written promises (2.2.166–171).

The Fool understands the paradoxical pertinence of Kent's ending up in the stocks:

> let go thy hold when a great wheel runs down a hill lest it break thy neck with following it; but the great one that goes upward, let him draw thee after. When a wise man gives thee better counsel give me mine again; I would have none but knaves follow it, since a fool gives it.
>
> (2.2. 261–266)

The Fool's riddling language attempts to go further than Kent's allegiance to the truth of service: indeed, his performance shows his words to be as wise as they are foolish, performing a rhetorical double-take on themselves. His careful witticisms ensure a kind of non-committal 'nothing' which is at the heart of his 'license': his standing as a 'witty' fool allows him to speak a paradoxical middle which articulates both conventional wisdom ('let go thy hold etc.') and its opposite ('give me mine again; I would have none but knaves follow it').[108]

Numerous critics, with good reason, find in the Fool's presence an aspect of salutary irony and level-headed skepticism in the play.[109] For Ewan Fernie, the Fool's role is nothing less than to bring about the salutary effect of a Christian 'shame', by presenting Lear with 'a parade of grotesquely degraded images of himself'.[110] Yet, this is perhaps to see him as too responsible, attempting to set Lear on a journey towards spiritual growth rather than, more simply and mysteriously, labouring 'to outjest/[Lear's] heart-struck injuries' (3.1.16–17).[111] Indeed, as Indira Ghose notes, the Fool's jests, witty and wise though they may be, are ultimately not the catalysts of any redemption.[112] It may also be tempting to see in the Fool a shade of 'learned ignorance', suggesting the Cusan and Erasmian roots of such a character.[113] But in the case of Erasmus, the praise of folly is ultimately turned on its head: it begins as an ironic encomium but finishes as a praise of the divine, implicitly developing the paradoxically ecstatic ground of Christian folly as the true praise of wisdom. It is *this* sort of transforming and transformative folly that ultimately provides an ascent to wisdom—one which Lear's Fool does not seem to generate.[114]

Indeed, in *Lear*, the speech of folly remains rooted to the tergiversations of a 'culture of paradox'. It persists as a subtle critique which is only and ever the reverse image of that which it seeks to mirror, as Rosalie Colie puts it: 'always challenging some orthodoxy', its goal is to provide 'an oblique criticism of absolute judgement or absolute convention'.[115] Here, Shakespeare accords no superior wisdom to such metatheatrical commentary—indeed the ultimate powerlessness of the Fool's words in the play may subtly mirror the powerlessness of the skeptical, witty commentator *tout court*. Caught in the dynamic of the 'ontology of violence', where speech has been usurped by force, Lear's courtly Fool can only emulate the reverse side of this power manoeuvre. Thus, the speech of witty critique only subtly mirrors; it does not *affirm*.[116] Just as with Kent's situation the oaths of service have been made groundless, the speech of witty wisdom, uprooted from its ground in Praise, is ineffective. If his own prudential sayings are short-circuited by his own clever witticisms, proverbial speech is a kind of 'nothing' that is reduced to nothing when confronting the forces of cosmic change that have been unleashed in the play.

Northrop Frye's elaborate archetypal criticism—which chronicles the downfall of the 'ironic' mode of literature—whose scope is precisely the critique of irresolvable breakdowns in social order, as coincident with a return to mythical forms, suggests a useful analogue to the passage from witty court speech to the kind of cosmo-demonic words uttered on the heath and in the hovel.[117] Indeed, sensing the coincidence between the oncoming of the storm and the decline of his professional foolery, the Fool sings: 'But I will tarry, the fool will stay,/And let the wise man fly' (2.2271–272). What the play seems to call for, as René Fortin argues, is a rift in speech that will permit a 'semantic of diabolism', a reading of language fit 'to enter the concepts of sin and diabolical energy into the calculus of the play'.[118] The speech of witty prudence beats against the gate of custom, but the cataclysm of *King Lear* rages outside court and castle. Words of wisdom will not do: words of pain, followed by words of love, are the way forward.

The Voice of the Skeleton Man

In the wild night, the storm rages—hard by is a hovel. The Fool's needling wit has not propitiated a turn to wisdom in Lear, whose own 'wits begin to turn' (3.2.66). Yet, this also initiates a turn to the Fool no longer as a professional entertainer—a recognisable social role in a King's court—but first as *another*, a fellow being in the tempest: 'How dost my boy? Art cold? I am cold myself' (67–68). Now Lear prays, no longer to gods and goddesses he once expected to be his own 'servile ministers', but *addressing* 'poor naked wretches, wheresoe'er you are' (3.4.28). Though still a 'whereso'er', space is no longer filled with commanding speech, curses and vengeful words, but begins to resound with words of genuine response. Consequently, words of prayer begin to discern the presence of sacred beings to whose very revelations Lear needs to listen and bear witness.

> take physic, pomp,
> Expose thyself to feel what wretches feel,
> That thou mayst shake the superflux to them
> And show the heavens more just.
>
> (3.4.33–35)

Invoking those who live at the margins of society, Lear's apostrophic speech is beginning to discern its own healing. Only through 'exposing' itself to fellow-feeling with 'wretches', Lear seems to feel, can 'pomp' become the manifestation of heavenly justice. Yet, as he himself had prophetically uttered, these are they who are 'in the poorest things superfluous'. Though he now wishes to conduct kingship with a just economy, it does not yet occur to Lear that the wretches might be able to 'shake the superflux' *to him*—to offer the superfluous, gratuitous yet vital *gift* of genuine insight and genuine words.

Yet, what is left to say with love banished, justice silenced and wisdom paralysed; if fathers have silenced their children, only for their children to seek to silence their fathers; if the very gods that one addresses seem to have fallen silent? 'If we cannot rationally predict or organize or guarantee some sort of reconciliation and healing', writes Rowan Williams,

> we have no choice but to approach it through *fiction* – not as a means of evading or denying an unpalatable present but as a form of acknowledging resources that are there in or for our present world, but to which we do not yet have straightforward access.[119]

Lear's call for 'physic' brings out such resources out of the world of fiction; the gods answer his prayer by way of the fictional, fiction-making medicine man that is Tom O' Bedlam.[120]

Kent had not succeeded in attempting 'to go out of his dialect'; but Edgar, significantly, does. Initially a very accommodated man, Edgar had in fact suffered the results of the Lear-world's deafness and dumbness: betrayed by a false letter and tried *in absentia* by his father, his own words had remained unheard. Proclaimed a traitor, he escapes by means of a dissolution of his identity, cloaking himself in nakedness (2.3.176–182). Yet, his being 'nothing' opens a space for a creative kind of language that is also genuine, a brand of *serioludere* that Larry Bouchard calls 'playing nothing for someone', a kenotic move 'where playing other roles may free us *for* one another'.[121] This mode of 'kenotic integrity' is, as Bouchard points out, a theatrical form where the requirements of authentic relationship blend together the realms of truth and fiction, of self and others, juxtaposing 'ideas and stories... without presuming to know their wholeness' and entering 'contingent spaces where others may enter as well'.[122]

Yet, playing this way, Edgar implicates himself in his own playing, worrying that genuine pain will overcome him and 'mar his counterfeiting' (3.6.58–59). Indeed, the language of Tom O' Bedlam, as Simon Palfrey shows in an adventurous phenomenological reading, offers a plurivocal collection of overlapping and contradictory voices, dissolving any traditional notion of stable human selfhood:

> Tom's idiom is radically indifferent to customary dialogical rules. It evokes some hobgoblin remainder—part ruined prose, part ruined verse, part ruined song. Verse is the mode of gentles like Edgar, prose of servants and beggars, and song of the suprapersonal community. All are at once recalled and scotched in Tom's vocative superflux. The effect is instantly to detonate decorum... Customary orders, affiliations, and relations of word to person or to deed are suddenly insecure...[123]

This 'detonation of decorum' may recall aspects of the Fool's speech. But Tom's 'vocative superflux' escapes the stable paradoxes of courtly wit because it is a *response* to Lear's invocation of a 'physic'. T. S. Eliot had sensed the requirement for a foolish kind of speech that is also medicinal in his reading of the Fool as 'a possessed; a very cunning and very intuitive person' who has 'more than a suggestion of the shaman or medicine man'—only perhaps, he had picked the wrong fool.[124] Mircea Eliade has written of the shamanistic 'skeleton condition', where the shaman, through a 'technique of ecstasy', can envision his own radical nakedness, beneath flesh and blood and to his bones: a 'naked fellow' who 'nothing' is. Such condition has a double aim: 're-entering the womb of primordial life' and an ascetic reduction of life as 'an ephemeral illusion in perpetual transformation'.[125] 'In so doing', Eliade writes, 'he must not use ordinary human speech, but only the special and sacred shaman's language', a language which voices both animal and spiritual beings, expressing energies that circulate beyond the scope of discursive reason.[126]

To be sure, Tom certainly hints at literary conventions of druids or wild men popular in medieval and early Renaissance literature.[127] But if Shakespeare does indeed make use of such tropes, it is not to offer an anti-humanist critique of the affectations of society, using a literary conceit in order to denounce conceitedness.[128] Rather, Tom's 'vocative superflux' may be paradoxically revelatory and decisive, the 'unnecessary' voice that is saying what it is most necessary to hear in order to 're-enter the womb' of words and reveal the 'skeleton' of language beneath the stranglehold of violence. Language overburdened by force creates a demonic surplus, which paradoxically articulates truth. Thus, 'what wretches feel', and not what they ought to say, will come from a voice that indeed reaches for the true words that, banished and betrayed, lurk beneath and beyond 'decorum'.

Before entering the hovel, Edgar had alluded to a register that would fluidly move from curses to blessings; to survive, he would have to speak, he tells the audience, 'Sometime with lunatic bans, sometime with prayers' (2.2.190). Here, he offers as 'physic' words which reverse Lear's curses on himself and his daughters: 'Bless thee from whirlwinds, star-blasting and taking' (59).[129] Yet, as Palfrey shows, the 'illocutionary certainty' of selfhood is modulated, primally haunted by other voices in need of speech.[130] Indeed, Tom also voices the non-human world: he 'speaks the poor creature of earth', becoming a tormented spokesperson for 'the sharp hawthorns', 'the cold wind', the 'ford and whirlpool', 'bog and quagmire' (46; 51–52), haunted even by 'the voice of a nightingale' (3.6.32), consuming what he becomes and, in turn, becoming the mouthpiece of what he consumes: 'he eats cow-dung for salads; swallows the old rat and the ditch-dog; drinks the green mantle of the standing pool' (3.4.127–129).[131] His multiple voices sound the protestations of a world whose thick rotundity has been spatialised into *res extensa*, rendered *mute* by the geometric logic of speech-as-power.

Attempting to expose himself to the superflux of such 'skeleton' revelations, Lear translates and rephrases Tom's suffering as caused by 'unkind daughters' (3.4.48–49; 62; 69–70) hesitating, as James Kearney notes, between genuinely 'exposing himself to alterity' and 'incorporating all difference into his narcissistic passion'.[132] Compelled to comprehend the mechanics behind his own present state, he asks: 'What has thou been?' (82). Here, Tom switches register: he now presents himself as a sometime sophisticated socialite, a courtly 'serving man, proud in heart and mind' whose being was crippled with duplicity, swearing 'as many oaths as I spake words and broke them in the sweet face of heaven' (86–87). Yet again, the register of the private confessional is inappropriate to contain the 'superflux': these words belong to a polyphony of voices that all expose the catastrophic underlay of 'gentlemanly' life, be it in Lear's court or in Gloucester's house. Likewise, the list of 'catechisms' and moral advice he speaks (92–96) could be spoken by demonic voices who manipulate Tom, casting spells by speaking outworn truisms which bear witness to the very same moral map that Lear and Gloucester abuse and Edmund manipulates.[133]

Seeing his father enter the hovel, Tom at once evokes 'the fould fiend Flibbertigibbet' who 'hurts the poor creatures of earth', obliquely suggesting Gloucester's implications in the state of things. Gloucester is shocked that Lear has 'no better company'; indeed, he attempts to silence Tom, requesting 'no words, no words' as they leave the hovel. But Tom's childish parting rhyme 'Childe Rowland to the dark tower came,/ His word was still Fie, foh and fum...' (3.4.178–179) through a kind of 'darkly poignant infantilism', evokes the hidden Edgar through the 'love and hurt that are expressible only through apostrophe'.[134] For Gloucester too, this shamanic *serioludere* is medicinal: 'My son/Came then into my mind', he will later admit of this fated encounter, even though his mind 'was then scarce friends with him' (4.1.35–37).

But if the language of conventional morality has become implicated in demonic speech, it is because it cannot fully contain, absolve or explain the sufferings of the Lear-world. That Tom's speeches should house forces that resist the linearities of language serves to reveal the skeletal agonies of speech and the call for words to return to their 'womb'. His words suggest the reach of the human voice when, pushed beyond its syntactical logic by the extremes of suffering, it allows other voices into its sway.

Hence, Edgar's 'I nothing am' (2.2.192) antiphonally echoes Cordelia's 'nothing': the 'middle' has transmuted into the hovel in the storm, a place separate from the socio-political order that paradoxically has become its theatre—in the sense of Peter Brook's 'empty space', a sacred stage for a ritual in which the invisible can be made visible, and the unspoken uttered.[135] Thus, Tom's voice too is a kind of middle-voice, which theatrically attempts to salvage genuine communication from the tyrannies of speech. With the pain caused by the banishment of love, Edgar also voices the torments of a muted, ravaged natural world, abandoned by the safeguard of human language as the 'Ark of Speech' and left to drown in a deluge of curse-words.

However, Lear's 'exposure' to Tom does not lead him to receive the 'superflux' but rather to philosophise about it, rebranding Tom 'the thing itself'—a free being not indebted to human or non-human orders (3.4.102). Owing nothing, Tom functions outside the circles of feudal sociality and, unlike the 'Pelican daughters' who renege their debts and are therefore cursed, Tom's freedom from this system of gift-exchange is his wisdom. Here, Lear interprets being human, as Rowan Williams puts it, to be the 'the pure *object*—a reality existing always and only in the third person, devoid of reciprocity'.[136] He admires in Tom what is impossible in humankind, to be free of mutual debt, mutual relationality.[137] Freedom for Lear is only possible when *not* in the sway of gift, of grace: it is to be 'unburdened' from relation, disentangled from the vulnerabilities of acknowledgement and response. Hence, Tom's status changes for Lear, from a 'wretch' to a 'philosopher' who could illuminate the

The Unsaying of the World 117

mystery of the 'cause of thunder' (150–151), a 'learned Theban' (153), 'good Athenian' (176), no longer 'unaccommodated' but dressed in rich 'Persian attire' (3.6.77). Though he starts with a disparaging of the three characters in the hovel that are 'sophisticated', he soon concludes that Tom is the greatest sophist of them all.[138]

Nakedness in Garments, or Fiction versus Justice

It has been my argument so far that the spatialisation of speech and the separating of *logos* from its doxological roots have tragic results for humans, things and beings. Locked into an ontology of violence, the language resources of the Lear-world continuously try to recover and re-articulate suitable conditions for the expression of love through words, whether through vociferous protection of the ancient ways (Kent), riddles of wisdom (The Fool) or even a shamanistic 'vocative superflux' (Edgar). Now, the multiple encounters in the hovel unleash a catastrophic series of events through which the underlying cruelty and barbarity of the stranglehold on speech get played out.

As many critics have noted, the play can be read as structured around a series of failed trials.[139] Act 3 presses this failure by juxtaposing a wholly theatricalised, 'mock' hearing in the hovel (3.6) with a political prosecution where Cornwall decides to ignore the 'form of justice' to violently assert his power (3.7).[140] We have seen that, through the Fool and Edgar/Tom, genuine speech tries to re-articulate itself through its 'serioludic', creative registers. In the 'mock' trial, however, these symbolic and imaginative forms of play are curbed since they now serve *only* to enact the King's wish for a vengeful justice. Indeed, the rhetorical enforcements of the first scene are replayed, since the daughters are reduced to 'joint-stools' who cannot speak for themselves (FOOL: 'Come hither, mistress: is your name Goneril?/KING: 'she cannot deny it' [3.6.49–50]), and the re-staging obtains the same result. The King had, perhaps, hoped for a more satisfactory spectacle; but this theatre of madness does not please him: his playful judges become 'false justicers' (55) whose garments need to be changed (77–78). The play ends with the King as its director and impresario calling for 'no noise; no noise' and to 'draw the curtain' (80). Without the openness to the gift of words that Lear has abjured, the parodic re-enactment of the love-trial is merely its mirror image: a ceremony without justice.

In Gloucester's house, conversely, ceremony—'the form of justice' (3.7.25)—is wholly abandoned, resulting in a barbarous act which inscribes on Gloucester's body the brutal writings of spatialising language.[141] What had begun as an attempt to leverage Gloucester's support (2.1.120–130) ends up in marking his life with an indelible imprint of ruthlessness. Likewise, the Servant's courage in attempting to defend Gloucester against such cruelty serves to show how justice can no longer manifest through any traditional social forms: 'I have served you ever since I was a child,/But better service have I never done you than now to bid you hold' (3.7.72–73). As with Kent, Cordelia and Edgar, the disobedience to social roles serves only to actualise the gift of a deeper obedience to a justice no longer inhabiting its earthly forms. Staging such an unspeakable violation of sociality contributes, paradoxically, to articulate something of the true nature of love as service.[142]

Act 3 features both a symbolic trial which brings no justice and, conversely, an unjust trial which, bereft of ceremony, degenerates into cruelty. For Lear, the question of justice is unresolved in the mock trial because it has become synonymous with a fruitless search for an immanent mechanics of the world; with the 'cause in nature that makes these hard hearts' (3.6.74–75) an attempt which, in Cavell's words, seeks to convert 'the human condition... into an intellectual difficulty, a riddle'.[143] But the wish to abstract from the fragility of this world coincides with its very foregrounding: the less language speaks in the mode of gift, the more bodies are made vulnerable to violence. As Valerie Traub notes, 'From "Give me the map there" to "let them anatomise Regan", the play's cartographic logic moves into an anatomical one, creating a powerfully allusive and alluring spatial style of reasoning'.[144] If the kingdom can be dissected, the body too must be mapped out: the desire to 'anatomise Regan' (3.6.73) coincides with the visceral brutality of gouging out Gloucester's eyes, both being consequent upon what Traub calls 'the logic of the grid', the transformation of nature, through the spatialising idiom, into a representable system of mechanical causes.[145]

With cruelty and reason allied against the creative modes of speech, Lear turns his initial obsession with the 'noble philosopher' into an attempt to reason out a nature wholly without justice. These famous scenes on the heath have led many to see signs of Lear's acquisition of a temporary salutary sanity, an insightful yet brutal wisdom ultimately fusing, in Harold Bloom's words, 'reason, nature, and society into one great negative image, the inauthentic authority of this great stage of fools'.[146] To be sure, Lear now perceives that the symbolic value of clothing hides unpleasant truths: 'Through tattered clothes great vices do appear;/Robes and furred gowns hide all' (4.6.160–161). However, he still dons one robe, that of the judge: for though authority is now nothing more than 'a dog's obeyed in office' (154–155), he still finds in himself the power to pass sentence and 'seal th' accuser's lips' (164–166): 'I pardon that man's life'; 'Let copulation thrive'; 'none does offend, I say none; I'll able them' (4.6.108; 112; 164). Lear still perceives in himself a moral authority called upon to dissect an authority-less world. 'Matter and impertinency' may be mixed in his speech (4.6.170), but the changing places of madness and reason proves to be a circular endeavour, for his new-found critical discernment does not, it seems, wholly apply to himself.

The Unsaying of the World 119

Yet, Lear also realises that his new-found pernicious cosmology coincides with having lost a sense of the ground of speech: 'to say "ay" and "no" to everything that I said "ay" and "no" to was no good divinity' (98–99). The bond between words and world had been sealed by his function as King: 'they told me I was everything', the centre of an immanent cosmos. Now, this power of speech, with its wager on immanence, has been proven fruitless, since 'the thunder would not peace at my bidding'. With his place in the order of things vanished, the very ground and bond of speech has been usurped: 'Go to', he complains, 'they are not men of their word' (101–103).

It is then the realisation of the contingency of his power of speech that leads to the figuring of a wholly unjust material world, and the affirmation of a natural order devoted not to creativity and regeneration but to lust and selfishness (106–127). Here, Lear plays judge again, and though his judgement of Gloucester turns to pardon, it is pardon in the name of a universal guilt which he sees as a totalising law of nature (106–119). He now re-maps the world according to the *aporia* of 'none does offend'—what he has anatomised and 'put in proof' (181) is that the justice of things is that there is no justice of things. It follows that Lear proposes a final, misogynistic and terminally dualistic picture of 'nature', in which the 'middle' is demarcated as a 'girdle' which parcels out the 'inheritance' of the gods and that the kingdom of demons, 'hell', 'darkness' and 'the sulphurous pit' (120–127). For George Steiner, these passages illustrate how the play's use of prose expresses its 'weight of suffering': 'having been unutterably wronged by fair but treacherous speech', he writes, 'Lear seeks to degrade language by steeping it in grossness and cruelty'.[147] Along with words, the world too is degraded, reshaped into a dual, flawed-because-feminine creature which is 'women above' and 'centaurs beneath' (121–125). Under the control of this nihilistic mode of reason and *without the salutary 'middle' provided by a mediation through the order of creative words*, nature can only appear as a cruel, monstrous divided divinity.[148] Lear's final poetic act, having fully negated the poetic capacities of speech, is to create a cosmic demon.

We have seen above that the language of proverbial wisdom in *King Lear* is a response that is by itself uncreative, bringing about no wisdom or insight because uprooted from its transcendent ground.[149] We saw, too, that the sacrificing of all moral rationality and the language of justice in the name of a grotesque theatrical playfulness leads to the same conclusion. Edgar also demonstrates traces of this split. After his performance as Tom O' Bedlam, he surprisingly returns to an optimistic moral posture, seeing himself at the bottom of a wheel of fortune whose cyclicality predicts that 'the worst returns to laughter' (4.1.1–6). Yet, soon this logic is abandoned, for the entrance of his blinded father makes him conclude that only 'hatred' of the world's 'strange mutations' adequately prepares one for old age and death (10–13)—before finally glimpsing that rationalising and moralising always falls short of his situation: 'The worst is not/So long as we can say "This is the worst"'(29–30).

His philosophical speeches are, in fact, shown to be premature throughout the play: attempts to give a moral context to a situation that seems to constantly slip out of his grasp, like a continuous deferral of 'poetic justice' that perforce escapes all ethical judgements.[150] In a play structured around the failings of ethical codes and forms of justice, it is moral speech *as such* that seems to lag behind, unable to bring about healing in the Lear-world. If, as Regina Schwartz suggests, the play gestures at a mode of justice which must be re-grounded and made translucent with love, this sense of moral inarticulacy may indeed speak to this overarching challenge.[151] For now, it seems that neither Lear's new position as the magistrate of the 'naked truth' nor Edgar's split between his theatricality and his moralising can fully respond to such a call. Reflecting on the ontological relation between love and justice, Paul Tillich writes: 'Love reunites; justice preserves what is to be united. It is the form in which and through which love performs its work'.[152] In *King Lear*, the ontological fracture between love and justice points in precisely this direction. Only a kind of human expression that arises from the wellspring of love can ultimately re-constitute the earthly formulations and institutions which protect and uphold justice. Only love can give justice new words.

Despite his reliance on proverbial wisdom to rationalise his own situation, Edgar's intuition is decisive: he attempts to preserve the registers of speech that are creative, theatrical and symbolic, seeking precisely to affirm the heuristic and revelatory functions of language, 'matter and impertinency mixed/Reason in madness' (4.6.170–171) through which something like the union of love and justice can once again be sensed, explored and affirmed. Thus, playing seriously to his own father, Edgar recreates a set of mythopoeic conventions and a narrative necessary for Gloucester's life to become intelligible again.[153] Through an ekphrastic description of an imaginary scene at the edge of a cliff, Edgar suggests to Gloucester's imagination a story of fall and redemption, encouraging him, after his 'fall', to 'Think that the clearest gods, who made their honours/ Of men's impossibilities, have preserved thee' (4.6.73–74). 'Thy life's a miracle', he enthuses as his father rises, 'Speak yet again' (55). The fiction he has created for him will provide, he hopes, a manner to make sense of things and speak a language that is doxological, oriented to the Good. Gloucester's later prayers give a sense that this is possible: he offers his life to the gods and a blessing to his disguised son: 'The bounty and the benison of heaven/To boot, to boot' (221–222). Much has been written over the metatheatrical 'delusions' that underscore this scene, as though the play staged the very dualism on which literary criticism thrives: 'the dichotomy between the falsely artful and the nakedly true'.[154] However, that the 'clearest gods' have acted through the creative aspects of human language does not discredit but rather substantiates the 'miraculous' element in Edgar's performance which, as Anthony Baker puts it, witnesses to 'an unveiling of the transhuman potencies lurking in human relationships', and pertinently to the play, 'in filial relationships in particular'.[155]

Despite these miraculous glimpses, however, Edgar himself does not possess the words to fully understand the fittingness of this imaginative counter-tactic: 'I know not how conceit may rob/The treasury of life, when life itself/Yields to the theft' (4.6.43–45). His artful use of fiction has been learnt through 'known and feeling sorrows' which have made him 'pregnant to good pity' (218–219). It is such an art which teaches him to continuously modulate parts to 'cure' his father's 'despair' (33–34): morphing from Tom into a voice-changing fiend, he re-scripts himself as a man who reveals the miracle of his spared life and as the West Country-accented 'justicer' who protects it.[156] In this fictive counter-system of theatricality and disguise, Edgar *resists* Lear's spatialising pursuit of an 'anatomical' 'naked truth'; his sense that there is a vicious, corrupt 'thing itself' locatable in space and measurable in time, accessible behind the theatrical symbolism of 'tattered clothes', 'robes' and 'furred gowns'. Edgar opposes this catastrophic vision precisely by deploying a poetic conceit, juxtaposing a 'myth of the given' with *fictive gifts*. Transcending this epistemological prejudice for a limpid and transparent kind of cognition, Edgar's disguised playing also alludes to a mysterious comingling of nakedness and garment, of 'nature' and 'art' (further discussed in Chapter 4) and adumbrates the revelation of the *logos* in a manner that contradicts Lear's epistemological sentences on the world as well as his own use of *sententiae*.[157]

We saw in Chapter 2 how liturgical performance produces a paradoxical form of speech that unites theatricality and truth—where the human voice, by becoming in some sense a 'work of art', becomes most itself. In *King Lear*, the reverse occurs: the fracture between truth and fiction makes it impossible for justice to take on an appropriate 'garment', since both forensic rhetoric and the symbolic dimensions of the trial are foiled in Act 3. Bereft of symbolic creativity, the Lear-world resorts in its final scenes to perhaps the *most* outworn form of justice: a chivalric medieval trial between Edmund and the masked Edgar, with numerous discussions on its appropriate rules and regulations—most of which are brought up, ironically, by the characters who violently sought to overthrow custom (5.3.90–118; 139–143; 149–154).[158] With this heavy regulation, the medieval trial also acts as a *substitute* for truthful speech: Edgar's real name is 'lost,/By treason's tooth bare-gnawn and canker-bit' (5.3.120), yet he urges Edmund to draw his sword, 'that if my speech offend a noble heart,/Thy arm may do thee justice' (125–126). Just as in the first act, force here substitutes words. When eventually fiction supersedes violence, however, *words of narrative* threaten to detonate the Lear-world: Gloucester's hearing of Edgar's tale results in his heart 'bursting smilingly' (198); Kent's account of his woes is so powerful that 'the strings of life began to crack' (215–216). The stories of love shatter the old order. The Lear-world groans for a salutary fiction, through which the 'form of justice' can be restored.

Insofar as it enfolds the beginning in its end, *King Lear* shows the pernicious circularity of a univocal, 'cartographic' cosmology by exposing its reliance on an ontology of power to the detriment of the full revelation of love. Insofar as word and world have been severed and with the possibilities of symbolic, fictional or creative speech having been radically curbed, nature and its things and beings is apprehended as a one-dimensional, spatialised battlefield in prey to force and counterforce, ruled by lust and bereft of justice.

Words without a Cause

Yet, as we have also seen, the play has opened a space where creative words and theatrical practice attempt to affirm and articulate insight. To do so, they are strangely left without an appropriate 'art', an appropriate garment, since the project of spatialisation has banished the symbolic language of love and rendered all words univocal, promoting a sterile, frozen cosmology. Without the marriage of truth and fiction, life and art, speech cannot be truly doxological, affirming *and* articulating the meanings present in the material world as a gift to the transcendent ground of all expression. Yet, because the 'middle' is the site of genuine speech, grounded in a gift of love and ultimately a gift to the ground of love, middle-speech *must* return if the world is not to simply fall silent. How then does this middle-voice return in the play?

Arguably, Kent's most powerful words are in letter form, for they succeed in piercing Cordelia to a 'demonstration of grief' (4.3.9–10) which, in turn, moves the King of France to pity (4.4.24–25). Thus, Cordelia is driven to become a political agent and take arms at the very moment when Lear begins to be liberated from concerns with politics. As Schwartz rightly notes, this action illustrates a cosmic principle: since in the Lear-world justice cannot in any way reach love, love must therefore go out of its nature in order to seek justice.[159] Cordelia is moved to action by grief; yet unlike Lear and Gloucester's agony, her sorrow, 'a rarity most beloved/If all could so become it' (4.3.24) is deeply generative. Awaiting to see her father once again, she prays to the fecund greenness of the earth to help her constitute a joint blessing, one comingling natural and human capacities:

> All blest secrets,
> All you unpublish'd virtues of the earth,

Spring with my tears. Be aidant and remediate
In the good man's distress.

(4.4.15–18)

These prayerful words, weaving a bond of alliance between the human and the material world, ultimately reveal the conditions under which Lear will recover new being and new speech. Here, Cordelia unsays the language of curse previously uttered by Gloucester, Lear and Edmund: no longer a vengeful, foreclosed 'nature', the ground of the earth is also the place for the Goddess' 'blest secrets' and 'unpublished virtues'. Cordelia here discerns how the goodness of the earth is also a kind of *disclosure*, alluding to a natural power as yet secret, that has not come to be said in words, and that can come forth through a mingling with generative tears. Unlike all previous attempts, her call on the Goddess is genuine, and something of the latter's voice comes to shimmer in her speech.

Lear awakens to Cordelia and perceives this co-mingled human-yet-divine nature in her presence and in her words. Thus moved, he turns to the religious reaches of speech to express the fracture that he feels in his being: 'Thou art a soul in bliss, but I am bound/Upon a wheel of fire that mine own tears/do scald like molten lead' (4.7.46–47).[160] But his subsequent encounter with the material world soon robs him of such words: a self-inflicted 'pin-prick' moves him to add 'I know not what to say' in seeking to be 'assured of his condition' (54–57). As we have seen, Lear has repeatedly cursed fertility, and material embodiment since "twas this flesh/that begot those pelican daughters' (3.4.74–75). Now, because he finds no appropriate language to respond to the totality of this experience, Lear's *body* takes over the functions of symbolic speech. As Cordelia tries to kneel to him to ask for a parental blessing, he is moved to kneel to her.

CORDELIA
O, Look upon me, Sir,
And hold your hand in benediction o'er me!
No, Sir, you must not kneel.

(4.7.58–60)

But he must; for in this paradoxical situation, the symbolic gesture of mutual kneeling *both* violates propriety *and* becomes its guarantor. The luminous space created between two awkwardly kneeling bodies, a gesture creatively articulating *because articulated by* love, offers the symbolic form appropriate for the kind of words that had been missing from the Lear-world: the language of mutual gift, mutual recognition, mutual

124 *Readings*

forgiveness. It is in thus giving a surprising, unprompted blessing to one another that Lear and Cordelia speak praise, bearing witness to the transcendent ground that blesses their encounter. Paradoxically said without words, this mode of middle-speech also rearticulates the relationship between the two; as Schwartz notes, 'Lear is here as much constituted by Cordelia's forgiveness as Cordelia is by her father's blessing'.[161] Becoming symbols of what is beyond themselves, they now have become most themselves. The gift expressed in the previous prayer to the 'blest secrets of the earth' has now resulted in a stuttering bodily expression that is paradoxically clear: a gift of mutual recognition and mutual blessing.

This gesture of authentic mutuality re-enacts a sense of connection between word and material world. The gravitational force that pulls Lear to touch the earth is not that of the play's turn towards death and despair; it is the salutary *weight* of recognition, not the 'burden' of power and destruction. This too is response to a call, a gift arising from Cordelia's prayer. The 'unpublished virtues' that have sprung out of the land meeting Cordelia's tears *also* bring Lear to touch to the earth and pay heed to 'the blest secret' that is 'aidant and remediate' to his being. Together with her, his kneeling on the earth briefly transfigures it as the place for this symbolic gesture, a sacred space, or an altar that both bears witness and consecrates an authentic and generative relationship.[162] 'Governed by [her] knowledge' and proceeding 'in the saw of [her] own will' (19–20), Cordelia has performed a kind of healing which, in turn, illuminates the 'jointure' between human speech and the land from which such words spring. It is thus, says the Gentleman, that the healing is performed, and 'the great rage' is spent in Lear (79–80).

However, this action has brought him to the recognition of Cordelia, and perhaps her full bodily presence is not clear to Lear until he sees for himself that her tears are wet (71). To him now, *her* sorrow is injustice; he doesn't need tears but poison. The logic of spatialisation guides him to the conclusion: 'I know you do not love me, for your sisters/Have, as I do remember, done me wrong./You have some cause, they have not' (72). Lear's anatomical enquiry into the causes of justice and evil has brought him to depict a world in which love simply has no reasonable place. But Cordelia's famous reply—'No cause, no cause' (75)—speaks words that flow from the previous symbolic revelation. Having opened the pyx, the poet-priestess speaks love as a causeless bond, *not* bound to 'the cause of thunder' which maps out the order of justice and justifies Kingship, nor to 'the cause in nature that makes these hard hearts' which attempts to subject the order of love to the dissections of human measurement. Such causeless origination transfigures the order of causality to reveal its analogical counterpart, as Catherine Pickstock notes:

> if finite things imitate and participate in transcendent realities, there need be no finite original, and one finds, in this world, a play of

repetition without original, where each variation is equally an original because it is equally a copy.[163]

Lear and Cordelia's encounter is thus a finite yet original repetition of an infinite and original form; or perhaps a finite yet original response to an infinite, original call. As we will see below, this insight is what will anchor Lear's concern with the repetition of their sacramental performance.

Indeed, because he has at last affirmed and articulated the Good, Lear becomes intent on its subsequent *repetition*. It will no longer matter who wins the war, or even whether the two of them are sent to prison: the vanities of the *realpolitik* of court have become for him nothing but a distant dream. Instead, he imagines a life grounded and re-grounded by the symbolic expression represented by mutual kneeling, where such an action can be performed again and again: 'When thou dost ask me blessing, I'll kneel down,/And ask of thee forgiveness' (5.3.10–11). With Cordelia he can, in his view, endlessly re-enact this economy of love which they both embodied. In this symbolic mode of speech that figures the economy of love, blessing and forgiveness become a mutual gift to one another of their own nature, a giving that is a receiving and a receiving that is a giving—an instance of genuine doxological speech. Hence, the modes of speech that emanate out of this ritual economy are for him no longer oaths, sentences and curses, but those associated with doxology: prayer, song, story-telling and listening, and the expression of true love that is to be found in poetic and symbolic speech: 'So we'll live/and pray, and sing, and tell old tales…/and hear poor rogues/Talk of court news, and we'll talk with them too…' (5.3.11–14). No longer needing 'space and liberty', genuinely free words can be spoken in a prison, a bounded place now appropriate to speak of what is unbounded. There is now another world available to Lear's imagination, *more real* because more generative than the one in which 'packs and sects of great ones' are condemned to intracosmic cyclicality, the cynical world reflected in Edmund's curt 'take them away' (17–19).[164]

Wishing 'to take upon's the mystery of things', Lear also alludes to the relevance of this new understanding of *weight,* a kind of 'assumption' felt through the kneeling gesture.[165] The ambivalence of the word 'mystery', referring both to the political nothings of the life at court and to the hidden and ponderous 'nothing' that grounds all genuine speech, gives a strange resonance to his insistence that they should become 'God's spies'. To be sure, the paradoxical image of Lear's being free even as his most condemned, fiercely insisting on the exclusivity of their love despite Cordelia's prompting to face his daughters, signals the dissonance between his evanescent insight and the brutal realities of the Lear-world.[166] Yet, the metaphor may rather suggest a cosmic situation in which love-speech can only and ever be a kind of counter-intelligence, a secret code whispered by a resistance that speaks for the well-being of all things, unintelligible to because uncontrollable by the language-networks of the established socio-political order. Assuming 'the mystery of things' means to speak, with Cordelia, a language that endlessly repeats the endlessly eloquent gesture of mutual blessing.

Even so, the language of forgiveness seems to be the foreshadowing of another, different world. The divorce between truth and fiction, nature and art, language and love results in a situation where even stories of mutual recognitions are mistimed: Edgar's tale of woe, Edmund's belated repentance and Albany's recognition of dread justicers above (5.3.170–255) all contribute to delay Lear and Cordelia's rescue. When Lear is once again 'burdened', it is with the body of the dead Cordelia, who had together with him found a way back towards genuine utterance. Now that he knows that truthful words are needed, words of blessing, of affirmation, words oriented to the Good, he finds that no one in the universe can appropriately speak them: 'O, you are men of stones!', he cries out, 'Had I your tongues and eyes, I'd use them so/That heaven's vault should crack' (255–257). No longer filling the void with monologic vengeful curses, he searches for appropriate fellow voices to intone a cosmic lament that would move the gods to descend to earth.

But paralysed by this scene, Edgar, Kent and Albany are silenced. They neither know if what they see is truth or art: it is unclear whether this is 'the promised end' or 'image of that horror' (261–262). Kent's desire to reveal himself and his service to his master (278–287) is counterpointed by Albany's vow to bring justice to the Kingdom, a vow which renders him deaf to the hidden revelations in the King's lament: 'he knows not what he says and vain is it/That we present thus to him' (291–292). Bereft of the fellowship of speech, Lear abandons the intuition of an eternal, creative repetition of sacramental gesture and instead returns to a sterile, punctiliar repetition in univocal space: like Edmund's 'bastardy' and Kent's 'knave', Lear's 'Howl, howl, howl, howl', 'no, no, no life' and 'never, never, never, never, never' (255; 302; 307) all resonate in an empty world devoid of its creative dimensions.[167] Thus, Lear dies looking on Cordelia's lips, hoping for her life to be a miracle and to hear her speak again.

What remains of Lear and Cordelia's sacrament is a new sense of the gravity of words that consequently illuminates the last lines of the play.

> The weight of this sad time we must obey
> Speak what we feel, not what we ought say.
> The oldest hath borne most; we that are young
> Shall never see so much, nor live so long.
>
> (5.3.322–325)

Nihilistic readings focus on these last lines as conclusive proof of the utter bleakness of the tragedy. Franco Moretti, for whom the above announces the reappearance of the 'obtuse assurance of sing-song proverb and of dead metaphor', sums up this sort of approach as he concludes that 'the close of *King Lear* makes clear that no one is any longer capable of giving meaning to the tragic process; no speech is equal to it, and there precisely lies the tragedy'.[168] In such an interpretation, tragedy overwhelms words in such a way as to condemn language to be mute in the face of its horror.

Yet, as we have seen above, this is not quite the picture in *King Lear*. However furtively, the play has staged the superabundance of language against the deadening of power-discourse. Words, it seems, can express *more* than pain could ever say. The world of *Lear* feels, perhaps, the gravity associated with a pregnancy that may bring to birth a new, frail but authentic *logos*. In Edgar's last words, the metaphor of 'weight' benefits from this new sense, for it signals an attention and bearing witness not to artificial ceremony but to an authentic speech that befits the quality of the *time* itself. It is thus a curious re-staging of the first scene, except that it is now possible to 'love, and be silent' and feel how love may be more 'ponderous' than tongue. Hence, 'the weight of this sad time' restores weight to language, making possible both speaking and hearing what must be said, away from what merely *ought* to be said, which would be a 'pious formulation' of poetic justice.[169] The piety of words means that the gods must no longer be invoked to justify or support merely human ends; instead, they must inhabit human speech, becoming the very dazzling and binding trans-human excess of words.

Thus, the Lear-world ends not without speech, but with its speech as *verbum infans*, a middle between no-longer speaking and not-yet speaking.[170] Such a world opens to its 'young' the far deeper challenge of re-articulating reality in words that can once again become luminous and attempt to re-weave the bond between word, world and *logos*, or Word.

In its portraying the speech of love as ineluctably woven into the symbolic, poetic and fictive orders of words, *King Lear* is also perhaps a subtle 'apology for poetry'. Yet, because human language extends well beyond even the bleakest sorrow, the play gestures at the excess of the Word itself over against the despair of finite human expression. If Beckwith is correct, Shakespeare will, after this play, turn to the world of the Romance precisely to stage ways to overcome the tragedy of inarticulacy.[171] As I have tried to show, this play chronicles how, even amidst the muting of the world, the middle-voice is obliquely preserved, every resource in human speech attempting to compensate for this lack. How such words can begin to sound anew is the spied promise of the Lear-world; Shakespeare takes up such a promise after this play.

Notes

1. Beckwith, *Forgiveness*, 89.
2. The word will be used with a capital 'N' when used with reference to its invocation in the plays.
3. Simone Weil, *Gravity and Grace*, trans. Emma Crawford and Mario von der Ruhr (London: Routledge, 2002), 2.
4. *Ibid.*, 4.
5. Elton, *Gods*, 272.
6. George Walton Williams, 'Invocations on the Gods in *King Lear*: A Second Opinion', *Shakespeare Newsletter* 51.4 (2002), 89–106.
7. Cox, *Knowledge*, 95–96.
8. Cf. Melinda Nielsen, '"Nothing Almost Sees Miracles/But Misery": Lucretian Philosophy and Ascetic Experience in *King Lear*', *Logos: A Journal of Catholic Thought and Culture* 19.4 (2016), 101–116.
9. On this theophanic aspect, see also Daryl Kaytor, 'Shakespeare's Gods', *LAT* 29.1 (2015), 3–17.
10. Baker, *Unstaged God*, 99.
11. *Ibid.*, 102.
12. *Ibid.*, 106.
13. Stanley Cavell, *The Claim of Reason: Wittgenstein, Skepticism, Morality, and Tragedy* (Oxford: OUP, 1999), 383.
14. *Ibid.*
15. *Ibid.*
16. Cavell, *Disowning Knowledge in Seven Plays of Shakespeare* (Cambridge: CUP, 2003), 58.
17. *Ibid.*, 46.
18. Listening to trusty counsellors was a recognisable mark of the good King 'type' in Early Modern moral literature. Cooper, *Medieval World*, 132.
19. Unless otherwise noted, all references to *King Lear* are to William Shakespeare, *King Lear*, ed. R. A. Foakes, Arden Shakespeare 3rd Series (London: Methuen Books, 1997).
20. Emphasis mine.
21. Stephen Booth, *King Lear, Macbeth, Indefinition and Tragedy* (New Haven, CT: YUP, 1983), 56.
22. As Cooper notes, referencing the emblematic and allegorical medieval traditions, 'Lear's division of his kingdom is in effect an emblematic dumbshow become literal'. *Medieval World*, 129.
23. See Harry Jaffa, 'The Limits of Politics: *King Lear* Act 1, Scene 1' in *Shakespeare's Politics*, ed. Allan Bloom (Chicago, IL: UCP, 1964), 113–145.
24. Paul Kahn, *Law and Love: The Trials of King Lear* (New Haven, CT: YUP, 2000), 16.
25. *Ibid.*, 4–7.
26. *Ibid.*, 16.
27. *OED*, 1a; 4d.
28. William Franke, 'Apophatic Paths', *Angelaki* 17.3 (2012), 8.
29. Notably, Robert Heilman, *This Great Stage* (Saint Louis, MO: Louisiana State UP, 1948), 41–64. This reading has persisted through numerous approaches: for a recent version with strong Catholic overtones, see Greg Maillet, *Learning to See: The Theological Vision of Shakespeare's King Lear* (Newcastle: Cambridge Scholars Publishing, 2016).
30. Valerie Traub, 'The Nature of Norms in Early Modern England: Anatomy, Cartography, *King Lear*', *South Central Review* 26.1 (2009), 45; 51.
31. *Ibid.*, 51.
32. Catherine Pickstock, *After Writing*, 69. See also Dupré, *Modernity*, 73.

33 *Ibid.*, 68.
34 Kahn, *Trials*, 60–62.
35 For the symbolism surrounding kingship, see Ernst Kantorowicz, *The King's Two Bodies: A Study in Medieval Political Theology* (Princeton, NJ: Princeton UP, 1957).
36 On the relationship between spatialisation and the power of number in *King Lear*, see also Michael Witmore, *Shakespearean Metaphysics* (London: Continuum, 2008), 61–89.
37 Kantorowicz, *Two Bodies*, 7–9. For the famous clothes pattern, see Heilman, *Stage*, 67–88.
38 Foakes' choice of the Folio's 'ponderous' (as opposed to the Quarto's 'richer') highlights the importance of weight in the play that Bradley also noted. See the latter's *Shakespearean Tragedy: Lectures on Hamlet, Othello, King Lear, Macbeth* (Charleston, SC: Bibliolife, 2007), 278n182.
39 13.19.10. The sense implied here is 'Aristotelian': a natural force which moves beings towards, and grounds them in, their natural habitation in the cosmos. Augustine, *Confessions*, trans. C. J. B. Hammond, 2 vols (Cambridge, MA: Harvard UP, 2014–16), ii. 352. Translation slightly altered.
40 On this aspect of rhetoric in the Renaissance, see also Debora Shuger, *Sacred Rhetoric: The Christian Grand Style in the English Renaissance* (Princeton, NJ: Princeton UP, 1988), 235.
41 *Confessions* 1.5., i. 8.
42 On the theological extensions of synaesthesia in Shakespeare, see Jennifer Waldron, '"The Eye of Man Hath Not Heard": Shakespeare, Synaesthesia, and Post-Reformation Phenomenology', *Criticism* 54.3 (2012), 403–417.
43 Hughes, 'Forgiveness', 281.
44 Samuel Taylor Coleridge, 'Lecture 6', in *Coleridge on Shakespeare (1811–1819)*, ed. Adam Roberts (Edinburgh: Edinburgh UP, 2016), 171.
45 Beckwith, *Forgiveness*, 90.
46 Ted Hughes, *Shakespeare and the Goddess of Complete Being* (London: Faber, 1993), 276.
47 *Ibid.*
48 *Ibid.*, 278. The 'tragic error' is discussed further in the next chapter.
49 *Ibid.*
50 Lancelot Andrewes, *Sermons on the Nativity* (Grand Rapids, MI: Baker Book House, 1955), 200–201.
51 *Ibid.* The theme of infancy is discussed further in the next chapter.
52 For the connection between the word 'nothing' and the womb, see David Wilbern, 'Shakespeare's Nothing', in *Representing Shakespeare: New Psychoanalytic Essays*, ed. Murray Schwartz and Coppélia Khan (Baltimore, MD: Johns Hopkins UP, 1980), 244–263.
53 Chrétien, *Répondre*, 24.
54 Linda Woodbridge, *The Scythe of Saturn: Shakespeare and Magical Thinking* (Chicago, IL: University of Illinois Press, 1994), 104–106.
55 John Kerrigan, *Shakespeare's Binding Language* (Oxford: OUP, 2016), 350.
56 *Ibid.*; see also 336–366.
57 See also Ted Hughes' etymo-mythological connection: 'Coeur de Lear'. *Goddess*, 276.
58 Philippa Berry, *Shakespeare's Feminine Endings: Figuring Death in the Tragedies* (London: Routledge, 1999), 136.
59 *Ibid.*, 152.
60 *Ibid.*
61 On the interest in the rhetoric of wonder as a counter-rationalist tradition, see for example Thomas Bishop, *Shakespeare and the Theatre of Wonder*;

130   *Readings*

  Peter Platt, *Reason Diminished: Shakespeare and the Marvellous* (Lincoln: University of Nebraska Press, 1997) and *Shakespeare and the Culture of Paradox* (Aldershot: Ashgate, 2009).
62 My argument only concerns the symbolic dimensions that an idea of 'authentic' Kingship requires. Shakespeare's interest in the idea of the King's *corpus mysticum* may well have been ironic or intended to support an argument for unifying rather than giving away land and thus, by implication, a critique of the 'divine rights' of kings. See Paul Raffield, *Shakespeare's Imaginary Constitution: Late-Elizabethan Politics and the Theatre of Law* (Oxford: Hart Publishing, 2010).
63 DVD, 19.86.
64 Ibid., 13.43.
65 Leah Marcus, 'King Lear and the Death of the World', in *The Oxford Handbook of Shakespearean Tragedy*, ed. Michael Neill and David Schalkwyk (Oxford: OUP, 2016), 422.
66 For this 'porous' aspect, see Gail Kern Paster, *Humoring the Body: Emotions and the Shakespearean Stage* (Chicago, IL: UCP, 2004).
67 Shannon, *Animal*, 129ff.
68 The field of Shakespearean literature and ecology is large and growing: for overview of its debates, see Gabriel Egan, *Shakespeare and Ecocritical Theory* (London: Bloomsbury Arden, 2015); Rebecca Laroche and Jennifer Munroe, *Shakespeare and Ecofeminist Theory* (London: Bloomsbury Arden, 2017).
69 Simon Estok, *Ecocriticism and Shakespeare: Reading Ecophobia* (New York: Palgrave, 2011), 27. See also Steve Mentz, 'Strange Weather in *King Lear*', *Shakespeare* 6.2 (2010), 139–152.
70 C.S. Lewis, *Studies in Words* (Cambridge: CUP, 2003), 24–64.
71 Ibid., 25.
72 See George Economou, *The Goddess Natura in Medieval Literature* (Notre Dame, IN: Notre Dame UP, 2002), 28–33.
73 See Pickstock, *Repetition*, 76.
74 Hughes, 'Forgiveness', 262.
75 John Danby figures the play as a conflict between a Thomist and a Hobbesian concept of nature. *Nature*, 15ff. For an opposing view, see Alex Schumann, *Rethinking Shakespeare's Political Philosophy: From Lear to Leviathan* (Cambridge: CUP, 2014), 97–124.
76 Kenneth Gross, *Shakespeare's Noise* (Chicago, IL: UCP, 2001), 162.
77 Hughes, 'Forgiveness', 263.
78 For the relationship between fertility, sterility and Shakespearean tragedy, see also Woodbridge, *Scythe*, 152–205.
79 See Jayne Elisabeth Archer, Richard Marggraf Turley and Howard Thomas, 'The Autumn King: Remembering the Land in *King Lear*', *SQ* 63.4 (2012), 518–543.
80 David Schalkwyk, *Shakespeare, Love and Service* (Cambridge: CUP, 2008), 218.
81 Ibid., 48.
82 Cavell, *Disowning*, 48.
83 Adelman, *Suffocating Mothers*, 105.
84 See Elton, *Gods*, 29–135. On the relationship between *King Lear* and the distinction between *nomos* and *phusis*, see Nic Panagopoulos, '"All's With Me Meet That I Can Fashion Fit": *Physis* and *Nomos* in *King Lear*' in *Shakespeare and Greece*, ed. Alison Findlay and Vassily Markidou (London: Bloomsbury Arden, 2017), 115–138.
85 As Phebe Jensen points out, 'Early modern astrology was not deterministic in the way Edmund describes, nor was the claim that the stars operated

The Unsaying of the World 131

by "necessity," "heavenly compulsion," or "enforced obedience" central to contemporary attacks or defenses of the art'. 'Causes in Nature: Popular Astrology in *King Lear*', *SQ* 69.4 (2019), 207.
86 Kerrigan, *Binding Language*, 351.
87 Andreas Höfele, *Stage, Stake and Scaffold: Humans and Animals in Shakespeare's Theatre* (Oxford: OUP, 2011), 186.
88 *Ibid.*, 184–185.
89 William Lynch, *Christ and Apollo: The Dimensions of the Literary Imagination* (Notre Dame, IN: Notre Dame UP, 1975), 160.
90 Bradley produces an extraordinary list of instances of 'lower animals' shape-shifting into human beings and actions. *Tragedy*, 222–223.
91 F. T. Flahiff, 'Lear's Map', *Cahiers Elisabethains* 30 (1986), 17–33.
92 Kerrigan, *Binding Language*, 355.
93 *Ibid.*, 354.
94 Cavell, *Disowning*, 122.
95 Gross, *Noise*, 177.
96 Paul Griffiths, *Lying: An Augustinian Theology of Duplicity* (Grand Rapids, MI: Brazos, 2004), 93.
97 For the Lear-world's 'immanent religion', see Knight, *Wheel of Fire*, 171–208.
98 Cf. Kathleen McLuskie, 'The Patriarchal Bard: Feminist Criticism and Shakespeare: *King Lear* and *Measure for Measure*', in *Political Shakespeare*, ed. Dollimore and Sinfeld, 88–108.
99 Berry, *Endings*, 162–163.
100 See Kahn, *Trials*, 14–15.
101 Schalkwyk, *Service*, 226–227.
102 I am grateful to Brian Edwards for this point.
103 Kenneth Graham, '"Without the Form of Justice": Plainness and the Performance of Love in *King Lear*', *SQ* 42.4 (1991), 445–446.
104 Giorgio Agamben, *The Sacrament of Language: Archaeology of the Oath*, trans. Adam Kotsko (Cambridge: Polity, 2013), 42.
105 *Ibid.*, 54.
106 See Pickstock, *Repetition*, 128–129.
107 Roland Barthes, *Roland Barthes by Roland Barthes*, trans. Richard Howard (New York: Noonday Press, 1977), 140.
108 Ghose, *Laughter*, 191.
109 See for example Jonathan Bate, 'Shakespeare's Foolosophy' in *Shakespeare Performed: Essays in Honour of R. A. Foakes*, ed. Grace Ioppolo (Newark: University of Delaware Press, 2000), 17–32.
110 Ewan Fernie, *Shame in Shakespeare* (London: Routledge, 2002), 197.
111 For a summary of the debate on the Fool and his motives in Shakespeare studies, see Robert Hornback, *The English Clown Tradition from the Middle Ages to Shakespeare* (Cambridge: D.S. Brewer, 2009), 143–182.
112 Ghose, *Laughter*, 197.
113 See John Evans, 'Erasmian Folly and *King Lear*: A Study in Humanist Intertextuality', *Moreana* 27.103 (1990), 3–24.
114 On this aspect of Erasmus' *Praise of Folly* see for example Michael Screech, *Erasmus: Ecstasy and the Praise of Folly* (London: Penguin, 1988). 'Wise folly' is further discussed in Chapter 4.
115 Rosalie Colie, *Paradoxia Epidemica: The Renaissance Tradition of Paradox* (Princeton, NJ: Princeton UP, 2015), 10. For the 'culture of paradox' see 3–40. See also Platt, *Paradox*, 17–56.
116 As Marjorie Garber notes; *Shakespeare After All* (New York: Anchor, 2005), 674.
117 See Northrop Frye, *Anatomy of Criticism* (Princeton, NJ: Princeton UP, 2000), 203–242.

118 René Fortin, '*King Lear* and the Anatomy of Evil', in *Gaining Upon Certainty: Selected Literary Criticism*, ed. Brian Barbour and Rodney Delasanta (Providence, RI: Providence UP), 232.
119 Williams, *Edge of Words*, 97. Emphasis mine.
120 My argument thus contradicts the common critical assumption that prayers in the Lear-world are left unanswered. See for example Joseph Sterrett, *The Unheard Prayer: Religious Toleration in Shakespeare's Drama* (Leiden: Brill, 2012), 123–145.
121 Larry Bouchard, 'Playing Nothing for Someone: *Lear*, Bottom and Kenotic Integrity', *LAT* 19.2 (2005), 176.
122 *Ibid.*, 162.
123 Simon Palfrey, *Poor Tom: Living King Lear* (Oxford: OUP, 2015), 69–70.
124 T. S. Eliot, 'The Beating of a Drum', *The Nation and the Athenaeum*, 34.1 (1923), 11.
125 Mircea Eliade, *Shamanism: Archaic Techniques of Ecstasy* (New York: Pantheon, 1964), 62–63.
126 *Ibid.*, 96ff.
127 For a suggestive reading of this trope, see Anne Barton, *The Shakespearean Forest* (Cambridge: CUP, 2017), 48–69.
128 Cf. Julián Jiménez Heffernan, *Shakespeare's Extremes: Wild Man, Monster, Beast* (London: Palgrave 2019), 86–108.
129 Cf. Lear's curse on Goneril, discussed above, his calling down wind and thunder, his 'blasts and fogs upon thee' (1.4.291) and his curse on Edgar's imaginary daughters, wanting to bring down 'all the plagues that in the pendulous air/Hang fated o'er men's faults' (66–67).
130 Palfrey, *Poor Tom*, 72.
131 *Ibid.*, 83–90.
132 James Kearney, "This is Above all Strangeness": *King Lear*, Ethics, and the Phenomenology of Recognition', *Criticism* 54.3 (2012), 459.
133 Palfrey, *Poor Tom*, 76.
134 *Ibid.*, 121.
135 Brook, *Space*, 49 and *passim*.
136 Williams, *Tragic Imagination*, 38.
137 *Ibid.*, 51.
138 Paul Cantor, 'The Cause of Thunder: Nature and Justice in *King Lear*', in *King Lear: New Critical Essays*, ed. Jeffrey Kahan (London: Routledge, 2008), 240.
139 See, for example, Adrienne Lockhart, "The Cat Is Grey": *King Lear*'s Mad Trial Scene', *SQ* 26. 4 (1975), 469–71; Paul Shupack, 'Natural Justice and *King Lear*', *Cardozo Studies in Law and Literature* 9 (1997), 67–105; Cantor, 'Cause of Thunder'; Kahn, *Trials*.
140 On this, see Kahn, *Trials*, 88–105.
141 On torture as an inscription of power on the body, see Elaine Scarry, *The Body in Pain: The Making and Unmaking of the World* (Oxford: OUP, 1985), 27–59.
142 Schalkwyk, *Service*, 241–242.
143 Cavell, *Disowning*, 138.
144 Traub, 'Cartography', 52.
145 *Ibid.*, 62.
146 Harold Bloom, *Shakespeare and the Invention of the Human* (New York: Riverhead, 1998), 515. See also Heilman, for whom Lear 'comes to his most penetrating vision' and that this scene 'is his most important in the play'. *Stage*, 197–198.

147 George Steiner, *The Death of Tragedy* (London: Faber, 1961), 258.
148 On this, see also V. Gerlier, "Recovering World-Welcoming Words: Language, Metaphysics and the Voice of Nature', *Religions* 12.7 (2021), 501.
149 See Michael Witmore, 'Shakespeare and Proverbial Wisdom', in *Religion*, ed. Witmore and Lowenstein, 210–211.
150 See Fortin, 'Poetic Justice in Shakespearean Tragedy', in *Gaining*, 179ff.
151 Schwartz, *Loving Justice*, 47.
152 Paul Tillich, *Love, Power and Justice: Ontological Analyses and Ethical Applications* (Oxford: OUP, 1954), 71.
153 See Kahn, *Trials*, 108–115.
154 As Judy Kronenfeld points out; see *King Lear and the Naked Truth: Rethinking the Language of Religion and Resistance* (Durham, NC: Duke UP, 1999), 90–91.
155 Baker, *Unstaged God*, 104.
156 For an attempt to read Edgar's fictions (and other fictions in the play) as Shakespeare's own 'apology for poetry', see Jean MacIntyre, 'Truth, Lies and Poesie in *King Lear*', *RAR* 6.1 (1982), 34–45.
157 On the coincidence of truth (*logos*) and garment (flesh) in Christ, see Cusa, *Sermo* 19.11.
158 For Shakespeare's paradoxical use of chivalric conventions in Edgar, see Michael L. Hays, '"What Means a Knight": Red Cross Knight and Edgar' in J. B. Lethbridge (ed.), *Shakespeare and Spenser: Attractive Opposites* (Manchester: Manchester UP, 2008), 226–241.
159 Schwartz, *Loving Justice*, 44.
160 Marjorie Garber, *Dream in Shakespeare* (New Haven, CT: YUP, 2013), 125.
161 Schwartz, *Loving Justice*, 44.
162 For the earth as an altar for the Mass, see Teilhard de Chardin, 'The Mass on the World', in *The Hymn of the Universe*, trans. Simon Bartholomew (London: Harper & Row, 1961), 6ff.
163 Pickstock, *Repetition*, 33.
164 Schwartz, *Loving Justice*, 46–47.
165 See Jason Crawford, 'Shakespeare's Language of Assumption', *JMEM* 49.1 (2019), 57–84.
166 Cavell, *Disowning*, 68.
167 Witmore, *Metaphysics*, 82–83.
168 Franco Moretti, *Signs Taken for Wonders: Essays in the Sociology of Literary Forms*, trans. Susan Fischer, David Forgacs and David Miller (London: Verso, 2005), 52–53.
169 Fortin, 'Anatomy', 241.
170 *Ibid.*, 249.
171 See Beckwith, *Forgiveness*, 85–103.

4 Words of Childlike Grace
The Winter's Tale

Introduction

In the previous chapter, I argued that *King Lear* concludes with a world awaiting true words. With the art of speech severed at is roots, every creative resource of language is called upon to rearticulate such bond; yet equally, bereft of praise as the ground of their utterance, no appropriate words of justice, no words of service and dedication, no wise sayings and poetic creations can *on their own* heal such a fracture. Without such affirmation and articulation, the material world too has been silenced, reduced to pure 'nature': an alien, hostile realm that is at odds with a wilful, distanced human voice that seeks domination and control. 'Those that are young' are left with a world that longs to 'speak again', feeling the weight of pregnancy of a language as yet unspeakable.

In this chapter, I will seek to show that the mending and reweaving of such bonds occurs through a gift of words made possible by the re-union of that which in *Lear* had been violently kept apart: 'art' and 'nature'. It is well known that *The Winter's Tale* stages a version of the ancient debate between *nomos* and *phusis*.[1] What I will suggest below is that the play re-presents the two realms as distinct yet mysteriously interwoven, a union that can be truly apprehended in the light of the transcendent principle towards which they point. The union of art and nature, I will show, is sanctified when speech becomes a gift back to God which glimmers with the affirmation and articulation of the Good.

Here, the theme of the language of praise coinciding with poetics and *possest*, the Cusan mystagogical name for God, will be reprised. Indeed, in *The Winter's Tale*, art is predominantly figured through *poesis*: it is a play that both narrates and is *about* narrative, both dramatises and is *about* drama—as such, it doubly circles around Shakespeare's own art. Yet, these allusions are oblique, for rather than effecting thereby a demystification of the poetic, the play in fact continuously accentuates its mysterious qualities—as Stephen Orgel notes, it 'speaks incomprehensibly'.[2] The 'incomprehensible' mysteriousness of poetics, as we will see, is paradoxically juxtaposed to the kind of genuine human art that the play affirms: a child's 'tale'.[3] Only such a wondrous and fabulous story,

I hope to show, can be the creative vehicle for authentic words and paradoxically affirm and articulate the natural world and its own mode of sacred creativity. It is such a union, at once fabulous and deeply natural, that can prepare for the possibilities of a final ritual that brings together lost loved ones, restores relationships and sanctifies the material world. In doing so, *The Winter's Tale* alludes to just the kind of authentic language which had been missing in *King Lear*: a mode of speech (or art) that performs the gradual re-enchantment of reality, just as reality (or nature) performs its own re-enchantment of language.[4]

It is precisely because of this quality of childlike enchantment that the critical tradition has long found the turn to Romance in 'late' Shakespeare puzzling.[5] Why should a profoundly gifted dramatist resort, in his later years, to such an outmoded genre? Is Romance, as Emma Smith terms it, 'part of the "retro" fashion of the Jacobean era, a consciously nostalgic deployment of a vintage form'?[6] Surely, after *Hamlet, Lear* and *Othello,* plays that have long enchanted the critical tradition, Shakespeare could return to this passé style only as a heavily satirised, self-conscious form of drama. Such a critical attitude has long persisted: for Arthur Quiller-Couch, for example, *The Winter's Tale* was a clumsy, 'bungled' attempt underway to creating a genre which Shakespeare would only master in *The Tempest*—a much more prominent critical favourite.[7] Lytton Strachey went even further: Shakespeare's late scribblings are but the final works of a bored poet crawling toward death, burdened.[8] Even as recently as 2004, such an eminent Shakespearean critic as Gary Taylor suggested that the turn to Romance was representative of 'an older man's anxiety or bitterness about his younger rivals… an increasingly grey, increasingly conservative man whose ego grows as his popularity shrinks'.[9]

But perhaps such views are based on a biographic notion of 'late writing', which as Gordon McMullan has shown, is largely a construct of the Romantic literary critical tradition.[10] Beyond such cultural and biographical evaluations, Shakespeare's late writings, almost outrageously skipping across genres and registers, seem in fact to resist easy classification. Raphael Lyne characterises such exuberant genre experiment as one in which 'remarkable and substantial things sit alongside notes of humour and skepticism'.[11] For Lyne, nothing of what is grand in Shakespeare is, in his late work, unaccompanied by irony.[12] Though one could make a case for this observation to apply to much of Shakespeare's work, the tonal tension between the remarkable and substantial and the sidelong and ironic is suggestive. One is here reminded of Socrates' suggestion, made to the stupefied Agathon and Aristophanes, that the greatest dramatist is one who is able to unify comedy with tragedy.[13] In fact, as Leo Strauss has shown, it is possible to witness even in Aristophanes' satirical account of Socrates how comedy concerns itself not merely with ironic portrayal, but with a distinctly 'poetical' preservation of wisdom, and an understanding of the comic form as inherently pointing towards what both grounds and lies beyond it.[14] The results of these transactions between the comic and the tragic, the grand and the ironic, are hinted at in *The Winter's Tale* itself. Seeking to describe a recognition scene that occurs largely offstage, a courtier comments: 'the wisest beholder, that knew no more but seeing, could not say if th'importance were joy or sorrow; but in the extremity of the one it must needs be' (5.2.15).

How then, does drama unite and transcend both joy and sorrow? One way to view this is, as Hans Urs von Balthasar and T. S. Eliot have variously suggested, that Shakespeare attempted to attune dramatic form to the surprising return of authentic language.[15] It is perhaps the concern for what shapes such drama might take on stage that led Shakespeare to a form that could marry comedy and tragedy under a 'magical' aegis.[16] We have seen in Chapter 2 how the orientation of the language of praise and its articulation in the liturgical explore this 'serioludic' register. Here, such a hyper-sophisticated form also paradoxically coincides with a return to the cultic roots of drama, a movement towards liturgical practice that enacts, beyond human concerns with good and evil, what Eliot calls the '"submarine music" of the deepest mystery of Being'.[17] These submerged 'ultra-dramatic' resonances, echoing the 'feasting' and 'marriage' of comedy and healing the despair of tragedy, are thus able to subtly allude to a source that is beyond both.[18]

The central claim of this chapter, then, is that *The Winter's Tale* is just such an 'ultra-dramatic' piece, staging a possible 'return' of language through a retrieval of such cultic roots, made possible by the unforeseen participation of *grace*. The theme of 'grace' is obviously ubiquitous in Shakespeare: Chris Hassel detects in his plays five basic 'religious' senses from which numerous inflections can be drawn.[19] But religious allusions reach for texts and contexts, words that are beyond the play. Instead, if something like 'grace' comes to glimmer *in* words, it is precisely because it is to some extent *of* words: as we have glimpsed through its absence in *King Lear*, 'grace' is possible only if the order of words is re-oriented to affirm and articulate the Good, thus becoming open to the gift of its love and insight. In this play too, Shakespeare is careful to keep the heuristic and open-ended dimensions of such a term, as Tom Bishop well notes.[20] Indeed, the word is used, in turn, to mean something like genuinely true speech (1.2.98; 105), a protective oath (1.2.80), the goal of a spiritual travail (2.1.121–122), an ineffable quality that accompanies physical beauty (4.1.24–25), fortune (4.4.739–740) and finally the blessed issue of cosmic theurgy (5.3.121–123).[21] In *The Winter's Tale*, 'grace' appears to be 'ecumenical', keeping open as many senses as possible, and its pinning down 'squarely risks closing down a highly flexible dramatic exploration of the concept'.[22]

As a way to sense this heuristic and generous 'grace' through my primary reading below, I will hold in general terms to what Rowan Williams reads as its particularly Shakespearean articulation: 'the advent of unplanned and uncontrolled insight, healing, or restoration', an occurrence that requires the framing of a unique kind of imaginative logic whose surplus pours through every aspect of the play, which itself becomes 'an increasingly uncontrolled imaginative world, in the sense of a world where the conventional plots of merit and reward have dissolved'.[23] Such an imagination also enlists the resources of the comic form, embracing notes of humour, irony and festivity to evoke something like what Anthony Baker calls 'unauthorised grace', a mode of speech which allows the surprising and the revelatory to shine through words even through their most comedic and chaotic formulations.[24] It is in allowing grace its creative freedom to employ every dramaturgic means at its disposal that we can imagine a Shakespearean turn to Romance, as a highly auspicious imaginative genre that opens spaces for what cannot be merely willed or controlled, nor merely spoken by the human self, but as 'middle-voiced', comes as gift to dwell with in human speech.

Finally, a word about thematic concerns. In the storm, Lear had stormed the order of words to rage about filial ingratitude. In *The Winter's Tale*, the gradual yet gratuitous rebirth of genuine words coincides with the return of a lost child who herself both bestows *and* fulfils the role of gift.[25] In *Lear*, the theme of 'weight' counteracts the terminal war between fathers and children, contributing ultimately to a sense of a world pregnant with true speech; in *The Winter's Tale*, such speech is given birth both through a lost child that is found again, and through the ultimate triumph of the childlike logic of the world of magical tales. These twin themes, 'gift' and 'infancy', will be developed throughout the following reading.

Turning the World to Stone

The theme of the 'the grace of words' has been anticipated throughout this book with my concern for the 'gift' as well as its coincidence with the donative nature of doxological speech. John Milbank's ingenious dialogue with *The Winter's Tale* offers fertile ground for his own thinking on the theme of 'the gift' and its 'fabulous' connection between ethics and poetics. For Milbank, it is ultimately an eschatological promise that grounds gift-exchange, because it responds to the hope 'for ecstatic communication, for "feasting" and for "marriage", which is the only viable paradigm for the Good itself'.[26] Because the gift of oneself is underwritten by the Good, it constitutes at once the surrender of oneself *and* the surprising return of oneself. For Milbank, Shakespeare offers in this play a theatrical figuration of the eschatological hope of a new innocence, where the world is itself returned as 'a transfigured earth', or 'the earth given back as manifest gift'.[27] In line with this approach, I will argue below that 'the transfigured earth' of *The Winter's Tale* is not the result of a divine bricolage unexpectedly patching-up a terminally broken human toy—it is instead, the world and its transcendent ground *praised*, re-affirmed and re-articulated as bearer of grace through and by its human dwellers. The gift that the Good promises is ultimately the gift of words.

The importance of these themes in the play makes its opening all the more pertinent, permeated as it is with an anxiety as to the nature of giving.[28] In this initial scene, the Bohemian courtier Archidamus, speaking with Leontes' trusty counsellor Camillo, worries over the 'great difference betwixt our Bohemia and your Sicilia' (1.1.4) which, he argues, the former will experience upon visiting the latter.[29] Camillo immediately corrects this sentiment: to him, Leontes will offer Polixenes 'the visitation he justly owes him' (7). But Archidamus does not seem to register the equivalence of this exchange; instead, he refocuses the conversation according to the difference he seeks to highlight: 'Wherein our entertainment shall shame us, we will be justified in our loves' (8–9). For him, 'entertainment' is not an occasion for 'ecstatic communication' and sharing, but only the outward masquerade of the 'difference' of power. It follows that Camillo's 'justly' becomes Archidamus' 'justified'; that reciprocity is seen by the Bohemian courtier as a terminal imbalance that is mortgaged by a transcendent principle.[30] Puzzled over the nature of giving, Archidamus' language over-compensates for the inequality he perceives: his courtly style is dense and pleonastic; yet, equally, he is at loss to express exactly *what* the nature of the exchange is:

> Verily, I speak it in the freedom of my knowledge: we cannot with such magnificence—in so rare—*I know not what to say*. We will give you sleepy drinks, that your senses, unintelligent of our insufficience, may, though they cannot praise us, as little accuse us.
>
> (11–16)

Unable to voice a counter-gift to hospitality, Archidamus proposes a situation where epideictic rhetoric is equalised and thus somehow nullified: no praise, no blame. Only a situation in which words and senses are made *mute* can adequately numb this initial sense of shame. 'You pay a great deal', Camillo remarks on this misappropriation, 'for what's given freely'; but Archidamus replies that he speaks in line with the binding purposes of speech: 'Believe me, I speak as my understanding instructs me, and as mine honesty puts it to utterance' (18–20). With Archidamus, Shakespeare creates an initial atmosphere in which gift and language are at odds: as with *Lear*, words are tangled in socio-political 'differences' that permit florid courtly speech but guard against genuine utterance.

Tellingly, Camillo modulates the conversation from the theme of gift to that of infancy. For him, equivalent exchanges coincide in what is founded in childhood and must grow naturally: the two Kings' boyhood love having been 'trained together', it is 'rooted betwixt them' and 'cannot choose but branch now'. Their being apart has been compensated by an 'interchange of gifts' in such a way that 'the heavens continue their love' (21–31). The vine metaphor speaks of two well-habituated natures, whose mature love *must* result from the careful early work of unnamed soul-grafters whose art is blessed by the gods. This will of course soon be challenged; but this image also introduces the dilemma through which the play works out its own logic: the overly *artful* Archidamus cannot receive the naturality of reciprocal hospitality and conversely, Camillo has too much hope in the *natural* foundations of the two Kings' friendship not to have been disrupted by the perilous sophistications of courtly life. Figured here is the opening of a 'gap' between art and nature, that distinguishes both terms *as if* they could be thus isolated. What both agree upon, however, is that Mamillius is a child who seems to be a gift, who brings 'unspeakable comfort' and 'physics the subject' (38–39). The hope of reciprocation between the two countries is represented by this son, who both images and furthers Leontes and Polixenes' boyhood love.

As Graham Holderness has shown, *The Winter's Tale* 'continually declares the necessity of a theatrical language other than the court itself'.[31] The play's representation of court life is not merely mimetic but questioning and self-reflexive.[32] Hence, as with *Lear*, the action in court quickly develops into a foreboding rhetorical contest: one that calls into question the relationships of speech, love and gift. Polixenes' opening words attempt to put into language a gratitude that is inexpressible. Speaking hyperbolically after a nine-month stay, Polixenes remarks that, even if another such period could be 'filled with our thanks', he still should 'for perpetuity/Go hence in debt' (1.2.1–6). But 'perpetuity' is for him arithmetical, because thanking means likening himself to a 'cipher' (zero), multiplying 'with one "we thank you" many thousand moe/That go before it' (8–9). Here, Polixenes echoes his courtier Archidamus' anxiety: the language of gratitude cannot compensate for the bonds of debt, except in a kind of self-muting. Thus, a 'thank you' is for him a neutral value, subject to the laws of an infinite of quantity. It is perhaps because of such anxieties, having imprisoned gratitude in rhetorical formulae, that Polixenes is anxious to leave.[33] Yet, if Leontes is set on convincing him to stay, such insistence is barely audible: despite Polixenes' assertion that 'there is no tongue that moves, none, none i'th'world/So soon as yours could win me' (20–21), Leontes makes no use of this supposed gift with words, turning instead to his consort for assistance with a curt 'tongue-tied, our Queen? Speak you' (28).

In fact, the following few lines show that it is Hermione, rather than the tongue-tied, vine-grown 'brothers', who seeks to compensate for such loss of language. She is put in the initial position *of giving the genuine gift of another,* substituting authentic utterance for what soon sounds like a rhetorical show. Showing the inverted image of Cordelia, yet an infinitely more talented rhetorician than the wooden Goneril and Regan, she enacts a word-combat with Polixenes' 'oaths' (2–29), and refuses to let the matter go even as the latter assures her he cannot stay: 'I may not', he puts it, 'verily' (45).

> Verily!
> You put me off with limber vows; but I,
> Though you would seek to unsphere the
> stars with oaths,
> Should yet say 'Sir, no going.' Verily,
> You shall not go: a lady's 'Verily' 's
> As potent as a lord's. Will you go yet?
> Force me to keep you as a prisoner,
> Not like a guest; so you shall pay your fees
> When you depart, and save your thanks. How say you?
> My prisoner? or my guest? by your dread 'Verily,'
> One of them you shall be.
>
> (46–56)

In playfully engaging in such jousting, Hermione dances around the truthfulness of words, testing the limits of veracity. She re-phrases Polixenes' 'verily' as a 'limber vow', only, in turn, to force the outcome of his utterance through a series of rhetorical questions, dismantling his oath by reframing its consequences into a binary choice: prisoner or guest.

This amounts to a situation which makes her, as Judith Wolfe notes, 'complicit in her husband's repudiation of the conditions of human discourse'.[34] Throughout this scene, Wolfe argues, Hermione fails to discern between play-acting and sincere utterance. Here, she cannot hear what may be genuine in Polixenes' words, translating his response into a further move in a language-game at which she is an expert, and in which, ultimately, 'nothing new is or can be said, because the game cannot be said to be "about" anything but itself'.[35] Thus, Leontes' later theatricalising of Hermione is also the result of her Cavellian 'avoidance': her refusal to fully *be* in her words.[36] As Wolfe notices, though 'ordinariness' and 'theatricality' are set at odds, the play ultimately suggests 'how such theatricality is to be integrated rather than excised'.[37] Theatrical words without genuine gifts amount to 'sophism', whereas a refusal to be exposed to the vulnerabilities of language amounts to a tragic avoidance of acknowledgement. In this case, however, Hermione's 'sophism' is the result of a language *already* unsettled by an imbalance in gift economy; for as we have seen, Polixenes has not in fact offered genuine gratitude; neither has Leontes' 'tongue' in any way 'moved' his childhood friend. Hermione's rhetoric is at once excessive and stunted because she takes the words of another: there has been, so far, no genuine gift and thus no genuine speech.

Hermione has imprisoned Polixenes in words, and while Mamillius plays, Polixenes agrees to stay, moving Hermione to ask about the two Kings' boyhood friendship.

POLIXENES
We were, fair queen,
Two lads that thought there was no more behind
But such a day to-morrow as to-day,
And to be boy eternal.

HERMIONE
    Was not my lord
The verier wag o' the two?

POLIXENES
We were as twinn'd lambs that did frisk i' the sun,
And bleat the one at the other: what we changed
Was innocence for innocence; we knew not
The doctrine of ill-doing, nor dream'd
That any did. Had we pursued that life,
And our weak spirits ne'er been higher rear'd
With stronger blood, we should have answer'd heaven
Boldly 'not guilty;' the imposition clear'd
Hereditary ours.

(67–74)

As is often pointed out, Polixenes here infuses an image of original, Edenic innocence with a suggestion of a sin permeated in sexuality. 'In longing to be boy eternal', Marjorie Garber summarises, 'he is protesting against the very cycle which gives life, against the necessity of experience before eternity'.[38] But here, Hermione questions him about the spirit of *difference*, about *which one* was the 'verier wag', to which Polixenes can only counter an image of *bland, mirrored identities*. For the two lambs are exactly alike: merely bleating at one another, their exchange of 'innocence for innocence' is no exchange at all, since what they receive is exactly what they give and does not flow from the distinct uniqueness of their being. This is not a genuine economy, but only a facsimile of gift-exchange—a safe-ground *away* from authentic giving and sharing. Only in such a way, Polixenes declares, does one avoid 'the doctrine of ill-doing': by exchanging bleat for bleat in a sterile paradise, refusing the densities of material life. Unsurprisingly, the image concludes with a movement from the bucolic to the forensic: for the 'answer' to heaven is not a bleat, neither a word of love or praise, but a bold, self-returned verdict, 'not guilty'; words which qualify the former sterile innocence as already secretly imbued with the thought of good and evil, and of legal transgression.

This remark, an inverted image of Hermione's later declaration of guiltlessness as Leontes' unjust trial (3.2.25) shows how Polixenes and Leontes both mistake genuine innocence with a preservation in formaldehyde away from infectious contact with 'blood' and with 'spirit'. Innocence, as well as related anxieties about blood and bloodline, will be themes developed throughout the play, only to be redeemed in its final scenes.[39] 'Temptations have since then been born to 's', declares Polixenes, because Hermione and his own wife have intersected with their 'innocent' lives. The first thing to be born of this situation of false innocence is thus 'temptation', the paradoxical offspring, it seems, of sterile boys made virile by 'demonic' women, an invocation from which Hermione defends herself with a semi-playful protective oath: 'Grace to boot!' (80).

Tellingly then, Hermione's rhetorical success in persuading Polixenes results in alienating Leontes from a homoerotic friendship conceived as a safeguard from femininity and the natural world. This is perhaps why he links word-prowess with sexuality, as J. D. Canfield remarks, and is haunted by his wife's 'verbal potency'.[40] Imagining that her erotically tinged rhetoric has redefined their worded bond to one another, he fears that verbal exuberance cancels out the troth-plight of marriage, that 'a new word has supplanted their previous word'.[41] This construal, however, flows from the groundlessness of language detached from its primary role as gift.

Hence, spurred on by Leontes' remark that she never spoke to better purpose 'but once' (89), Hermione demands an inauthentic rhetorical counter-gift: 'cram's with praise', she requests, 'and make's/As fat as tame things. One good deed, dying tongueless/Slaughters a thousand waiting upon that' (91–93). Praise is here either surfeit or famine: to be 'crammed' like 'tamed things' brings the praised one to the slaughterhouse, yet to leave goodness unpraised ensures the same faith. Here, praise becomes entangled in a moebius strip of death. It is the converse image to Polixenes' 'ciphers': whereas his thanks nought themselves in a mathematical infinite that paradoxically cancels out the grateful speaker, the praise-giver in Hermione's image, to avoid the slaughter, can neither speak *nor* remain silent—suggestive of the same situation the Fool points out is the rhetorical ambience in Lear's court.[42] Though she gently recognises that having given her word of marriage to Leones was her truest word, 'grace indeed', she subsequently flattens out two modes of speech, the spiritually binding and the rhetorical, remarking

'I have spoke to th'purpose twice./The one for ever earned a royal husband,/Th'other, for some while a friend' (105–107). As Wolfe notes, it is precisely this misappropriation of two analogically related registers of speech that sets off Leontes' unsettling reaction.[43]

In the first scene, the anxiety over gift and language had found resolution in the hopes offered by Mamillius. Yet, with language uprooted and gift cancelled-out, children are no longer thus intelligible. Hence, Leontes' own mental torment, as Cavell notes, coincides with a struggle to 'count' Mamillius as his son. For Cavell, this exemplifies Leontes' 'skepticism': a loss of ability to ascertain *what* counts as evidence leading, ultimately to a failure to count *anything* as meaningful.[44] 'She was as tender/As infancy and grace', Leontes will later recall, facing the lost Hermione's statue in Paulina's chapel (5.3.26–27). This belated recognition of the correspondence between childhood and gift shows the tragic consequences of their severance. Here, Mamillius becomes a sign of Leontes' own vulnerability, his indebtedness to mutuality and materiality, to the very 'gift of life'.[45] This is why, argues Cavell, 'the sense of revenge upon life, upon its issuing, or separating, or replication' becomes also 'the solution of a problem in computation or economy, one that at a stroke solves a chain of equations, in which sons and brothers are lovers, and lovers are fathers and sons, and wives and mothers become one another'.[46] Counting and recounting are movable objects: the vulnerability that comes with indebtedness provokes in Leontes the need for an impregnable tale of vengeance. As we will see below, it will become the business of the play to untangle tale telling from tall tales and from retaliation.[47]

Now, however, Polixenes' suspect tale of Edenic infancy is beginning to permeate Leontes' language. Recalling Polixenes' sterile lamb bleats, Leontes attempts to find solace in an account of human 'multiplying' (Gen 1:22) that favours repetition *without* differences: 'they say we are/Almost as like as eggs – women say so,/That will say anything' (129–131). The word of women is here both clung onto yet recast, in the light of Hermione's earlier performance, as mere gossip. Mamillius, perhaps sensing his father's confusion, seeks to reassure him with a sense of identical repetition: 'I am like you, they say' (207).[48] But now Leontes only has women's words for this. Indeed, the mere sensing of Mamillius' separation from his own generation triggers in Leontes a series of unsettling puns: 'bawcock' (121), 'neat... wanton calf' (126), 'sweet villain', 'most dear'st, my collop' (137), 'my young rover' (175) phrases which, as Simon Palfrey observes, are 'always close to dissevering or dehumanizing Mamillius' body', giving his language 'a tantalizing literalism, magnetic and kinetic, to the physical contiguity of father and son'.[49] As Leontes himself later intimates, he is imagining Mamillius as the boy Leontes, who himself was wrenched away from the barren, disinfected paradise he shared with Polixenes (153–160). Indeed, his reflections on a broken innocence he sees as foreshadowed in his son bring his distrust of words to a head:

> Come, sir page,
> Look on me with your welkin eye: sweet villain!
> Most dear'st! my collop! Can thy dam? May't be
> Affection?—Thy intention stabs the centre:
> Thou dost make possible things not so held,
> Communicat'st with dreams—how can this be?—
> With what's unreal thou coactive art,
> And fellow'st nothing. Then 'tis very credent
> Thou mayst co-join with something, and thou dost,
> And that beyond commission, and I find it,
> And that to the infection of my brains
> And hardening of my brows.
>
> (135–147)

It is Leontes' difficulty in recognising his own son while demeaning the physical continuities between the two that move his meditation on 'Affection'. Indeed, this famously difficult speech is a powerful instance, as Joel Altman notes, of the wilful confusion of probability and truth, which turns 'that which is not into that which may be, then into that which is likely to be, then into that which is—making what is "unreal," real—that is, *res*'.[50] In fact, Leontes sees 'Affection', because it arrives from without and hence is not under wilful control, as able to be 'coactive' with non-being, thus effectively 'fellowing' nothing *into* being—a misappropriation that Northrop Frye glosses as a 'parody of a creation out of nothing'.[51] The fracture between gift and language renders suspect the creative aspects of physical and mental life alike. For Leontes, a covert alliance between the powers of creation and a secret *nihil* somehow able to copulate with and inseminate reality justifies how 'Affection' could 'co-join' or mate with things.[52] Just as his son is interchangeable with another's, now 'something' and 'nothing' are interchangeable ontological co-ordinates, both malleable to and contingent upon the intention of a power from without. Tinged with *nihil*, what is given *must* be tainted, sinister. Likewise, the analogically related registers of 'creative' playfulness are collapsed into one; Leontes' 'Go play, boy, play. Thy mother plays and I/Play too' (186–187) reduce childlike innocence, sexual transgression and the tragic role of the powerless cuckolded husband to a demonic collaboration with nothingness. If the registers of praise are oriented to God who is *possest*, the mysterious ground of both being and potency alike, Leontes (like Lear) attempts a freezing of *esse* into a static and infertile 'pure' act, 'disinfected' from *posse*, which becomes the possession of his isolated self. Shakespeare is here phrasing a parody of doxological language.

Predictably then, it is not 'something' but 'nothing' that soon permeates his speech. If the 'nothing' he has now turned into truth turns out to be nothing, truth itself, indeed the whole cosmos, turns out to be nothing as well:

> Why, then the world and all that's in't is nothing,
> The covering sky is nothing, Bohemia nothing,
> My wife is nothing, nor nothing have these nothings,
> If this be nothing.
>
> (290–294)

If such clamour discloses, as Janet Adelman puts it, 'the anguish of a masculinity that conceives of itself as betrayed at its point of origin' it soon becomes, like in *King Lear*, the key protest about the nature of creation, and thus the ground of a dualistic cosmology. For Leontes, the immanent cosmos itself is flawed by Venus, the 'bawdy planet' that spreads the power of the *nihil* (197–203).[53] Re-imagined in this way, it becomes imperative to destroy the agent of this sin: Hermione, whom he now calls 'the cause' (2.3.3). Bereft of feminine creativity, Sicilia will soon be reduced to a perpetual 'landscape of tragedy, an endless winter of barrenness and deprivation'.[54]

But to affirm this vision of things is for Leontes more than misogyny: it is a matter of spiritual, and therefore linguistic, hygiene: he *must* get his trusty servant Camillo who 'priest-like' has 'cleansed [his] bosom' (235–236) to turn the occasion of confession into slander: 'say my wife's a hobby horse' (274); 'say't, and justify't' (276). Camillo's warning of the danger in such words only convinces Leontes to proclaim him a liar (298–304). When eventually, he condemns Hermione, Leontes asserts that his language wholly depends on his dual cosmology: 'If I mistake/In those foundations I build upon,/The centre is not big enough to bear/A schoolboy's top' (2.1.100–104). He sees himself 'accursed/in being so blest' with his 'true opinion'; truth being a curse, all genuine knowledge is also a form of infection (42), the same infection with which all reality is pregnant. Losing at a stroke Hermione, Polixenes and the trusty Camillo moves him to proclaim that 'all's true that is mistrusted' (48). Here, the play produces something like that which Howard Felperin terms 'linguistic indeterminacy', a condition where 'it is not only sexual innocence… that has been lost, but a kind of verbal innocence as well' a 'fall' into a condition of 'multivocality or equivocation' where duplicity enters the fabric of language itself.[55]

Unsurprisingly, Hermione's recall of the quality of faith in words is powerless: 'I'd be sworn you would believe my saying' (63), she counters him incredulously. At the play's opening, Hermione had been a rhetorical champion: yet now, the words to respond to Leontes' accusation of adultery are simply unavailable:

> Should a villain say so,
> The most replenished villain in the world,
> He were as much more villain—you, my lord,
> Do but mistake.
>
> (78–81)

Hermione's fruitless repetition of 'villain' reveals her inability to speak to such an affront. Because 'Leontes has denied the very grounds of Hermione's intelligibility', Beckwith comments, 'though she can mouth words, she cannot so much as tell him anything'.[56] Yet, this repetition also chimes with the powerlessness of genuine speech in the Sicilian world. Conversely, Leontes' equation of speech with mistrust allows him to redouble his accusation: her crime, as he sees it, threatens to break the social order, 'should a like language use to all degrees', thus imposing a regime of barbaric univocity (82–86)—which is, ironically, exactly what Leontes himself performs. If words cannot be given because gifts cannot be worded, the ends of language are thwarted. Thus, she tells Leontes, 'you speak a language that I understand not' (3.2.78).

The Rescue of Words: Fools, Counsellors, Oracles

As in *Lear*, an initial situation in which the language of love is avoided produces a situation in which the world is denied. Yet, as David Schalkwyk has remarked, *The Winter's Tale* explores how 'disobedience, critical opposition, and judicious counsel' are all 'shown to be of the essence of service'.[57] Thus—again as in *Lear*—those who at court *give* service employ various linguistic strategies to respond to this imbalance. But Sicilia is now permeated with an ontology of death, and so neither words of service nor counsel can steer it from this course. Accordingly, Camillo chooses to fulfil his oath of service precisely by breaking it (1.2.348–360); whereas like Kent and the Fool in *Lear*, Antigonus and Paulina explore, in a courtly context, the available registers of language to detonate this ontology.

Highlighting that speech and service are bound together for him—'It is for you we speak, not for ourselves' (2.1.140)—Antigonus attempts to exaggerate to its logical conclusion the birth-curse implied in Leontes' accusation: yet in doing so, his own language becomes submerged by the latter's creation-denying utterance: if Hermione is indeed 'honour-flawed', he tells him, his three young daughters will 'pay for 't'—'by mine honour', he swears chillingly, 'I'll geld them all' to avoid bringing into the world 'false generations' (2.1.143–147). Once again, the brutal image here consolidates the sense of powerlessness of promissory speech that comes hand in hand with the rejection of femininity and the suspicion of children. This finally results in Leontes' resolution to refuse to listen to *any* counsel (162–169) yet also, paradoxically, to adopt a misdirected aspect of imagination *not even fit for young children*, as Paulina reminds him (3.2.178–179), unsuited even to feature in a sad tale that is best for winter.

Like Leontes, Antigonus is bound to a system of oaths that, not underwritten by love, is caught in a circular and deathly self-curse and thus cannot speak in a manner that brings renewal. Imprisoned in his ethic of his service, he nonetheless wishes to save the baby, but *only* as far as 'my ability may undergo/And nobleness impose' (2.3.163–164). His unwillingness to transgress his social standing, despite Paulina's prophetic warning that this will result in an everlasting curse (75–78), attracts the power of Leontes' curse on himself: forced to swear he will abandon the baby on a distant shore, he recognises that 'a present death/Had been more merciful' (2.3.182–183). Accordingly, the dreamlike vision of Hermione he receives as he sails to Bohemia merely consolidates the curse for him: he neither hears the truth of the oracle, knows he has inadvertently saved the new-born or sees his wife again (3.3.15–45). Antigonus' implication in Leontes' wilful tyranny of language can also bring light upon what is perhaps the most famous stage direction in English theatre. With reference to 'the ancient Greek wild' on which this play continually draws, the Bear can be understood, as Michael Steffes has suggested, as an earthly agent of Artemis/Diana, its entrance in pursuit figuring nothing less than a vengeful aspect of the goddess' protection of fertility and of wronged women. The Bear's agency is a tragic result of the curse upon the wrongful perception of nature and femininity, a transgression condemned both by Apollo and by Artemis/Diana, Apollo's twin.[58]

Antigonus' bond in words makes his words bound to death; but his wife Paulina loosens her speech from the ethic and etiquette of court in order to bring about goodness. For her, the scope of language is healing, and healing is equated to truth itself: she is resolved 'to bring words as medicinal as true' (2.3.36). From the outset, the audience hears how the dedication of her being to the Good will become palpable in her words: 'I'll use that tongue I have. If wit flow from't/As boldness from my bosom, let't not be doubted/I shall do good' (2.2.51–53). Indeed, she soon diagnoses that courtly speech is articulating the reverse: being 'honey-mouthed', therefore, must now be overwhelmed by righteous 'red-looked anger' (2.2.32–34). The 'art' of speech spoken at court, as Paulina intuits, is no longer in conjunction with either 'law' nor 'process of Great Nature' (2.3.59) but has become bound with the threat of non-being, dragooned into upholding a polity of death. Perceiving that 'the office/becomes a woman best' (2.2.30–32), she inaugurates the transformative action of the play by anticipating its gathering around three feminine figures.

As Anthony Gash has shown, Paulina's performance at court can be read in the light of the Erasmian tradition of 'serioludic' foolishness, a tradition which reaches back to Plato and St Paul (and, as we have seen, extends through Cusa).[59] Gash offers a Bakhtinian reading of this trope to show how Paulina evolves from a Rabelaisian 'verbal and physical transgressor of the decorous, claustrophobic world of the royal bedchamber' to, in the second half of the play, a 'priestess-like' character who demands absolute obedience to Apollo.[60] For Gash, Shakespeare superimposes Paulina's carnivalesque role to the stock character of the 'midwife' in both its comic conventions and as a practitioner of Socratic *spiritual* midwifery.[61]

Here, to move Leontes, Paulina performs her 'comic' guise, appearing at court with the unwanted baby, violating court etiquette, refusing traditional gender roles and playing fool to her King (2.3.25–128).[62] Despite a shower of insults from Leontes (68–69; 90–91), she takes over the court with both 'wit' and 'boldness', fuelling his rage while neither husband nor lords can silence her. Like Lear's Fool, Paulina plays on the knife-edge of what licensed language allows: she both acknowledges *and* overturns the 'rule' of her husband Antigonus (46–50); she dangerously alludes to Leontes' tyrannical behaviour precisely by affirming she would never use such a title (114–119); and reinforces the idea that her truth-telling is mostly due to her mere foolishness (3.2.226–229).

Combining aspects of the Fool and Edgar's playing, then, Paulina tries to invoke a kind of 'carnivalesque' grace, trusting that turning the world upside down can somehow bring it the right side up.[63] To Leontes' incredulous 'Good queen?' (2.3.57) Paulina responds by breaking the rules of court and of pentameter alike with her powerfully trochaic 'Good queen, my lord, good queen, I say good queen' (60). In this case, the Good is emphatically affirmed and preserved but, like in the world of *Lear*, cannot be articulated. Here again, the repetition of words has a tragic aspect: it entails an ungenerative identity, a sameness that words without inspired resonance is prone to establish. 'Betake thee to nothing but despair', warns Paulina when Leontes finally ignores the Oracle and Mamillius dies:

> A thousand knees,
> Ten thousand years together, naked, fasting,
> Upon a barren mountain, and still winter
> In storm perpetual, could not move the gods
> To look that way thou wert.
>
> (3.2.209–214)

Such words pre-empt, in Tom Bishop's apt words, 'the gelid theatre of repetition', a religious action of repentance in which the gods refuse to participate; hence Paulina prophesises 'a ghost-theatre, the permanent ossification of remorse'.[64] As words and gift have been ontologically divided, even the resources to produce an appropriate spiritual response to such tragic events are no longer available—in becoming terminally detached from its orientation as praise, Sicilia's art is terminally cursed, locked in perpetual winter.

Yet, the saving language, here, is the word of the gods. Indeed, the reaches of human speech are juxtaposed to the clear and limpid utterance of the Oracle, received through an appropriate and revelatory human performance. It is a distinct aspect of Shakespeare's late art that divine agency becomes staged (in *Pericles* and *Cymbeline,* for example); yet, in this play, crucially, the speech of the oracle is *reported*, and thus relies on an understanding founded on *human mediation* as well as *trust*, an assent of the heart, rather than aural proof.[65] Indeed, Cleomenes and Dion, messengers sent by Leontes to Apollo's oracle at Delphi, report a scene of divine communication at once awesome and wondrous: a 'sacrifice' offered in 'ceremonious, solemn and unearthly' guise (3.1.6–7), performed by some who wore 'celestial habits' (2) in a temple which words of praise cannot describe (3). Above all, Cleomenes seems to still shake with the thunderous voice of the god-speakers: 'the ear-deafening voice o'th' oracle,/Kin to Jove' thunder, so surprised my sense/That I was nothing' (9–11). This oracular utterance saturates the senses as much as it benumbs common sense: Cleomenes and Dion seem sure that, when the reported speech of the oracle will be heard, 'something rare... will rush to knowledge' (20–21).[66] Despite their ignorance as to the content of the prophecy, they know that the gods have articulated in divine terms something that is also already latent in human hearts.[67] The fact that Cleomenes and Dion are *theoroi,* a word which can mean 'envoys', but also 'spectators' and ultimately, 'beholders of god' is suggestive:[68] Shakespeare here highlights the importance of *reported* against direct speech: because it must be received *on trust*, only the latter can communicate clarity when the former has become misdirected. As we shall see below, the second half of the play will highlight the importance of trusting *mediation* and report—figured in the trope of 'tale'—as a crucial aspect in the rebirth of speech.

Hence, in contrast to the florid, equivocating rhetorical manoeuvres of courtly speech, it is the Oracle that, through human mediation, rescues and protects the simple truth.

> Hermione is chaste, Polixenes blameless, Camillo a true subject, Leontes a jealous tyrant, his innocent babe truly begotten, and the king shall live without an heir, if that which is lost be not found.
>
> (3.2.130–133)

Speaking through prophets and messengers, Apollo re-sacralises words as truth-finders by rescuing clear speech to counteract its forensic abuses. In contrast to such lapidary diction, however, the conditions for the possibility of rebuilding a genuine community are given with an enigmatic, elliptical utterance: 'if that which is lost be not found'. The magical aura surrounding such prophetic words, combined with the reported nature of the visit to the temple, already adumbrate that whatever magical thing is 'to be found' will carry the quality of a gift from another world. With the Oracle's intervention, truth must now go undercover from language and re-appear as gift. Henceforth, the play modulates to a dynamic powered by these prophetic words.

The final sense is one in which the play, bereft of 'that which is lost' has neither words of sorrow nor of repentance. Moved too late by the dreadful results of his refusal to heed the Oracle, Leontes now re-imagines the scope of language only as an instrument of shame: as he tells Paulina, 'Thou didst speak but well/When most the truth, which I receive much better/Than to be pitied of thee' (230–231). But Paulina intimates that the 'truth' has now gone beyond what language can do:

> Now, good my liege,
> Sir, royal sir, forgive a foolish woman.
> The love I bore your queen—lo, fool again!—
> I'll speak of her no more, nor of your children.
> I'll not remember you of my own lord,
> Who is lost too. Take your patience to you,
> And I'll say nothing.
>
> (225–229)

Still speaking with an overtone of 'Erasmian folly', Paulina mentions what she ought not to say but ought instead to be burnt in Leontes' memory, intimating that words can now no more act except to cause wounds.

Like in *Timon of Athens*, the tragic part of this play buries language in the grave (*TIM* 5.2.105), the stone of which will publicly speak of Hermione's and Mamillius' unjust deaths. Leontes' last vow is to attend such words there, in perpetual sorrow (237–239). Indeed, the entire cosmos has become unable to sing its most natural expression, that of comfort and joy to infancy: it threatens to perform a 'lullaby too rough' (3.3.53). The depth of despair is come in accordance with the world losing the voice with which it can sing to children.

Interlude: From Time to Tale

In *King Lear*, Edgar attempted to produce a kind of redemptive fiction that could bring about the recovery of the world. In *The Winter's Tale*, as will be seen below, it is the world itself that is reconfigured by fiction: as the real begins to appear strange, the strange and dreamlike becomes ever more fully real. The second part of this chapter explores this idea, introduced by the figure of Time (4.1), whose rhetoric signals a transition from a reality locked in endless chronological becoming into a world where fiction begins to administer the action—a movement from 'time' to 'tale'. This metamorphosis does not simply figure the enchantment of reality necessary for the success of the Romance form, but explores the resources of 'tale' precisely as a redemptive resource of language. For this to occur, several stories, mis-told in the first half of the play, will now have to be told aright: the story of Edenic innocence, of true kinship, of intimate love, and the story of 'nature', of the material world. As I will seek to show, the healing of reality occurs when the right kind of 'art' begins to flower, an art which, because oriented to the Good, can again affirm and articulate the world, thus creating the conditions for the theurgic ritual enacted in the play's final scenes to bear witness to the grace of words.

As was noted above, Cavell remarks on how the play turns on the question of 'counting' and 'recounting', offering the narrative act itself as the 'offspring' of an imperative to '[count] again... either as retribution or as the overcoming of retribution we know as forgiveness and love'.[69] The devaluing of embodiment and the petrifying fear of 'indebtedness' that turns the world to stone will seek its own solutions through the story-telling act. Henceforth, to count will be to recount; to tell a story *and* tell anew *what counts*, what is ultimately of *meaning*. The death of Mamillius and the loss of Perdita will need to be counter-acted by a 'recounting' of the world as gift, where children can once again be received as gifts.

When the pivotal figure of Time appears to announce the action moving forward 16 years, he articulates both the continuity and discontinuity between counting and recounting: figuring himself as a blind counter in the first half of his speech he becomes, in its second part, one who witnesses and recounts.[70] As is often pointed out, Time requests of its audience a dramaturgical indulgence, the violation of the famous Aristotelian 'unities'—but theatrical license may here also serve a deeper reason.[71] To begin with, Time proclaims himself unique spinner of his own immanent metaphysic. Far from being Plato's 'moving image of eternity', Time claims no descent from a prior eternal, but presents himself as a self-begetting creature, ever the same 'ere ancient'st order was/Or what is now received' (4.1.10–11).[72] This eternal cyclical repetition generates hours that are 'self-born', who have the power to 'overthrow law' (begging the question of the 'laws' of temporality) and who can 'plant' as well as 'overwhelm' culture (8–9). His control on the real mirrors his control on words, and he begins his speech with a meticulous aphorism;

152   *Readings*

'I, that please some, try all'; ruling the world by indifferently administering good and evil: 'both joy and terror/Of good and bad; that makes and unfolds error' (1–3).

But his clock-like precision soon begins to be unsettled by his own metaphysics: 'Let me pass/The same I am' (9–10), he requests, asking to dissimulate his dual nature as one who stands for unchanging change yet whose dynamic it is perpetually to disappear. Despite his truistic claims, in fact, Time struggles to assert himself as complete master of the story. With the turning of the hourglass half-way through his speech (16), he switches from cosmological pronouncements to attending to the 'growth' of Perdita (16–32), announcing that he will 'give my scene such growing/as you had slept between'(16–17).[73] He now asks for the audience's indulgence in loosening his grip on the story, moving forward 16 years in the space of a dream. Perdita, it seems, *precisely because* 'untried' by Time, has 'grown in grace/equal with wondering' (24–25). The lexicon of 'growth' suddenly disrupting his sterile metaphysical speech foreshadows that, as we will see below, the creative powers of nature in the play are not merely bound to cyclicality but somehow also overcome it. Indeed, Time's concern is now an 'argument' that, contrary to the sequence that seems to ensue from his cosmology of eternal repetition, he 'list not prophecy' (26), because only true as a unique *event* appropriate only 'when 'tis brought forth' (27). Time's strange rhetoric, moving from chronological metaphysics to tale telling, mirrors a structural movement of the play: from the mode of time that ensures from 'transformation of mere successiveness' into one immersed with significance: in other words, from *chronos* to *kairos*.[74] Indeed the play, as will be discussed below, culminates in the truth of an ending that, from any other perspective than those concerned, might be 'hooted at/Like an old tale' (5.3.116–117; also 5.2.27–28; 60). It is an old tale, it will turn out, that has the power to turn Time's hourglass and overthrow its unchanging logic of change. The violations of the 'unities' turns out to be a dramaturgic irony, for narrative truth shows itself not bound to Time's erratic metaphysical pronouncements but coincides with an old story that, paradoxically, will give time a new shape.

The Art of Storytelling; or Cutpurses, Courtiers and Clowns

For Nicholas of Cusa, as we saw in Chapter 2, our linguistic engagement with reality coincides with our shaping of it. This creative component of language derives 'from the Infinite Divine art', which ultimately seeks to shape reality as a form in which its gift can 'shine forth fittingly'—thus becoming a name for God. It is especially pertinent, then, that the second half of *The Winter's Tale* highlights how the creative possibilities of human language participate in the appearance of grace as 'insight,

Words of Childlike Grace 153

restoration and healing'. As I will argue below, Shakespeare explores three modes of language as fiction-making before turning to a final moment in which it is the real *itself* that seems to offer its own mode of fiction.

As Rawdon Wilson has noted, *The Winter's Tale* 'makes the possibilities of story (whether retrievable or irretrievable, true or false) a central preoccupation' and is ultimately 'a play that is stunningly reflexive about narrative'.[75] This 'reflection', inaugurated by Time, is furthered in the appearance of Autolycus, the con-man narrative artist, in the 'green world' of Bohemia. Time had claimed to be the master of an art which shapes the destinies of others, and something of this logic also seeps through Autolycus' language.[76] His time is 'the time that the unjust man does thrive' (4.4.677–678) because it is always ripe for spinning false tales. As the cutpurse narrative-forger, Autolycus will not, until the close of the play, let the powers of storytelling slip out of his control.

Autolycus' associations with the poet as trickster figure have long been noted: they suggest, as W. H. Auden observes, a role in line with the Biblical overtones of the pastoral world, that of a 'comic serpent' in a 'comic Eden'.[77] Others have read in this counterfeiting ballad-maker an ironic Shakespearean self-portrait; one who can, in Louis MacNeice's words, slitting 'Purse-strings as quickly as his maker's pen/Will try your heartstrings in the name of mirth'.[78] Perhaps falling for such a trick, some more recent voices have complicated Autolycus into a hero of postmodern indeterminacy, exemplifier of metadramatic resistance to logocentrism.[79] Perhaps he himself suggests his shape-shifting, hermetic duplicity: 'When I wander here and there/then do I get most right' (4.3.17–18); yet, he performs his first identity scam on his audience: for while he refers to the lupine mythological parentage of his name ('lone-wolf'), and claims to be 'littered under Mercury' (24–25), he sings about 'lies' and an 'account' of himself he would 'avouch in the stocks' (22). In fact, he never publicly acknowledges his name except in the third person, as part of a story he has spun (24; 92–98). The effects of this kaleidoscopic identity undermine attempts to make Autolycus' metatheatre a token for authorial identity or an argument for post-authorial indefiniteness and hence, by pickpocketing them, satirise both modern and postmodern positions. Rather than an ironic self-portrait or satirical commentator, his significance to the play is that of *a thief of language*—yet one whom, as we will see, is ultimately *given* his true identity by his own art, the art of storytelling. In the last scenes, as we will see, Autolycus' disruptive energy is enfolded into the language of the real in such way that, as Richard Hillman puts it, it is 'the dramatic universe' that out-tricks the trickster.[80]

In line with the theme of sophistry that dominated the first half of the play, Shakespeare presents Autolycus as a roguish master of words. 'My traffic is sheets', he claims, punning on a word which also suggests printed songs and ballads (4.3.21–22).[81] Indeed, as the play soon shows, ballads in Bohemia are a means to truth: 'I love a ballad in print, alife, for then we are sure they are true' (4.4.245), exclaims Mopsa, the young shepherdess in love with the Clown (the Shepherd's son). Autolycus easily sells his 'sheets' to them, as the printed word and its seemingly secure hold on veracity baffles the rustics. Since for them printed material must coincide with an accurate account of things, Autolycus masterfully masks recounting with counting. Mopsa's question 'is it true, think you?' is met by Autolycus' echoing of Time's chrono-ontology, 'very true, and but a month old' (266–267). In fact, Autolycus makes abundant use of numerical examples to report his stories, giving details of time, quantities, number of witnesses, such as 'one mistress Tale-Porter, and five or six honest wives that were present' (270–271).[82]

As the Shepherd's own servant reports, 'he has points more than all the lawyers in Bohemia can learnedly handle, though they come to him by th' gross; inkles, caddises, cambrics, lawns—why, he sings 'em over as they were gods or goddesses' (206–210). Like lawyers (frequent butts of Shakespeare's jokes),[83] Autolycus is able to make the weaker argument stronger just as he can transform knickknacks into vessels for divine presence. For Leontes, law is used as a solemn dissemblance to mask the worst injustice; Autolycus' parody reveals law as mere spin that flows from wit at the service of appetite. Parodying Leontes' lugubrious forensic propensities, he has no hesitation in appealing to 'judges' and 'witnesses' as corroborators of his ballad's improbable tales (283–284).[84] While in *Lear*, fiction and justice were seen to be terminally at odds, Autolycus shows how a storyteller can set laws at the service of fiction. This parodic kinship with Leontes extends to its sexual undertones, for Autolycus' songs are counterpointed with unsettling bawdy (193–197) and a spinning of the very event of 'birth' as monstrous (263–265).[85] As he links word-thieving with cutting purses, he soon compares both even to male and female castration (612–618). As in *Lear*, the generativity of words and that of nature are inextricably mingled. But the blood that, for Leontes and Polixenes, carries primal sin (1.1.73) becomes, in this 'comic' context, the energy for the circulation of wayward and amoral productivity. Words and purses being both in his power, there is no genuine gift-exchange for Autolycus: everything is potentially 'boot' (678–680).

As Russ MacDonald notes, these scenes help foreground the play's ironic relationship to storytelling: 'we ourselves have hooted at the tabloid-style fictions Autolycus has been peddling to the Bohemian rustics, and yet we ourselves are emotionally engaged with and moved by the old story of the stone that came to life'.[86] Unaware of the lone wolf preying on their innocence, the 'rustics' easily believe the truth of ballads: yet precisely in doing so, they release the spiritual potencies of this play. In fact, their innocent faith in tales, while hinting at the felicitous conclusion of the drama, also suggest that Polixenes and Leontes' assessment of Edenic innocence as homosocial and pre-sexual is mistaken: though malleable to the powers of sophistry, the community in Bohemia is in every way earthly and 'adult' and maintains its own coherent relationship to reality. It is in the juxtaposition of simple faith in tales with sophisticated rhetorical manipulations that Shakespeare, as I will show, corrects the erroneous account of innocence that lay beneath the action in Sicilia, making use of the wisdom of the Bohemian community to subtly and non-didactically explore the question of poetics.

As Autolycus realises, 'Though I am not naturally honest, I am so sometimes by chance' (4.4.715). The gifts of good fortune he happens to pass on to others, providing Florizel and Perdita with means of escape and the Shepherd and his son with a passage to Sicilia, are for him by-products of Fortune 'dropping booties in his mouth' (836). But Fortune does eventually *stop* his mouth, when in the ante-final scene, the linguistically promiscuous Autolycus witnesses the rhetorically agile Sicilian courtiers attempt to report an off-stage Shakespearean 'recognition scene' (5.2), at once extoling yet limiting the reach of *ekphrasis* and *energeia*.[87] Here again, as with the visit to the Oracle, the focus is on how this event is *recounted*.

When describing the multiple recognitions, the courtier and servants create a sense of the wondrous (5.2.4; 11; 15–16; 23) which elicits religious and sacramental allusions: for them, the re-union of Leontes and Camillo resonates with ambiguous apocalyptic overtones, alluding to 'a world ransomed, or one destroyed' (14–15) while their communication become quasi-liturgical: 'there was speech in their dumbness, language in their very gesture' (5.2.14). Likewise, the story of Hermione's plight already foreshadows its resolution: 'Who was most marble there changed colour. Some swooned, all sorrowed. If all the world had seen't, the woe had been universal' (89–90). As in the beginning of the play, the courtiers exercise a monopoly on language yet equally, they are at pains to communicate that what they have witnessed is simply beyond the powers of their eloquence (41–42; 56–57), since it resembles an old 'tale' (28; 60), yet one that has the power to speak beyond time: 'though all credit be asleep and not an ear open' (60; 61). Such a story, to them, will defy even the powers of poetry as 'ballad makers cannot be able to express it' (23).

In Autolycus' cutpurse poetics, ballad makers *can* express all things, since all words are essentially manipulation. But this unbelievable story that could well have been matter for his traffic of sheets now paradoxically becomes the story which is about to give him new life. The pull of the dramatic action makes Autolycus retreat from his metatheatrical role as conspiring commentator into a receiver of the gifts that come through this wonder-filled story. His manipulations of the 'innocent' rustics and the sway of words has been absorbed by the forces of the tale of which he is no longer the forger, but the *agent*. This is why the Shepherd and the Clown, for all their innocent malapropisms, actually turn out to be the masters of language. Anxious for Autolycus to admit that he is a 'gentleman born', the Clown exclaims, on the former's finally recanting his opinion, that he has been so 'any time these four hours'.

> but I was a gentleman born before my father, for the king's son took me by the hand, and called me brother, and then the two kings called my father brother, and then the prince my brother and the princess my sister called my father father, and so we wept, and there was the first gentleman-like tears that ever we shed.
>
> (136–141)

Precisely through such a comical account, the story told by the Shepherd's son *reveals* the essence of the un-witnessed recognition scene in a more authentic and metaphysically astute way than those before him. Humorously, he is *able* to affirm *and* articulate—that is, to praise— what constitutes a genuine community and how renewed bonds of kinship with one another gives birth to an authentic family forged by the healing which expresses *both* joy and sorrow.[88] The giving of new names and the jumbling of birth-chronology further suggests that such bonds do not cancel or supersede but indeed *redeem and transform even the ancestral past*. In his being gentleman born 'before' fatherly begetting, the Clown restores an Edenic image that had become sullied: having encountered his true nature in the gift of the name 'brother', he articulates rightly what it means to *be* such a nature, a genuine 'boy eternal'.[89] His account, for all its comic simplicity, is cosmically accurate: the true account of a gifted child-storyteller undoes Time's stunted metaphysics. The triumphant mode of storytelling turns out to be one of innocence.

Michael Witmore has shown the connection between children and the particular kinds of narratives proper to Shakespeare's Romances, how 'their almost wilfully naïve intelligence' intimates 'not so much an expression of authorial regression as it is part of an ongoing attempt by the author to explore the affective force of fiction'.[90] Lacking adulthood's sense of prudential self-reflexivity means, Witmore argues, that children's 'actions are tinged with a quality of incomprehension that Shakespeare links with the immanent potency of theatre itself'.[91] This particular non-comprehending comprehension, recalling Nicholas of Cusa's layman, also paradoxically pictures 'innocence' as its own complex mode of knowledge, just as it ultimately justifies *The Winter's Tale* being a 'tale' and not any other kind of story, since only those kinds of narratives possess the register to adequately figure the theological logic of gift-exchange, as John Milbank has argued.[92]

Thus, when Autolycus attempts to further his interests by begging to be given 'good report', the Clown does not hesitate in granting it; he will 'swear to the prince' that Autolycus is 'as honest a true fellow as any is in Bohemia':

> If it be ne'er so false, a true gentleman may swear it in the behalf of his friend: and I'll swear to the prince thou art a tall fellow of thy hands and that thou wilt not be drunk; but I know thou art no tall fellow of thy hands and that thou wilt be drunk: but I'll swear it, and I would thou wouldst be a tall fellow of thy hands.
> (159–185)

Here, the Clown simply suggests that language is permitted to do anything in the name of friendship: even turn truth itself upside down. If here the oath has lost its illocutionary power, it is only in order to become charged with the founding power of words: a gift that is a dedication and desire to the Good that friends have in common.[93] This cannot be construed as a unilateral gift, since Autolycus has paradoxically given the Shepherd's son the means to this new birth.

Just like in the underground workshop where an uneducated craftsman had outshined both philosopher and orator, it is here through its most unlikely spokesperson that speech shimmers with grace. Rather than Autolycus' word-thievery and the courtier's *admiratio* and *energeia,* it is the simple recognition of the orientation of words and the re-founding of the community that truly prepares the conditions for the final scene. By foiling and transcending both court and country, both sophistication and roguery, Shakespeare gathers ecstatic seriousness and equivocal laughter into the play's comedic conclusion—thus gesturing to the paradoxical, 'serioludic' mode of the doxological dimension of speech. If Shakespeare, as Beckwith argues, explores in this play a 'new grammar of theatre', it seems that his last move consists in upholding the naïve, comedic, yet deeply revelatory speech of an adult-like second innocence as its highest human expression.[94] It is this register that comes closest to the consummation of the oracular, in which the gift of the gods and the language of humans will somehow coincide. By giving *verbum infans*, which in Lear had been 'unable to speak a word', a paradoxical, non-sensical yet true speech, Shakespeare can move beyond the limits of sterile language and towards the doxological. If it is this innocent form of narrative that ultimately triumphs in this storyteller's contest, it is because it most truly reflects the deepest grammar of existence, describing the impossible transfiguring of the world as though it were child's play.

The Queen of the Flowers, or the Voice of Nature

The two worlds, Sicilia and Bohemia, seem exceptionally far apart: indeed, the latter seems to have no existence in Sicilia's courtly imagination—for Leontes, it is merely 'some remote and desert place'

(2.3.176). In Bohemia, conversely, the tragicomic death of Antigonus precipitates the play's sudden mood-jump with the Shepherd's entrance, whose amusing comments at the vagaries of the young provide a comical summary of the action in the Sicilian court: 'I would there were no age between sixteen and three-and-twenty, or that youth would sleep out the rest; for there is nothing in the between but getting wenches with child, wronging the ancientry, stealing, fighting' (3.3.58–62). What, in Sicilia, was the 'adult' reality of a tyrannical court can, in Bohemia, be rendered as a youth's restlessness on the way to a different kind of coming of age. Indeed, if Bohemia fulfils the role of an archetypal 'green world', it is not, as I hope to show below, to offer a timely break from the *realpolitik* of court into joyful bucolic rusticity but rather, as was intimated above, as a challenge to the former realm's claim upon reality.[95] In the following, I will argue that Perdita and Florizel fulfil the elliptic end of the Oracle's prophecy, the finding of 'that which is lost', by creating the possibility *for a new kind of language*, a human art which affirms and articulates the creative potencies of nature; what Ian McAdam terms as 'the grand Shakespearean theme: the sanctification of Nature and the natural'—a sanctification that, I argue, only occurs through the meeting of natural and divine spheres.[96]

To suggest this is to see Perdita as a key speaker in the world of the play bringing, like Paulina, words 'medicinal as true'. For Ted Hughes, as we saw, Cordelia does not succeed in opening the sacred pyx and letting the magical alphabet of Being permeate the language of *King Lear*. The returning Perdita demonstrates the converse aspect of the mythic deep structure of Shakespeare's *oeuvre*: she figures the triumph of sacred love over a death-bound loveless tyranny.[97] Hughes reads reasons for this through his Shakespearean 'tragic equation', a kind of 'contrapuntal' play between the myths underlying the long poems *Venus and Adonis*, in which an erotic goddess pursues a puritanical God who rejects her advances, and *The Rape of Lucrece*, where the latter is reborn as the lustful and savage Tarquin who, in turn, ravishes Venus in her 'chaste' aspect as Lucrece.[98] Recalling Cavell's analyses, Hughes sees in Adonis' rejection of Venus the symbol of a 'type of rational, moral intelligence' which in its refusal of sexual love becomes consummated by a desire to violate its sacred aspect.[99] Hughes' mythopoetic enjambments, tying the rejection of Venus the Queen of Heaven with a deeper rejection of Mary, show that it is the denial of a universal sacred feminine principle that is, for him, the true Shakespearean sin.[100] Attacked by a divine boar, Adonis' death figures the tragic consequences of a rationalist intellect that shuns the transformative powers of love and repudiates—while attempting to control—nature.

Applying this myth to *The Winter's Tale* means reading Leontes as driven by this double-sided masculinity, in turn puritanically reticent and savagely destructive. But it is also, by extension, seeing Perdita as

Leontes' healing soul-double. Despite his earthly exit pursued by a boar, the memory of Adonis' soul is, in the poem, taken up by Venus, transformed into a flower that will thereafter eternally dwell in her heart. For Hughes, the flower becomes, in Shakespeare, the symbol of the rebirth of love in the world, a rebirth that occurs through distinctly feminine, 'Sophianic' figures: for this reason, Hughes attends especially to floral symbolism in the Romances.[101] Thus, Perdita's first appearance as Flora is decisive, and even the homonymic resonances between 'Flora' and 'Florizel' suggests that the latter is born, in some sense, from the heart of the former: hence Florizel is 'the redeemed one (the reborn self of Polixenes), who springs, so to speak, from the flowers, which are the reborn nature of Perdita'.[102] Perdita is, then, a giver and partaker of mystic rebirth: a lost child resulting from Leontes' repudiation of sacred love, she returns to the play as an unlikely goddess-maid; through her flowering *and* her flowers, new life flows to both lovers alike.[103]

Visited by visions and foresight, Antigonus had laid the unwanted baby down on Bohemian soil, 'the earth of its right father' and prophetically named its spiritual quality: 'Blossom, speed thee well!' (3.3.44–45). Fittingly, Florizel's first words in the play are words of praise for Perdita that also coincide with a recognition of this other nature:

> These your unusual weeds to each part of you
> Do give a life: no shepherdess, but Flora
> Peering in April's front. This your sheep-shearing
> Is as a meeting of the petty gods,
> And you the queen on't.
>
> (4.4.1–5)

Like many young men in love in Shakespeare's plays, Florizel makes ample use of encomia (40–51; 375–383). Though Perdita herself gently rebukes him for 'praises too large' (147) that can easily result in wooing 'the false way' (151), she also responds deeply to his words: 'I cannot speak so well' she feels, yet 'by th'pattern of my own thoughts I cut out/ The purity of his' (385–388). Here, in praising Perdita by also strangely recognising Flora through 'unusual weeds', Florizel's encomium seems to spring from a kind of mythic seeing, something like what Northrop Frye, following William Blake, terms 'The Double Vision': a mode of seeing material and spiritual aspects of reality as distinct yet intertwined.[104] Manifesting, through an 'artful' disguise, what is paradoxically a deeper part of her own nature, Perdita's subsequent 'defence' of nature will thus speak a kind of double-speech, voicing Perdita by voicing Flora.[105] Yet, this double nature also means that Perdita does not fully allow the pre-eminence of Florizel's poetic gaze. Paradoxically, she is mistrustful of artful conceits, of being 'most goddess-like pranked-up'

(10). Yet rather than a 'profound ontological unease with festive play' motivated by iconoclastic tendencies,[106] this concern with the respect of sacred differences will be articulated in her defence of nature, as we will see below.

Amidst the festivities of Sheep Shearing, Polixenes and Camillo too appear disguised: they visit the Shepherd's hut precisely to investigate Florizel's absence from court. After welcoming the visitors with flower offerings, Perdita informs Polixenes that she cannot supplement these with the flowers in season, 'the streaked gillyvors', 'Which some call Nature's bastards' (82–83), because 'There is an art which in their piedness shares/With great creating Nature' (87–88). Polixenes retorts that 'Nature is made better by no mean/But nature makes that mean'; through grafting, artists can create 'nobler' out of 'baser'.[107] Such a production, Polixenes argues, is an art 'Which does mend Nature—change it, rather—but/The art itself is Nature' (96–97). There is here, of course, a chink in the armoury of Polixenes' courtly language: for he hesitates between an art that *is* and one that *changes* nature. Whereas the former conveniently effaces the distinction, the latter espouses it while secretly affirming a wish for control.[108] Such a 'Freudian' slip, as Jeremy Tambling notices, recalls that the notion of art, in the poetics of Sicilia, is haunted by the idea of artfulness as mere disguise, mere 'mock'.[109] Mamillius had perhaps recognised the contrived nature of his nurse's stories as well as her cosmetics: 'Nay, that's a mock' (2.1.13).[110] But as we have seen, even children in Sicilia were construed as a kind of 'mock', here in the sense of 'identical copy'; Polixenes suggests it through 'boys eternal', Mamillius says so precisely to appease his father—'I am like you, they say'—and even Paulina appropriates this logic of repetition to show in the baby Perdita 'the whole matter/And copy of the father' (96–101). Up to the last scene in fact, art seems understood as mere freezing, petrifying or identically copying, making 'mocks' of nature, just as Giulio Romano, the supposed sculptor of Hermione's statue, is understood to be nature's 'ape' (5.2.97).

Yet, as Shakespeare shows, this sterile and uncreative cultural expression results in situation in which nature, in its turn, 'mocks' art. Recalling the diluvial rains and thunder of *Lear,* the storm which caught the sailors on their way back to Sicilia 'mocked' them and the Bear, in eating him, 'mocked' Antigonus (3.3.96–99). The hybridisation championed by Polixenes speaks of such a possibility: for it signals that certain noxious cross-fertilisations between nature and art can result in situations in which nature, mocked, itself counter-mocks humans, that is, by fundamentally unsettling human culture *and* redirecting its 'arts' to address such a situation—as one can see, in a contemporary key, in the instance of global warming, where the effects of art in nature are a call to human art to 'mend', rather than 'change' our perception of the real.

Like the Bear and the Sea, the material world, if improperly articulated, re-inserts itself in human expression as a warning from the gods.

This is why, maintaining distinctions that sophisticated philosophers might mock, Perdita will not plant gillyvors, regardless of what Polixenes says, 'No more than, were I painted, I would wish/This youth to say 'twere well, and only therefore/Desire to breed by me' (101–103). Here, as Tambling remarks, 'she echoes Mamillius' because 'supplementing nature with cosmetics makes nature simply a thing of use, employed for breeding, a harnessing that does not respect nature's difference'.[111] An art that 'changes' nature permits the detachment proper to an instrumental mentality to seep into the dynamics of love. She spots the 'instrumentalism' behind his defence of an art that 'displaces nature' because she perceives that nature, like love, thrives on the mode of sacred difference.[112] Willemien Otten reads precisely this aspect of nature's difference as an important motif in the Western metaphysical tradition: 'nature inserts itself indelibly into the human imagination, all the while resisting preconceived models of thought and, in the end... remaining irreducible and intractable'.[113] It is only in terms of this difference that nature can come to appear as a dialogic partner in the human imagination, not merely as a generative matrix nor in the mode of passive victimhood, but as a nonhuman voice that speaks in and through human speech.[114] As we will see below, Perdita's speech coincides with such a voice.

Hence, Perdita's curt 'so it is' (97) to Polixenes' patronising (mocking?) *apologia* resembles Cordelia's 'nothing': they both convey a sense that such language simply has no counter-language, or rather that an artless but resolute inarticulacy seems the only appropriate response to such words.[115] Perdita's point, then, is not a wholesale condemnation of grafting, but a sense that such an art must be practiced in accordance with the sacred speech that belongs to the order of nature, that nature already speaks. To make cannot be to mock: like love, language must not be cosmetic but cosmic: it must affirm and articulate the invisible densities of the cosmos itself. Tellingly, Polixenes soon reveals what is concealed in this 'slip' in his anger at the young couple's attempt at a secret marriage. There, he will condemn Perdita's beauty as 'unnatural': a 'fresh piece of excellent witchcraft' (427–428), whose beauty will be 'scratched with briars and made/More homely than [her] state' (430–431).[116] For him, her authenticity is a dark 'enchantment' (439) which distorts the forces of the world and, what is more, curses his own son. Yet, even then, Perdita declares herself unafraid to speak and respond with the 'plain' truth (446–451); unabashed at his sophistications before, she is unmoved by his anger now.

The theme of a language tangled up in a sterile, ungenerative art also affects Camillo whose pun upon seeing Perdita, 'I should leave grazing, were I of your flock/And only live by gazing' (109–110), echoes Leontes'

162   *Readings*

'use of the aesthetic stance as a way of resisting human connection', as Tom Bishop notes, "freezing" 'both himself and Perdita into the postures of statuary'.[117] Perdita's response to such an attitude is an appeal to Proserpina, the goddess who was ravished by Dis and swallowed into the underworld. Here, however, the energy of Perdita's speech gathers, in an apostrophic call, the verdancy of life *over against* the petrifying reach of Dis' death.[118]

> O Proserpina,
> For the flowers now, that frighted thou let'st fall
> From Dis's waggon! daffodils,
> That come before the swallow dares, and take
> The winds of March with beauty; violets dim,
> But sweeter than the lids of Juno's eyes
> Or Cytherea's breath; pale primroses
> That die unmarried, ere they can behold
> Bright Phoebus in his strength—a malady
> Most incident to maids; bold oxlips and
> The crown imperial; lilies of all kinds,
> The flower-de-luce being one. O, these I lack,
> To make you garlands of, and my sweet friend,
> To strew him o'er and o'er.
>
> (116–129)

As Bishop argues, Perdita here does not become Proserpina's 'mock': her invocation is in fact a subtle *reversal* of the myth, voicing a call that conjures up powers to *preserve* emerging life *against* the icy touch of the underworld.[119] Whereas Proserpina lets the flower fall from Dis' wagon, Perdita, Flora's earthly double, specifically calls them *to* her. The lively, disjointed syntax expresses the unique boldness of these early flowers, who spell out the incomprehensible hinge between dying winter and the risky, audacious opening of the spring-world.[120] What is more, her call makes clear that the potency of this incomprehensible threshold also extends over the divine realm. Thus, daffodils do not bow but *triumph* with beauty over the winds of March (the month of Mars), violets, though dim, *exceed* potencies of both Juno and Venus (divinities who, in the myth, are complicit to Dis' abduction), the beauty of 'pale primroses' is singular precisely in that it *escapes* the summer-rule of Phoebus. Rather than rehearsing the classical allusions associated with Proserpina, Perdita is here calling for *another story*: one that voices nature as no longer simply associated with the decline that results from a contract with the underworld, but as forever inhabited by the potencies of spring—unlike Ceres and Proserpina, she will not barter with but 'overcome' Dis.[121] Affirming the natural world against Polixenes and Camillo's freezing gaze, she suggests an eschatological symbol: a world where the cycles of

Words of Childlike Grace 163

time are not merely seen as an equilibrium between life and death but as manners of glimpsing nature's own privileged relationship to the divine. This glimmer of the organic in the world of speech shines with the responsibility of response to affirm and articulate the material world—the very moment of an 'Ark of Speech' floating over the lapidifying action of death-language.

Florizel's response, echoing Camillo's frozen courtly rhetoric, bears the latter's imprint—'what, like a corse?'(129)—and cannot quite distinguish this quality. Here Perdita's triumph mingles life and death together to affirm the power of love over both:

> No, like a bank for love to lie and play on,
> Not like a corse - or if, not to be buried,
> But quick and in mine arms.
>
> (130–133)

From the praise of the created world of spring which has shone in her speech, Perdita is able to distinguish love's kinship with yet overcoming of death: love copies death insofar as it images the 'corse' but it 'mocks' it by transforming mere lifelessness into a quickening embrace.[122] Hence, her reticence towards artifice is paradoxical, since Perdita knows that by 'lying and playing' on the bank of time, love's art mingles with nature and performs its miracles amidst the densities of matter. The uniqueness of the spring-world, then, is that it expresses in incomprehensible ways the material energies proper to love. Here, nature and words coincide to bear witness to the love that gives birth to them both. Thus, fittingly, Perdita's praise of nature engenders Florizel's artful praise of her:

> What you do
> Still betters what is done. When you speak, sweet,
> I'ld have you do it ever; when you sing,
> I'ld have you buy and sell so, so give alms,
> Pray so, and, for the ordering your affairs,
> To sing them too: when you do dance, I wish you
> A wave o' the sea, that you might ever do
> Nothing but that, move still, still so,
> And own no other function. Each your doing,
> So singular in each particular,
> Crowns what you are doing in the present deed,
> That all your acts are queens.
>
> (135–146)

This is a speech which, as Russ McDonald points out, exemplifies the musical sophistication of late Shakespearean style: while the rhythmic instabilities express harmonies, the harmonious images create pace and unstable energy, a dancing flux of chaos and order.[123] By its reaching beneath and beyond syntactical linearity and the predictable steps of iambic music, Florizel's speech attempts to affirm the 'singular particularity' that arises from participations into a 'stiller' and thus mysterious, inaudible harmony. By playing on both meanings of 'still', Florizel 'de-freezes' Perdita, praising her nature as a work of art which, paradoxically, is ever in motion. His repetition of conditionals ('I'ld have you'/'I wish you'/'That you might' etc.) suggest, rather than the 'aesthetic stance', a baffled, continuous wonderment at the ungraspable energies of Perdita's being.[124]

For Florizel, furthermore, Perdita's voice enables a transformed economy of *gift*. Her speaking and singing turn 'buying and selling' into 'giving alms' and finally into 'prayer'. Here, he senses that there could be an 'ordering of affairs' that such speaking and singing intones and reflects. In fact, her speech and her song give to everything a 'singular particularity' which manifests an authentic majesty that is ungraspable in its motions and so beyond the powers of this world. What began as Perdita's praise of the singularity and sacred difference of nature becomes in Florizel a praise of Perdita' own sacred difference. The sacred and incomprehensible element in nature celebrated in Perdita's words coincides with Florizel's apprehension of the sacred and incomprehensible element in art, which is the lure of the mystery that is the beloved.

In the tongue-tied world of Sicilia, there had been no such language. Instead, these words are said in the Shepherd's house, as part of a feast which will culminate in an attempted marriage (361–422)—the very symbols of 'ecstatic communication' which as Milbank has suggested, grounds the possibility for the ethical in the symbol of donative ritual. Here, the genuine gift of hospitality to the unknown strangers establishes the communal possibilities for such ceremonies and undoes the ambiguous and rhetorically stunted gift-giving practices of the courtiers.

In this way, Florizel and Perdita *speak* what Polixenes' courtly *apologia* can only sophistically *reference*: they voice what glimmers in the middle-commerce between art and nature. Between Perdita's 'divine' affirmation of the natural world and Florizel's erotic wonder-filled praise whose dynamic unsettles syntactical stability, the two intimate a middle-voiced expression which their being affirms and grammar merely approximates. What shines between their two modes of speech alludes to the divine ground of nature and art that illuminates their love, somehow establishing them as wonder-begetting, 'gracious couple' which keep Mamillius' memory alive, as Leontes will both see and intuit (5.1.132–133).

Thus, the pastoral, 'natural' world does not ironically celebrate a kind of bygone, bucolic 'artlessness' so much as it generates a dynamic which re-affirms both nature *and* art, by giving the former a voice for praise and the latter an appropriate *telos*.[125] Here, Shakespeare also re-deploys the Edenic motifs of genuine exchange mis-appropriated by Polixenes. In arising in conditions of genuine human community, the ecstatic speech of praise, in its *élan* of love, discovers something of its divine source, and the Sheep-Shearing feast does indeed become, for an instant, 'a meeting of the petty gods'.

The Grace of Words and the Ground of Language

As I have argued above, the play performs a gradual metamorphosis of the world from a reality bound to the rhythms and ravages of time to a world fictionalised, yet paradoxically made *more real* by the regenerating energies of 'tale'. *The Winter's Tale* performs this transformation, I have suggested, because only a reality shaped *as fiction* can more fruitfully and mysteriously ground the logic of gift. Just as the Shepherd's son offers a new Edenic vision grounded in gift as the restitutions of genuine relations and is able, in turn, to give such a gift to the word-thief Autolycus, Perdita affirms and articulates the incomprehensible powers of the natural world, giving to nature a new story, in a mode of speech that solicits Florizel's gift of ecstatic admiration. The Sheep-Shearing feast then results in an attempted marriage, but one that Polixenes, here playing Leontes' double, cannot grant, threatening instead the dissolution of both lovers' oaths and family bonds (4.4.824–826). The couple embark on a voyage at sea, suggested by the artful Camillo, anxious to return to his native land.

In Sicilia, meanwhile, there has been no gift and no regeneration. The 'gap of time' of 16 years has passed in penitence and sorrow. The winter's tale of a man who dwelt by a churchyard having become reality, the language of Sicilia is permeated with Mamillius' and Hermione's absent presence: though commemorated in courtly poetry (5.1.100–104), Hermione's voice is only encountered as ghostly, 'soul-vexed' shrieks (59–60; 65–67); the name of Mamillius, on the other hand, cannot be spoken, for its very utterance re-enacts his death (118–119). The atoning Leontes, daily visitor to their graves, now recognises Paulina as a genuine counsellor, whose 'boundless tongue' (2.3.90) is an instrument of truth-speaking (5.1.55). As one 'who hast the memory of Hermione... in honour' (49–50), she is to him the priestess of a sacred order founded on a holy but irretrievable past. Yet, in guarding the primacy of such a memory, Paulina establishes the sovereignty of her own counsel against those at court who would have Leontes marry again 'for royalty's repair' (31). In fact, 'royalty's repair' is what she is truly minding: she protects the uniqueness of the gift of love, refusing to reduce it to the transactional nature of political marriages (1–55).[126] In giving authority to Paulina, Leontes, as David Schalkwyk notes, now 'subscribes wholly to the paradox that service is freedom': he recognises that giving away his power entails the possible return of a counter-gift: his own nature, and through it, the beginnings of a genuine community.[127]

Nevertheless, Paulina's guardianship entails a kind of archaic past that is haunted by indelible sin: 'Whilst I remember/Her and her virtues', Leontes despairs, 'I cannot forget/My blemishes in them' (7–9). What had happened to courtly language in the first acts now permeates the language of the sacred: it has become sterile and uncreative, dedicated to a frozen memory that is understood as ontologically prior to presence and seems interminably laced with pain. This cult of Hermione to which Paulina demands absolute obedience relies on an ancestral past that can only figure the sacred as memorialised but *not re-enacted*: thus, mourning supplants doxology.

And yet—for the regeneration of Sicilia to occur, the Oracle of Apollo needs to be fulfilled (34–49). Paulina carefully protects Apollo's utterance (36–40) all the while stressing that the return of 'that which is lost' is an occurrence that can only be 'monstrous to our human reason' (41). Hence, she leads Leontes, despite the protestation of his lords, to swear that he will not marry except by her leave (5.1.70), all the while knowing that such marriage is inconceivable: 'That/Shall be when your first queen's again in breath./Never till then' (83–85). Here, Paulina brings Leontes to expect an unhoped for gift that is, to recall Cusa, both necessary *and* impossible, and thus leads beyond the law of non-contradiction.[128] This paradoxical dream of an impossible gift serves also, as Scott Crider argues, to rehabilitate the binding language in Sicilia as no longer founded on fealty and allegiance but on *trust and hope*.[129] Thus being faithful to Apollo's oracle, Paulina is able to perform a regeneration that Kent could not, both in service and (therefore) in words: 'Now by Apollo, King/thou swear'st thy gods in vain', he had bellowed in Lear's court.[130] Like Kent, her service is constant and dedicated, but unlike him, she has married 'that tongue she has' to the language of the heavens, and is able to modulate her words according to the situations proceeding from the Oracle's prophecy.

To be sure, the play's final scene has been a constant focus for scholarship on Shakespeare and religion. As well as debating whether it is to be experienced within the texture of a Christian poetics, critics have long touched on confessional and iconographic issues.[131] Though these readings are in their own way suggestive, I suggest that the play's final scene forges an appropriate doxology out of its *own* language, motifs and themes—indeed, it is *speech itself* which is, as Carol Neely puts it, both 'the means by which Hermione's life is restored' *and* 'the mark of this restoration'.[132]

After many recognitions fit for an old tale, the time comes for the reunited ones to visit Paulina's house and view a mysterious artwork that memorialises an irretrievable past. Paulina had already brought Leontes to understand and trust that salvific grace somehow dwells beyond the reach of human reason. Now, as they wander down her gallery of artistic wonders, she tells him that Hermione's 'dead likeness' exceeds the reach of human knowledge and vision (14–17). Małgorzata Grzegorzewska has suggested that Paulina's drawing of the curtain to reveal the statue evokes a Shakespearean 'space of revelation', in which the audience's ocular attention is called both with and beyond what they can see.[133] Hence, she proposes, there is in such a gesture an oblique reference to the severing of the veil in the Temple in the Gospels which reveals, for a moment, the sustaining union of the domain of the hidden with the manifest.[134] Like those gathered in Paulina's house, she suggests, the audience must 'let their inner sight sink into the impenetrable abyss of the empty grave'.[135]

We have seen in Chapter 3 that a mode of listening that is hospitable to true words requires a synaesthetic mode of attention, with love acting as its *sensus communis*.[136] Here, those in the chapel are enveloped in a silence pregnant with words which, in 'showing off' wonder (21–22), is the appropriate quality to receive the words which will follow. If the rhetorical manipulations of the first scene in *King Lear* had created a stifled, violent silence which had made true speech inaudible, the silence of the last scene in *The Winter's Tale*, to recall Jean-Louis Chrétien, alludes to something like 'the first hospitality' of speech, the gift of wondrous and welcoming attention that makes all word-gifts possible.[137]

Leontes had sworn his allegiance to Paulina invoking in his oath a new mode of vision: 'all eyes else, dead coals!' (5.1.68). Now, Paulina invokes the coincidence of the senses appropriate to the doxological register: the words spoken here will have to resonate with the Divine creative 'speaking gaze' which Cusa invokes—'Behold', she commands, 'and say "tis well' (20).

> LEONTES
> Her natural posture.
> Chide me, dear stone, that I may say indeed
> Thou art Hermione - or rather, thou art she
> In thy not chiding, for she was as tender
> As infancy and grace.
>
> (23–27)

Leontes breaks from his speechlessness to call forth speech from the statue. But the first words he wants to hear are his own: he desires language only as an exchange of retributive justice, only willing to say ''tis well' if Hermione's authenticity coincides with an inevitable doom. Yet, caught like Florizel by the 'Double Vision', he also spies in the stone something of Hermione's *nature*: an eloquent silence that binds together 'infancy' and 'grace' and which he praises as life-giving: *'thou art she/In thy not chiding'*. By revealing something of Hermione's nature, the speech of praise here gently supersedes the speech of opposition. However, her silent eloquence causes him to hesitate, and he cannot by himself move beyond the shame which overwhelms him: 'does not the stone rebuke me/For being more stone than it?' (37–38).[138] Here, words of self-wound merely ricochet on the statue; shame turns his speech to marble. Yet, as we will see, something in the stone calls from him further response in a mode of speech that, while not revoking shame, constantly *exceeds* it.

Turning to his daughter, Leontes surmises in Perdita's stone-like stance the same loss of life he feels (42); yet she, unlike him, has become petrified with *wonder*. Theirs are two different modes of being stone: matter as the boundary of death, which is where Leontes' shame leads, and matter as shimmering with sacred life, which is what Perdita has already affirmed. Now, in a reverse image of the 'men of stones' in *Lear*, Perdita is stone come to life with speech: 'give me leave… that I kneel and implore her blessing' (44), 'give me that hand of yours to kiss' (46). But Paulina asks for 'patience!' (46), because all healing words and all words of praise and gratitude have not yet been said.

Indeed, Camillo and Polixenes too must participate in the rite: the former now recognises and forgives Leontes' trials; he sees them as a pigment, a 'sorrow too sore laid on', a kind of paint that pains nature, going beyond the 'natural' terms of *both* joy and sorrow only by 'mocking' them (50–54). Hermione's colour is but freshly painted, but Leontes' is laid on by an unnatural art which, unmoved by the lure of the Good, can only entomb reality. Surprisingly, Camillo's remark now moves Polixenes to a prayer which *joins together* sorrow and joy: 'Let him that was the cause of this', he entreats, 'have power/To take so much grief from you as he/Will piece up in himself' (54–56). The art he desires to practice is a kind of gift which will carry the weight of his brother's sorrow: 'mending', this time, rather than 'changing' nature. Tongue-tied by the 'ciphers' of impossible gifts at the beginning of the play, Polixenes now offers a gift which could heal the breach in their friendship.[139]

For Leontes, however, the terminus of art remains that of a 'mock' of unredeemed life (68). Here, Paulina resumes her wise-foolish tactics, but in a different key. Indeed, this scene, as Kenneth Gross points out, stages a trial that is also 'purificatory rite',[140] thus atoning for by reversing Hermione's unjust arraignment in 3.2 which had offended even the gods. Hence, Paulina now tests Leontes: she threatens to draw the curtain: 'lest your fancy/May think anon it moves' (61) or 'lives' (69), prompting from Leontes the desire to stay in the gaze of the statue whose very eyes seem alive (67). Paulina here overturns Leontes' initial anxieties over 'Affection', suggesting how the 'truth-bearing' imagination participates in appropriately discerning both movement and life in a 'poor image' (57).[141] It is here that Leontes finally *affirms* how the lure of the vision overwhelms his shame: no matter how 'monstrous' to human reason, he finds that he *must* praise the impossible vision since 'no settled senses of the world can match/The pleasure of that madness' (72–73). The statue has lost the status of 'artwork' and is no longer an 'it' but a 'her' (66; 68). Rather than retreat in shame and death, he decides to advance and kiss her, because 'the very life seems warm upon her lip' (66). If before he marvelled at how art could be so lifelike, he now wonders how anything so lifelike could be art.[142]

Again, however, this is too sudden: Paulina's 'you'll mar it if you kiss it', 'stain your own/With oily painting' (81–82) *tests* Leontes and Polixenes with a reference to their former understanding of sin as a 'stain' which passed on through 'their own' bloodline and had so paralysed the language of the first scene. They are challenged to renounce that view, to see blood as pigment, beyond the seeming difference between life and art: 'shall I draw the curtain?', Paulina asks audaciously (82). Now, Perdita and Polixenes inhabit a liminal state between stone and flesh: unable to touch or kiss her, they would outdo the statue in its statuesque state, contemplating not for 16, but 20 years (84–85). Paulina thus demands a kind of amazement that moves beyond petrification and learns to speak the language of praise: but this, she reminds them, entails the necessary fulfilment of the impossible and unhoped-for (91–92). Using both passive and active forms, she commands an action that is paradoxically unperformable: 'it is required/you do awake your faith' (95–96). The cosmic decree, like the Oracle earlier, remains impersonal ('it is required') but nonetheless bestows personhood, a coming out of the statue-state, in the paradoxical action of awakening a kind of love, 'faith', a trust that, by overcoming the doubt and deceit that had stifled all relationships in the first half of the play, is *itself* a kind of awakening. Thus, only because Hermione has somehow *already moved* Leontes, Perdita, Camillo and Polixenes is she herself able to move; only because it has already paradoxically given life can the stone itself surge into life.

In reading this central motif, it is imperative, as Peter Platt has argued, to encounter it as 'a key-text of the Shakespearean paradoxical project' that stages a dialogue between 'the naturalistic and the marvellous' as 'participating in a tense, paradoxical dynamic'.[143] The logic of non-contradiction that wants to settle the issue of Hermione's life or death must, as Paulina warns us, be surrendered: instead, the theurgic rite performed here is now transforming our perception of what life and death actually *are*.[144] In doing so, Shakespeare chooses doxology over comedy or tragedy: as Kenneth Gross suggests, it 'not only questions a purely comic end but demands that we also relinquish any hidden wish for the specious "realism" of a tragic economy'.[145] Challenging the audience's expectations for both comic or retributive wish-fulfilments amounts to moving beyond *mimesis* into a creative *re-presentation* of the real (in Williams' sense), an affirmation and articulation of the deep grammar of grace that incomprehensibly yet fittingly underscores existence. Hermione's sudden animation, a Gross rightly notes, 'retains a starker mystery in its having so little dialectical shape. That the closing scene allows us neither self-evident faith in magic nor the quiet comforts of disenchanted irony is its real difficulty'.[146] In the middle of this difficulty, as I have argued in this chapter, is a simplicity: the tale of the second infancy of speech shaping itself around the unplanned, uncontrolled, original energies of grace.

With all the watchers silenced, caught in the posture of statuary, Paulina's chapel has also paradoxically become the court of Dis, peopled with a host of stone which her priestly poetic powers seek to captivate: 'those that think it is unlawful business I am about', she warns, 'let them depart' (95–96). In the guise of the lord of the underworld, Leontes performs his final command as King, abolishing the rule of epistemic doubt that would find Paulina's action illicit: 'Proceed' he decrees, 'no foot shall stir' (96–97).[147] The law now implicitly pronounced as both fulfilled and overthrown by its lawgiver, Paulina is able to performs her Orphic incantation[148]:

> Music, awake her, strike!
> 'Tis time; descend; be stone no more; approach.
> Strike all that look upon with marvel. Come,
> I'll fill your grave up. Stir, nay, come away;
> Bequeath to death your numbness, for from him
> Dear life redeems you.
>
> (98–102)

Paulina first invokes the fittingness of the moment: 'tis time'. Because, as I suggested above, 'tale' has given 'time' a whole new shape, it is not the time of chronology, but the time of 'music' that awakens, gathering past and future into a harmonic present. Rather than the previous attempts to 'freeze' material life into art, which had been the scope of courtly speech in the play's earlier scenes, Paulina here shows how genuine art 'stirs' matter into life.[149] Hence, 'tis time' also means *this* miracle is what time, in its fulfilled form, *is*: the ecstatic dimension of gift-giving, the interruption of the diachronic *by* the synchronic, an event that bestows to time *itself* its own concentrated nature.[150]

We saw earlier how the Shepherd's son had understood time as a mode of gift, and thus was able to bless genealogy by reversing its flow: being a 'gentleman born' before his father was the only manner in which a community scarred by the breaking of all kinship could once again call one another 'sister' and 'brother' (5.2.136–142). Such a mode of time, being the 'moving image of eternity' and reaching at once into irredeemable past and unhoped-for future could guarantee a genuine economy of gift. Paulina calls to such a poetic vision when she alludes to the creative participation of the senses and the mind in the liturgy ('*you perceive* she stirs' [103]). Such participation is required to seal the appropriateness of the rite and show that 'her action shall be as holy as/You hear my spell is lawful' (103–104). Beyond strained early modern anxieties about

Words of Childlike Grace 171

'magic', the word 'spell' here resounds with a sense of the cultic, incantatory roots of language itself, with its etymological cognates, 'riddle' and 'charm' but also 'tale' and 'song'.[151] Paulina's spell is one which will *make words and action one thing,* binding words through the sacredness of the enacted gift.

To do so, Paulina's 'purificatory rite' must address the curse on birth and generation that haunted the world of the play from the beginning, thereby also hinting at the ritual dimension missing in *King Lear*. Here, the purification must be that of corporeal love as the carrier of sin, as announced in the play's initial distorted Edenic image. Hence Hermione's movement from stone to life provides an inversion of the laws of courtship: 'Nay, present your hand./When she was young, you wooed her; now in age/Is she become the suitor?' (108–109). Paulina's question, though rhetorical, suggests the recapitulation of a marriage that will upturn its first iteration. Thus, it is *only upon touching Hermione* that Leontes can undo the curse. His stirring 'O, she's warm!' is his first passing of Paulina's test, since before he can speak *to* Hermione, he *must* affirm and articulate the goodness of the coursing sap of material life. Here then, the blood which warms Hermione's veins, but which had at first had been synonymous with the circulation of death, is now the very sign which can *redeem* the past.[152]

Initially powered with 'wit' and 'boldness', Paulina's own words had become charged with full priestly powers *only after* the gift of the return of the lost one. In accordance with the Oracle that preserved language, words will return to Hermione when 'that which is lost' is found, and thus the 'interposition' of Perdita is vital: 'kneel', Paulina commands, 'and pray your mother's blessing' (119). The daughter safeguarded by the earth becomes the interposed *middle* between the community in the chapel and the mother-queen preserved through the word of the gods. It is she who affirmed and articulated the goodness of nature that can give *words* to she who had been everlastingly numbed by a death-bound art. The sway of praise that began with Florizel and Perdita comes at last to give its word-giving force in the paradoxically silent gesture of seeking for grace. It is then Perdita's kneeling—a gesture beautifully yet briefly attempted in *Lear*—that will bring Hermione to her theurgic utterance:

> You gods, look down,
> And from your sacred vials pour your graces
> Upon my daughter's head! Tell me, mine own,
> Where hast thou been preserved? Where lived? how found
> Thy father's court? for thou shalt hear that I,
> Knowing by Paulina that the oracle
> Gave hope thou wast in being, have preserved
> Myself to see the issue.
>
> (121–128)

Hermione's first words are prayer, asking the gods to pour a libation on the death-defying 'issue': they must, in other words, perform a heavenly rite that will fittingly correspond to the earthly miracle. On earth, life has been redeemed from the dead; now, Hermione completes the theurgic practice by praying to invert heaven and earth: the two must mingle in participatory ritual.[153] She asks that the grace that courses from above commune with the prayer that ascends from below. This cosmic rite, mixing the pouring down of grace with the rising up of words, ensures the final participatory blessing that re-founds the community: heaven and earth for an instant in accord, becoming likenesses of one another, meet in this ecstatic middle. Brought back from the dead by Perdita, words of prayer, which once were fruitless (3.2.204–211), can now be said no more in vain (140–141).

As Hermione approached, Paulina had promised to 'fill her grave up', an action which returns soil to an original site, from the tomb of the dead to the womb of the living. But 'filling the grave up' also means, paradoxically, to *elevate* the gravestone of Hermione to its status as living monument, a cultural artefact which paradoxically remembers Hermione's death as an integral part of her movement back to life.[154] Thus, Perdita was right: art permeates life only if it validates and celebrates the gift of love. The filled gravestone becomes here, paradoxically, a monument to the myth of the surprising, grace-filled return of life.[155] As we have seen, *The Winter's Tale* affirms just such a poetics of the gift, which is why it stages a transformation of the real into fiction, and mere fiction into the truly real. The 'holy gift' memorialised by the filled grave, yet enacted and brought to life by the ceremony of 'lawful spells', must now re-enter the world through the form of *story*.

This is why, after liturgy and prayer, the words required are those of the tale: 'Tell me, mine own', asks Hermione of Perdita, 'Where has thou been preserved?/Where lived?/How found/thy father's court?' (123–125)—and she promises in turn to recount her own story. As Paulina again points out, the rite itself, in 'awakening faith', has enacted the impossibility of such 'old tales' (115–117). Such original stories of gift, which strike the distant hearers as improbable, are calling for new words, words that can bear witness to the event of grace. Paulina notes that this desire to overwhelm life with tale now offers the sweet danger to 'trouble/Your joys with like relation' (129–130). The energy of true speech having been released throughout the cosmos, all others, audience and actors alike, having sensed the grace of words, may be moved to perform their own holy actions, and tell such stories, again and again. For now, it is *their* story which must be recounted: 'Go together,/You precious winners all; your exultation/partake to everyone' (130–132).

Lastly, Paulina's own nature transmutes: the vessel of Apollo is touched again by earthly old age; the great priestess retreats into a former presence, an 'old turtle' looking for 'a withered bough', with no oracles to her available and no old tales that prophecy the return of Antigonus, 'that's never to be found again' (131–133).[156] Her last words, she tells us, will be Orphic: a 'lament' of her mate 'till I am lost' (134). But here, Leontes, the redeemed King, becomes priest for an instant, and his nature exchanges with hers: 'Thou shouldst a husband take by my consent/ as I by thine a wife. This is a match,/And made between's by vows' (137–138). Uniting Camillo and Paulina who truly served, he becomes himself, for a moment, at their service.

The event of the gift of redeemed life and love has, as Nicholas of Cusa might put it, been made possible in and through impossibility coinciding with necessity, where

> I come to that which is unknown to every intellect and which every intellect judges to be very far removed from the truth, there You are present, my God, You who are Absolute Necessity. And the darker and more impossible that obscuring haze of impossibility is known to be, the more truly the Necessity shines forth and the less veiledly it draws near and is present.[157]

This is the coincidence that, ultimately, vindicates the utterly gratuitous donative register of doxology; for the ritual performed here is the response to the gift of life that is also the birth of language. Grounding ethics with poetics—that is, creatively affirming and articulating the Good—this gratuitous event performs the rebirth of speech. Indeed, we might suppose that this story will to them become *the* story, *the* founding myth of their redeemed community, providing new symbols and new language in order to tell another time the ever-new story of infancy and grace. If the final image is eschatological, it is also, paradoxically, archetypal: *the end of language is also its beginning.*[158] The story of the wondrous gift of life is the story of the return of words. The close of *The Winter's Tale* then, articulates the beginnings of a new world, by showing how doxological participation founds all genuine speech, articulating the primordial precedence of grace over necessity, of the excessive over the useful and of the gift over the given.

Through the gradual, spiral-like transformation of the world of time into a tale of redeemed life, the energies of poetry come to seep through the material world, just as matter subtly draws sacred words to itself. Beginning with a movement of recoil at a nature interpreted as irredeemably fallen, *The Winter's Tale* performs a surprising re-vivifying of erotic love and of the death-defying energies of creativity alluding to, as this study has suggested, the mysterious revelation that the Word has been made flesh, language and matter brought into one in expression of the divine mystery.

Whereas the social order of Sicilia is, like that of *Lear,* terminally haunted by a language that resists love, shuns nature and therefore becomes subordinate to a death-bound mistrust, it is with words that praise, partly animating, and partly animated *by* 'Great Creating Nature' that the social order is transformed and genuine relationships are restored. It is because the fragile miracles of love and the creative densities of the material world have been affirmed that something of God's voice has come into speech, 'Beholding' and saying "'tis well'. Such words are timeless and musical, but also medicinal and thus material: they can only and ever be spoken in and through time and with and through one another. Hence, the poetics of *The Winter's Tale* do not offer an aesthetics of fairy-tale sentimentality, but a continuing story that must also come to terms with the wound of the world—that must tell of Mamillius' death, of the disappearance of Antigonus, and the silence of Hermione towards Leontes. Like language itself, the nature of forgiveness is at once given yet also always deepened, always underway, as a gift to the past that is to be redeemed and transformed, not forgotten.[159] Thus, Leontes ends:

> Good Paulina,
> Lead us from hence, where we may leisurely
> Each one demand an answer to his part
> Perform'd in this wide gap of time since first
> We were dissevered.
>
> (151–155)

Suggesting ever further reciprocal questions and answers, the play reverberates with the antiphonal unfinishedness of the doxology: something more can and must be said, another story told, another miracle recounted.[160] The poetic world of the word, where Word is continuously made flesh, is left unfinished, open to be retold, represented, recounted. Shakespeare prefers the salutary incompleteness of genuine incarnate words to a totalising, idealised complete picture. As art and life awaken one another on the stage, the poet too, perhaps, awakens in his audience a taste for such paradoxical life-giving and life-redeeming speech. Shakespeare's post-tragic words, then, celebrate the fragile courage and death-defying joy of authentic speakers that evermore seek to affirm and articulate the Good—perhaps the audience too might be visited by the surprising, restoring and insight-bestowing gift that is the grace of words.

Notes

1. Stephen Orgel, 'Introduction', in *The Winter's Tale*, ed. Stephen Orgel (Oxford: OUP, 1996), 46.
2. *Ibid.*, 10.
3. I understand 'tale' as a story which bears the trope J. R. R. Tolkien terms *eucatastrophe*, 'a sudden and miraculous grace: never counted on to recur';

a kind of literature that is 'the higher form of art, indeed the most nearly pure form, and so (when achieved) the most potent'. J. R. R. Tolkien (ed.), 'On Fairy Stories', in *The Monster and the Critics and Other Essays* (London: Harper Collins, 2006), 153, 139.

4 There is evidence that *King Lear* may well have been re-written for the First Folio precisely around the time of the composition of *The Winter's Tale*. Emma Smith, '*The Winter's Tale*', *Approaching Shakespeare*, University of Oxford podcasts: https://podcasts.ox.ac.uk/series/approaching-shakespeare (June 2019).

5 I accept the term 'Romance' as a convenient qualifier for Shakespeare's late works, in particular because of its references to the medieval imaginary and its 'magical' world: see Barbara A. Mowat, '"What's In A Name?": Tragicomedy, Romance, or Late Comedy?" in *A Companion to Shakespeare's Works*, vol 4., ed. Jean Howard and Richard Dutton (Oxford: Blackwell, 2003), 129–153.

6 Smith, '*The Winter's Tale*', *Ibid*.

7 Arthur Quiller-Couch, 'Shakespeare's Later Workmanship: *The Winter's Tale*', *The North American Review*, 203.726 (1916), 754.

8 Lytton Strachey (ed.), 'Shakespeare's Final Period' in *Books and Characters* (New York: Harcourt and Brace, 1922), 64.

9 Gary Taylor, 'Shakespeare's Midlife Crisis', *The Guardian*, 3 May 2004: https://www.theguardian.com/stage/2004/may/03/theatre.classics (February 2020).

10 Gordon McMullan, *Shakespeare and the Idea of Late Writing* (Cambridge: CUP, 2007).

11 Raphael Lyne, *Shakespeare's Late Work* (Oxford: OUP, 2007), 6.

12 *Ibid*., 6–7.

13 Plato, *Symposium*, 233d.

14 See Leo Strauss, *Socrates and Aristophanes* (Chicago, IL: UCP, 1966).

15 See Aaron Riches, 'The Shakespeare Music: Eliot and von Balthasar on Shakespeare's "Romances" and the "Ultra-dramatic"', in *Postmodernity*, ed. Lehmann *et al.*, 195–213.

16 For an argument that Shakespeare's late writings are 'tragicomedies' rather than Romances, see Johan Hartwig, *Shakespeare's Tragicomic Vision* (Baton Rouge: Louisiana State UP, 1982).

17 Riches, 'Music', 198.

18 *Ibid*., 203.

19 Chris Hassel, *Shakespeare's Religious Language: A Dictionary* (London: Continuum, 2007), s.v. 'Grace', 146–150.

20 Thomas Bishop, 'Sacred and Theatrical Miracles in the Romances', in *The Cambridge Companion to Shakespeare and Religion*, 276.

21 *Ibid*.

22 *Ibid*.

23 Rowan Williams, 'Afterword: Finding the Remedy', in *Ibid*., 290.

24 Baker, *Unstaged*, 111–136.

25 For more on this gift-like quality of 'magical' characters in 'tales', see Milbank, 'Fictioning Things', whose themes are also discussed further below.

26 Milbank, *Reconciled*, 157. My concern here is not Milbank's notion of the gift in general, but only how and why his thematic thinking on the gift arises in conversation with *The Winter's Tale*. For a clear yet lapidary summary of Milbank's thinking of the gift, see 'The Transcendentality of the Gift: A Summary in Answer to 12 Questions', *Revista Portuguesa de Filosofia* 65 (2009), 887–897.

27 *Ibid*.

28 For a Derridean reading of the *topos* of gift in this scene, see David Ruiter, 'Shakespeare and Hospitality: Opening *The Winter's Tale*', *Mediterranean Studies* 16 (2007), 157–177.
29 All references are to *The Winter's Tale*, ed John Pitcher, Arden Shakespeare 3rd Series (London: Methuen, 2010).
30 It is tempting to read 'justified' in terms of an anxiety perhaps present in a Calvinistic doctrine of grace. See Pitcher, 1.1.8–9n and 1.2.80n.
31 Graham Holderness, '*The Winter's Tale*: Country into Court', in Graham Holderness, Nick Potter and John Turner, *Shakespeare: Out of Court* (Basingstoke: Macmillan, 1990), 235.
32 *Ibid.*
33 He seems to give, as Hermione points out (34–37), no fully convincing reason.
34 Judith Wolfe, 'Hermione's Sophism: Ordinariness and Theatricality in *The Winter's Tale*', *Philosophy and Literature* 39.1 (2015), 86.
35 *Ibid.*, 88.
36 *Ibid.*, 91.
37 *Ibid.*, 86.
38 Garber, *Dream*, 164.
39 Andrew Moran, 'Synaesthesia and Eating in *The Winter's Tale*', *Religion and the Arts* 9.1 (2005), 46. See for example 1.2.330; 2.1.57; 4.4.693–695.
40 J. Douglas Canfield, *Word as Bond in English Literature: From the Middle Ages to the Restoration* (Philadelphia: University of Pennsylvania Press, 1989), 61.
41 *Ibid.*
42 See previous chapter, 99.
43 Wolfe, 'Sophism', 89.
44 Cavell, *Disowning*, 206.
45 *Ibid.*, 211.
46 *Ibid.*, 213.
47 *Ibid.*, 211.
48 Here, the Folio reads 'I am like you say' which suggests an even closer, darker connection between Leontes' language and Mamillius' being.
49 Simon Palfrey, *Late Shakespeare: A New World of Words* (Oxford: Clarendon, 1997), 206.
50 Joel Altman, *The Improbability of Othello: Rhetorical Anthropology and Shakespearean Selfhood* (Chicago, IL: UCP, 2010), 365–367.
51 Northrop Frye, 'Recognition in *The Winter's Tale*', in *The Winter's Tale: Critical Essays*, ed. Maurice Hunt (New York: Routledge, 1995), 114.
52 Carol Thomas Neely, '*The Winter's Tale*: The Triumph of Speech' in *Ibid.*, 244.
53 Adelman, *Suffocating Mothers*, 222.
54 *Ibid.*, 228. Though Adelman reads the 'pastoral' in the play as the return of feminine generativity, she is mistaken in my view to argue that the former order is merely restored and that 'the female agents of restoration turn out to have been good patriarchalists all along' (235).
55 Howard Felperin, *The Uses of the Canon: Elizabethan Literature and Contemporary Theory* (Oxford: OUP, 1992), 43–44. However, I dispute Felperin's overall claim that '[b]y foregrounding the fallen nature of human speech and backgrounding any divine or redemptive "reality" to which it refers, Shakespeare dramatizes, in linguistic terms, the condition of secularity within which we all, wittingly or not, inescapably dwell', 53.
56 Beckwith, 'Are There any Women in Shakespeare's Plays?: Fiction, Representation, and Reality in Feminist Criticism', *New Literary History* 46.2 (2015), 251.

57 Schalkwyk, *Service*, 263.
58 Michael Steffes, 'The Ancient Greek Wild in *The Winter's Tale*', *RAR* 27.4 (2003), 35–40.
59 Anthony Gash, 'Shakespeare, Carnival and the Sacred', in *Shakespeare and Carnival: After Bakhtin*, ed. Roland Knowles (Basingstoke: Palgrave, 1998), 180. For Paulina's 'Pauline' background, see for example Roy Battenhouse, 'Theme and Structure in *The Winter's Tale*', *SUR* 33 (1980), 123–138; Huston Diehl, '"Does Not the Stone Rebuke Me?': The Pauline Rebuke and Paulina's Lawful Magic in *The Winter's Tale*', in *Shakespeare and the Cultures of Performance*, ed. Paul Yachnin and Patricia Badir (Farnham: Ashgate, 2008), 69–82; Daniel Knapper, 'Thundering, Not words: Aspects of Pauline Style in *Pericles* and *The Winter's Tale*', *Shakespeare Studies* 47 (2019), 169. See also footnote 131, below.
60 Gash, 'Sacred', 189ff.
61 *Ibid.*, 190. For the theme of Socratic midwifery in Shakespeare, see also V. Gerlier, 'The Word of Love: Poetic Truth and Socratic Midwifery in Shakespeare', *Temenos Academy Review* 18 (2015), 71–90. Paulina's Socratic midwifery is discussed below.
62 On Paulina as midwife, see also Caroline Bicks, *Midwiving Subjects in Shakespeare's England: Women and Gender in the Early Modern World* (Aldershot: Ashgate, 2003), 141.
63 Gash, 'Sacred', 195.
64 Bishop, *Wonder*, 148.
65 The late plays also make use of temples as staging places for divine communication (if we accept that the Island in *The Tempest* bears the quality of a sacred space). Bishop, 'Sacred and Theatrical', 281n3.
66 Altman, *Improbability*, 368.
67 John Baxter, 'Reported Speech in *The Winter's Tale*', *RAR* 36.3 (2013), 131.
68 Bishop, 'Sacred and Theatrical', 270.
69 Cavell, *Disowning*, 211.
70 The capitalisation of 'Time' is used here only when referring to the 'character' in the play.
71 On the suggestive 'Incarnational Aesthetic' behind the violation of such unities, see Groves, *Traditions*, 43ff.
72 Plato, *Timaeus* 37c-e.
73 As Orgel notes, it is Perdita and not 'Truth as the daughter of Time' (as in Greene's *Pandosto*, a source of this play) that is the subject of Time's argument. 'Introduction', 42.
74 William Engel, 'Kinetic Emblems and Memory Images in *The Winter's Tale*', in *Late Shakespeare: 1608–1613*, ed. Andrew J. Power and Rory Loughlane (Cambridge: CUP, 2013), 75ff.
75 Rawdon Wilson, *Shakespearean Narrative* (Newark: University of Delaware Press, 1995), 102.
76 Jeremy Tambling, '*The Winter's Tale*: Three Recognitions', *Essays in Criticism* 65.1 (2015), 48.
77 W. H. Auden, *Lectures on Shakespeare* (Princeton, NJ: Princeton UP, 2019), 284.
78 Louis MacNeice, 'Autolycus', in *Collected Poems*, ed. Peter McDonald, (London: Faber, 2007), 274–275.
79 See for example, Palfrey, *Late*, 119–120; Richard Hillman, *Shakespearean Subversions: The Trickster and the Play-Text* (London: Routledge, 1992), 222–225.
80 Hillman, *Subversions*, 223.
81 OED, 5a.

82 Michael Witmore, *Pretty Creatures: Children and Fiction in the English Renaissance* (Ithaca, NY: Cornell UP, 2007), 162.
83 Famously in *2 Henry VI*, 4.2.; but see also Kerrigan, *Binding Language*, 67–96.
84 For Carol Thomas Neely, Autolycus functions as Leontes' 'parodic double'; *Broken Nuptials in Shakespeare's Plays* (New Haven, CT: YUP, 1985), 203–204.
85 Cavell, *Disowning*, 215.
86 Russ McDonald, *Shakespeare's Late Style* (Cambridge: CUP, 2006), 232.
87 On the paradoxical relationship between *ekphrasis* and narrative in the play, see Richard Meek, *Narrating the Visual in Shakespeare* (Farnham: Ashgate, 2009), 147–180.
88 Here fulfilling what Baker calls 'unauthorised grace'; see above, 137.
89 The action in Bohemia suggests a curious jangling of chronological time, since it appears to take place in several timeframes: April (4.4.3), Whitsun (4. 4. 134), during the summer 'shearing' festival, and autumn (4. 4. 79–81).
90 Witmore, *Creatures*, 138.
91 *Ibid.*, 144.
92 Milbank, 'Fictioning'.
93 See Plato, *Phaedrus*, 279c.
94 Beckwith, *Forgiveness*, 130.
95 For a suggesting reading of this reversal, see Garber, *Dream*, 163–186.
96 Ian McAdam, 'Magic and Gender in in Late Shakespeare', in Power and Loughlane, *Late*, 243.
97 The following attempts to briefly summarise the labyrinthine argument of *Goddess*.
98 Hughes, *Goddess*, 82; for the equation, see 49–86 and *passim*.
99 *Ibid.*, 510.
100 For a reading of the Marian motif in the play, see also Ruth Vanita, 'Mariological Memory in *The Winter's Tale* and *Henry VIII*', *Studies in English Literature 1500–1900* 40.2 (2000), 311–337.
101 Hughes, *Goddess*, 406–417.
102 *Ibid.*, 410.
103 *Ibid.*
104 See Northrop Frye, *The Double Vision: Language and Meaning in Religion* (Toronto: University of Toronto Press, 1991).
105 Cf. Jonathan Bate, *Shakespeare and Ovid* (Oxford: OUP, 1994), 239ff, for whom Florizel, precisely by naming Perdita 'Flora', performs an appropriation of her being. Such reading assumes that Florizel's language of love is prey to an ontology of power: it gives Perdita less life, not more.
106 Jensen, *Revelry*, 218.
107 For a representative discussion of these two themes, see for example Derek Traversi, *An Approach to Shakespeare*, vol. 2 (London: Hollis & Carter, 1969), 282–302; Harold S. Wilson, '"Nature and Art," in *Winter's Tale* IV, iv, 86 ff', *Shakespeare Association Bulletin* 18 (1943), 114–120.
108 A. D. Nuttall suggests Polixenes here follows a 'stoic' argument that assimilates nature *with* reason; *Shakespeare the Thinker* (New Haven, CT: YUP, 2007), 354–356.
109 Tambling, 'Recognitions', 30–52.
110 *Ibid.*, 43.
111 *Ibid.*
112 *Ibid.*
113 Willemien Otten, *Thinking Nature and the Nature of Thinking: From Eriugena to Emerson* (Stanford, CA: Stanford UP, 2020), 16–17. On this

Heraclitean aspect of nature which 'loves to hide', see also Pierre Hadot, *Le voile d'Isis: essai sur l'histoire de l'idée de nature* (Paris: Gallimard, 2004).
114 Otten, *Thinking*, 13–125 and *passim*.
115 In fact, this courtly manner of speaking about 'nature' is parodied by Autolycus at 4.4.749–751.
116 On the connection between early modern, 'Polixenian' views of nature and witches, see Carolyn Merchant, *The Death of Nature: Women, Ecology and the Scientific Revolution* (San Francisco, CA: Harper, 1990).
117 Bishop, *Wonder*, 154.
118 *Ibid.*, 155.
119 *Ibid.*
120 *Ibid.*
121 *Ibid.*, 156.
122 This transformation, as Jensen notes, echoes that of Hermione in the final scene. *Revelry*, 225ff.
123 McDonald, *Late Style*, 203–204.
124 Bishop, *Wonder*, 157.
125 See Nuttall, *Thinker*, 232–233.
126 Schalkwyk, *Service*, 284.
127 *Ibid.*, 285.
128 See *DVD*, 9.38.
129 Scott Crider, *With What Persuasion: An Essay on Shakespeare and the Ethics of Rhetoric* (New York: Lang, 2009), 156.
130 Schalkwyk, *Service*, 284.
131 This literature is considerable. For examples of a Protestant reading, see Diehl, "Rebuke"; Grace Tiffany, 'Calvinist Grace in Shakespeare's Romances', *CAL* 49.4 (2000), 421–445. For Catholic readings, see Beauregard, *Catholic Theology*, 109–123; Wilson, *Secret*, 246–270. On the issue of idolatry, see Shell, *Religion*, 18; Michael O' Connell, *The Idolatrous Eye: Iconoclasm and Theatre in Early Modern England* (New York: OUP, 2000), 141–144. Julia Lupton attempts to read this scene in a Pauline key while moving beyond confessional issues; see *Afterlives of the Saints: Hagiography, Typology, and Renaissance Literature* (Stanford, CA: Stanford UP, 1996), 175–218.
132 Neely, 'Triumph', 252.
133 Małgorzata Grzegorzewska, 'Shakespeare's Curtain: The Stage Revealed or the Stage Re-Veiled', *Cahiers Elisabethains* 20.1 (2019), 1–10.
134 *Ibid.*, 7.
135 *Ibid.*
136 See above, 95.
137 See Chapter 2.
138 On the relationship between rebuke, justice and forgiveness in Shakespeare, see Schwartz, *Loving Justice*, 103–117.
139 See Pitcher, 5.3.56n (341) and Cf. 1.2.155n. (163).
140 Kenneth Gross, *The Dream of the Moving Statue* (Ithaca, NY: Cornell UP, 1992), 104.
141 See above, 145.
142 Neely, 'Triumph', 253.
143 Platt, *Paradox*, 200–201.
144 On Shakespeare's poetic 'quasi-resurrections', see Sean Benson, *Shakespearean Resurrection: The Art of Almost Raising the Dead* (Pittsburgh: Duquesne UP, 2009), 149–163.
145 Gross, *Statue*, 109.
146 *Ibid.*

180 Readings

147 On this scene's movement beyond epistemic doubt, see James Kuzner, *Shakespeare as a Way of Life* (New York: Fordham UP, 2016), 80–105. For the associations between Leontes and Dis, see Bishop, *Wonder*, 151–152.
148 See Plato *Cratylus*, 428e–429b, where the lawgiver is the one whose art is to properly name things.
149 Neely, 'Triumph', 254.
150 Milbank, 'Fictioning', 241.
151 Northrop Frye, 'Charms and Riddles', in *Spiritus Mundi* (Brighton, MA: Fitzhenry, 2006), 123–147.
152 Neely, 'Triumph', 254.
153 For a reading of the play in the light of Renaissance Hermetic philosophy and theurgy, see Engel, 'Kinetic'. My reading accords less with specifically Renaissance inflections and more with the Neoplatonic sense of a transformation of the whole cosmos into a temple for sacramental practice. See Shaw, *Theurgy*, 56 and *passim*.
154 See Milbank, 'Stanton Lecture 8'; Catherine Pickstock, *Repetition and Identity*, 79. This is also the preoccupation of many of Shakespeare's Sonnets.
155 Lori Newcomb reads in the play a similar paradoxicality between the monumental, which commemorates 'what is lost', and the spectacular, which celebrates that which is found. Lori H. Newcomb, "'If That Which Is Lost Be Not Found': Monumental Bodies, Spectacular Bodies in *The Winter's Tale*" in *Ovid and the Renaissance Body*, ed. G.V. Stanivukovic (Toronto: University of Toronto Press, 2001), 239–259.
156 Kuzner, *Way of Life*, 100.
157 DVD, 9.38.
158 On this, see Eric Voegelin, 'The Beginning and the Beyond: A Meditation on Truth', *in What Is History? and Other Late Unpublished Writings*, ed. Thomas A. Hollweck and Paul Caringella (Baton Rouge: Louisiana State UP, 1990), 173–232.
159 Cox, *Knowledge*, 24.
160 At least 14 of Shakespeare's plays end with the call for further narrative—a common trope of Renaissance literature. See Barbary Hardy, *Shakespeare's Storytellers: Dramatic Narration* (London: Peter Owen, 1997), 72–90.

Epilogue
Shakespeare, Metaphysics and 'Theology and Literature'

This book has been animated by a central claim, that a theological reading of literature can approach language as kind of gift, encountering *verbum* and *donum, logos* and spirit, as profoundly intertwined and grounded in the simple yet profound act of affirmation and praise. In reflecting the First Praise, the divine 'speaking gaze' alluded to by Cusa, human language as praise is a mode of expression which aligns with God's vision in Genesis that sees all things as good, and so truly 'beholds' and is given the words to truly say "tis well'—as Shakespeare shows. This account of language, it seems to me, can make sense of my initial theological wager that the mystery of the incarnation is somehow always already intimately involved with linguistic expression. Yet, as we have also seen, this is a mode of language which is not spoken in a vacuum, but as a response that bears the imprint of an always already prior address. From this point of view, words are not speech-acts uttered in a univocal and unidimensional reality. Being enharmonically related to the incarnation, rather, they become aligned with and oriented to a spiritual quest to redeem of all things and beings by affirming and articulating their fundamental and enduring goodness. To see language in this way suggests an ontology shaped by such an orientation: the doxological approach, ultimately, entails a poetic vision of the real.

In Chapter 1, I articulated possibilities for a doxological reading of Shakespeare as emanating from both the literary-critical and theological traditions. With regard to religion, however, the former is caught in an *aporia*: for while it wishes to celebrate the creative liberty of literature uncurbed by oppressive ideologies, it struggles to move beyond the hegemony of a hermeneutic of suspicion grounded in an implicit ontology of power. Shakespeare scholars who have sought to negotiate this difficulty are still dealing with its consequences. Hence, there seems to be no stable category for religion, other than as a vestigial or transitional expression in the face of an impending secular culture: while theatre 'competes' with or 'fills the void' left by the church, religion is reduced to political manoeuvring, or equated to a kind of 'existential' expression, or an antique mode of social thought, or a residual imaginary lurking in a semi-secular poetics. In line with such perspectives, poetic language too

DOI: 10.4324/9781003223276-7

is often encountered as second-degree speech, either as allegory of or escape from a prime-order reality which remains nakedly socio-political. These are views which affirm something very close to the ontology that paralyses the first part of *The Winter's Tale*: an account of the real as the merely 'given', in which grace is at most an epiphenomenon—rather than a theological-poetic apprehension of the real as gift, in which, no matter how elusive, paradoxical or elliptical, grace is somehow the *central* phenomenon.

Yet, undoubtedly, literary scholars are right to be wary of the 'baptising' of literature, which restricts its adventurous modes of creative re-presentation by attempting to force texts into pre-established theological frameworks. To be sure, this warning should also be heeded by theologians who approach the poetic as a secular expression onto which one can 'superimpose' a theological lens—theology being understood as an unrelated form of words which merely bears intriguing comparisons with literature. 'Farming' poetry or plays in order to make sense of scripture ignores the full theological dimension of language itself, the dynamic, surprising and non-reducible revelations that linguistic expression continuously unfolds. The Cusan reading of Shakespeare outlined by Hoff and Hampson provided an insightful way to resolve some of these difficulties, insofar as it showed that the 'doxological reduction', being both prior to *and* the consummation of discursive reason, proposed an understanding of language as a kind of cosmic gift, in a manner that could also stay true to Shakespeare's poetic freedom. On this view, the poetic is both sub-theological *and* ultra-theological, a creative component primordial to human linguistic expression that is nonetheless also an indelible aspect of the deepest theological reflection.

Hence, while remaining wary of literary criticism's bracketing out of theology in the name of suspicion and *also* suspicious of the theological impulse to make literature instrumental to religious doctrine, I have tried to approach the interdisciplinary venture of 'theology and literature' by making language *the* phenomenon at play for both fields of study. As I have tried to show, a doxological approach to literature presents language not an instrument of communication but as a kind of primordial speech of the soul, whose expression participates in a reality permeated with divine utterance. The metaphysics I sketch out throughout this work portray reality as a cosmic instantiation of the creative word spoken 'in the beginning', an utterance palpably present in all things, calling and directing the soul towards love and goodness, thus being also 'redeeming'. To be sure, this metaphysical continuity between Cusa and Shakespeare could be seen as historically problematic: historians of ideas anxious to demarcate a clear line between the medieval synthesis of words and world and the early modern breakdown of medieval metaphysics may feel that a deep cultural fault-line severs Cusa's early Renaissance world from Shakespeare's early modern culture. Though my argument was not historical, I have nevertheless tried to suggest deep continuities between the two worlds, and this study certainly suggests further readings of cultural history that could place both Cusa and Shakespeare as exponents of a tradition, or set of traditions, that can broadly be seen to belong to the Christian Platonic corpus—a tradition that stretches back before and extends well beyond their work. Whereas it may be overly ambitious to represent Shakespeare as a 'metaphysician', his work, as I hope to have shown, shows strong creative convergences with Cusa's participatory metaphysics. Cusa wove an original synthesis of a pre-modern, participatory analogical cosmology with a uniquely modern sensitivity to poetic creativity grounded in a manifest concern to show that wisdom can playfully 'roam free'. For him, then, linguistic creativity was more than an aesthetic flourish serving to illustrate metaphysical and theological questions: rather, it offered specific *solutions* to the cultural problems of his day. Accordingly, literary scholars, who perhaps are more instinctively attuned to the ambiguous vagaries and unrestrainable creativity of language than theologians, might benefit from Cusa's approach, and be brought at least to consider the possibility that religious thought may not always be powered by a ploy to organise, control or suppress creative freedom. Rather, as Cusa and Shakespeare both show, it is possible to attend to literature 'religiously' insofar as it constitutes an attempt to discern and respond to the creative intelligence under the aegis of which such creativity arises. Similarly, theologians working with literature, I suggest, are called to deepen this sensitivity to the gift-like, daring unpredictability and instability of the wisdom that moves through and with poetic language.

Ultimately, this brings up the larger question of the difficulty of understanding literature within a universe that is both predisposed to spiritual flourishing *and* open to unpredictable, creative linguistic freedom. In other words, it brings into question an ontological confluence between order and play, between structure and freedom, between metaphysics and poetics. What I hope to have shown is that 'theology and literature', more than an ill-defined comparative discipline, unfit to qualify either as literature or theology proper, is in fact at heart a kind of metaphysical pursuit that articulates something of this 'ontological confluence'. For theologians interested in literature, I have suggested, this means reading literary works as manifest responses to a cosmos felt, experienced and understood linguistic all the way down, that the Word both creates and redeems; that is, whose creative roots and origins and spiritual energies are also both linguistic in nature. Poetry, as Shakespeare shows, cannot be reduced to a movement out of real into a nebulous fantasy realm, or to an instrument for political allegory, or to mere melancholic, rhetorical decoration of a brute world or objective reality 'standing out there'. Instead, Shakespeare offers a unique case of 'theology and literature' insofar as he shows that fiction is not an escape from life, a fugue into the fantastical, but rather is an attempt to re-imagine, re-envision, indeed 're-present' the real as envisioned in the light of this primordial linguistic ontology.

So much for my initial venture into the literary aspects of the 'Word made flesh', but what about its reverse and equally important sense of flesh being made Word? The relationship between praise and the natural world that I touch upon in this book bring us back to the sense in which this approach to reality as linguistic ties together matter and spirit, or things, beings, bodies and words. The final scenes of *The Winter's Tale* offer a clear instantiation of the 'middle-voiced' relationship between the material and the poetic; for while they figure reality as ethereal and translucent, they also articulate a deep affirmation of natural life and embodied relationships, acknowledging their unfinishedness and complexities, their unexpected, grace-filled joys—but also their unresolved sorrows. Conversely, I showed that *King Lear*, and parts of *The Winter's Tale*, chronicle a downfall of language that coincides with a refusal to allow words to become praise-gifts to the material world. *King Lear*, in particular, shows how the severance of language from its roots coincides with encountering the world as a dumb and mute 'given'. In this way, our participation in the real, our inhabitation of its material dimensions, can be transformed into the positing of an isolated, wilful selfhood over against a death-bound material sphere. For Shakespeare, the manipulation of matter coincides with the manipulation of words.

Yet *King Lear* also explores the creative superabundance of language over the speechlessness of pain and death, staging situations in which human speech seems to call on its every resource to touch its own sacred ground. Language's liturgical and doxological roots remind us that the creative and poetic sway of words is always irreducibly embodied. It is such energy that powers Kent's visceral anger at the breakdown of an ethic of love and service felt to be a cosmic truth; or inhabits Tom's skeletal vision and 'vocative superflux' at the edge of society and of words; or dwells in the last gesture of Lear and Cordelia, who perform an embodied blessing which, in turn, becomes the symbol of the restitution of a genuine 'gravity' of words. In this play, it is the human body that overcomes a situation where sophistry has made the world inarticulate, just as it is an encounter with nature in its 'wild' aspect, rather than in its suspect courtly iteration, that offers to Lear, Gloucester and Edgar possibilities for regeneration. Even the last scene ascribes to the weight of Cordelia's dead body in Lear's arms the inverted measure of Cordelia's sense, at the play's opening, of the true gravitational pull of linguistic expression. Indeed, the last scene returns to the first, calling to obey the weight of 'this sad time' with appropriate sentient expression, with grief, lament and prayer, with honest and heartfelt words, 'speaking what we feel'.

The Winter's Tale too offers final moments in which human language returns to its own roots by re-affirming and re-articulating the world in terms of the great gift of life, the flower of 'Great Creating Nature'. In order for human words to re-harmonise with the 'First Praise' that sees all things as good, *The Winter's Tale* shows, deeply and ambiguously, that the language of praise must also be a response to the lure of material life: that to praise is to praise all the things and beings of 'Great Creating Nature' in the light of their divine origin *and* (consequently) their material origin. Thus, Perdita's affirmation of nature vitally contributes to the gift of Hermione's return to natural life. Yet, Hermione's tale-like return does not cancel out the weight of Mamillius' absence, Antigonus' death or the Queen's 'tongue-tied' response to Leontes. The play does not stage an unambiguous or triumphalist victory of redeemed life over bodily death. To simply avoid the significance of bodily suffering as though it had never occurred would mean to lessen a crucial aspect of embodied life: its vulnerabilities, its fragilities and its risks. It would mean, in other words, that the call to praise the created world had not been properly responded to.

If the doxological approach always suggests the entanglement between the natural, the material and the linguistic, one consideration might be that the specifically theatrical aspect of Shakespeare's art has been under-considered in this study. These works are primarily play-texts, it could be said, intended to be performed and embodied. Does not this book's emphasis on metaphysics elide the complicated densities of embodied performance? What might the significance of my approach be for theatrical practice? As someone with many years' experience in the performing arts, this difficulty has not escaped my attention. It seemed to me, however, that the interdisciplinary crossover between theology and literature needed detailed metaphysical elucidation, corroborated by patient readings, and that such a project was already ambitious enough without venturing into full exploration of its dramaturgical consequences. The primordial connection between theatre and liturgy, assumed in this study throughout, will require further work to be properly developed. Yet I hope to have sketched out a theo-literary *imaginary* which can at least provide ground for reflection as well as for performance.

A final word might be offered with regard to the kind of interdisciplinary scholarship I have tried to practice in this book. The characters encountered in this study, the layman, crafting spoons and names in his underground workshop, the Cardinal on the hunt for wisdom, the banished daughter and the estranged son on the heath, the councillor turned spiritual midwife and the miraculous returning child, all turn to the creative extensions of human speech to craft words 'medicinal as true'. It became clear, as I explored my themes, that one could only elaborate an account of praise through a writing practice that was, to some degree, *itself* performative.[1] The argument that runs through this study is not linear: it circles around an energetic centre from which it weaves a multitude of patterns, seeking to evoke the very reality towards which it points—perhaps also inviting the readers to enter into its world rather than simply follow its logic. What emanates from this book, then, is also an attempt to imagine scholarship in 'theology and literature' as, in some sense, a kind of doxology. In this sense, I have tried to learn from insights that both Cusa and Shakespeare seem in their own way to uphold: that the search for wisdom always begins with the creative affirmation of the goodness of all being.

Note

1 For a recent account of theology as craft, see Elizabeth Powell, *David Jones and the Craft of Theology: Becoming Beauty* (London: Bloomsbury T&T Clark, 2020).

Bibliography

Adelman, Janet. 1992. *Suffocating Mothers: Fantasies of Maternal Origins in Shakespeare's Plays*. London: Routledge.
Aers, David, and Sarah Beckwith. 2003. "Introduction: Hermeneutics and Ideology." *Journal of Medieval and Early Modern Studies* 33 (2): 211–213.
Agamben, Giorgio. 2013. *The Sacrament of Language: Archaeology of the Oath*. Translated by Adam Kotsko. Cambridge: Polity.
Albertson, David. 2006. "That He Might Fill All Things: Creation and Christology in two Treatises by Nicholas of Cusa." *International Journal of Systematic Theology* 8 (2): 184–205.
Altman, Joel. 2010. *The Improbability of Othello: Rhetorical Anthropology and Shakespearean Selfhood*. Chicago, IL: University of Chicago Press.
Anderson, Judith. 2005. *Translating Investments: Metaphor and the Dynamic of Cultural Change in Tudor-Stuart England*. New York: Fordham University Press.
Andretta, Helen Ruth. 1997. *Chaucer's Troilus and Criseyde: A Poet's Response to Ockhamism*. New York: Peter Lang.
Andrewes, Lancelot. 1955. *Sermons on the Nativity*. Grand Rapids, MI: Baker Book House.
Archer, Jayne Elisabeth, Turley Richard Marggraf, and Howard Thomas. 2012. "The Autumn King: Remembering the Land in King Lear." *Shakespeare Quarterly* 63 (4): 518–543.
Armstrong, Philip. 2016. "Preposterous Natures in Shakespeare's Tragedies." In *The Oxford Handbook to Shakespearean Tragedy*, edited by Michael Neill and David Schalkwyk, 104–119. Oxford: Oxford University Press.
Ashley, Kathleen. 1978. "Divine Power in Chester Cycle and Late Medieval Thought." *Journal of the History of Ideas* 39: 387–404.
Asquith, Clare. 2005. *Shadowplay: The Hidden Beliefs and Coded Politics of William Shakespeare*. London: Perseus Books.
Auden, W. H. 2019. *Lectures on Shakespeare*. Edited by Arthur C. Kirsch. Princeton, NJ: Princeton University Press.
Augustine. 2014–2016. *Confessions*. Loeb Classics Library. Translated by C. J. B. Hammond. 2 vols. Cambridge, MA: Harvard University Press.
Baker, Anthony. 2020. *Shakespeare, Theology and the Unstaged God*. Abingdon: Routledge.
Barber, C. L. 1967. *Shakespeare's Festive Comedy: A Study of Dramatic Form and Its Relation to Social Custom*. Princeton, NJ: Princeton University Press.

Barthes, Roland. 1977. *Roland Barthes by Roland Barthes*. Translated by Richard Howard. New York: Noonday Press.

Barton, Anne. 2017. *The Shakespearean Forest*. Edited by Hesther Lees-Jeffries. Cambridge: Cambridge University Press.

Bate, Jonathan. 2000. "Shakespeare's Foolosophy." In *Shakespeare Performed: Essays in Honour of R. A. Foakes*, edited by Grace Ioppolo, 17–32. Newark: University of Delaware Press.

———. 2019. *How the Classics Made Shakespeare*. Princeton, NJ: Princeton University Press.

Batson, Beatrice, ed. 2006. *Shakespeare's Christianity: The Protestant and Catholic Poetics of Julius Caesar, Macbeth, and Hamlet*. Waco, TX: Baylor University Press.

Battenhouse, Roy. 1980. "Theme and Structure in *The Winter's Tale*." *Shakespeare Survey* 33: 123–138.

Baxter, John. 2013. "Reported Speech in *The Winter's Tale*." *Renaissance and Reformation* 36 (3): 127–151.

Bearman, Robert. 2005. "John Shakespeare: A Papist or Just Penniless?" *Shakespeare Quarterly* 56 (4): 411–433.

Beauregard, David. 2008. *Catholic Theology in Shakespeare's Plays*. Newark: Delaware University Press.

Beckwith, Sarah. 2011. *Shakespeare and the Grammar of Forgiveness*. Ithaca, NY: Cornell University Press.

———. 2015. "Are There any Women in Shakespeare's Plays?: Fiction, Representation and Reality in Feminist Criticism." *New Literary History* 46 (2): 241–260.

Benson, Sean. 2009. *Shakespearean Resurrections: The Art of Almost Raising the Dead*. Pittsburgh: Duquesne University Press.

Berry, Philippa. 1999. *Shakespeare's Feminine Endings: Figuring Death in the Tragedies*. London: Routledge.

Bethell, S. L. 1944. *Shakespeare and the Popular Dramatic Tradition*. London: King and Staples.

Bicks, Caroline. 2003. *Midwiving Subjects in Shakespeare's England: Women and Gender in the Early Modern World*. Aldershot: Aldgate.

Birns, Nicholas. 2010. *Theory After Theory: An Intellectual History of Literary Theory from 1950 to the Early 21st Century*. Peterborough: Broadview.

Bishop, Thomas. 1996. *Shakespeare and the Theatre of Wonder*. Cambridge: Cambridge University Press.

Bloom, Harold. 1998. *Shakespeare and the Invention of the Human*. New York: Riverhead.

Blumemberg, Hans. 1983. *The Legitimacy of the Modern Age*. Translated by Robert M. Wallace. Cambridge, MA: MIT Press.

Boitani, Piero. 2013. *The Gospel According to William Shakespeare*. Translated by Vittorio Montemaggi and Rachel Jacoff. Notre Dame, IN: University of Notre Dame Press.

Bond, H. Lawrence. 2004. "Mystical Theology." In *Introducing Nicholas of Cusa: A Guide to a Renaissance Man*, edited by Christopher Bellitto, Thomas Izbicki and Gerald Christianson, 205–231. New York: Paulist Press.

Booth, Stephen. 1983. *King Lear, Macbeth, Indefintion and Tragedy*. New Haven, CT: Yale University Press.

Bouchard, Larry. 2005. "Playing Nothing for Someone: Lear, Bottom and Kenotic Integrity." *Literature and Theology* 17 (6): 159–180.
Bouwsma, William. 1990. "The Two Faces of Humanism: Stoicism and Augustinianism in Renaissance Thought." In *A Usable Past: Essays in European Cultural History*, 19–64. Berkeley: University of California Press.
Bradley, A. C. 2007. *Shakespearean Tragedy: Lectures on Hamlet, Othello, King Lear, Macbeth*. Charleston, SC: Bibliolife.
Brook, Peter. 1996. *The Empty Space*. New York: Touchstone Books.
———. 2014. *The Quality of Mercy: Reflections on Shakespeare*. London: Nick Hern Books.
Buber, Martin. 1959. *I and Thou*. Translated by Ronald Gregor Smith. Edinburgh: T&T Clark.
Burrow, J. A. 2008. *The Poetry of Praise*. Cambridge: Cambridge University Press.
Burrows, Mark, Jean Ward, and Malgorzata Gregorgzewska, eds. 2017. *Poetic Revelations: Word Made Flesh Made Word*. London: Routledge.
Byassee, Jason. 2007. *Praise Seeking Understanding: Reading the Psalms with Augustine*. Grand Rapids, MI: Eerdmans.
Canfield, John Douglas. 1989. *Word as Bond in English Literature from the Middle Ages to the Restoration*. Philadelphia: University of Pennsylvania Press.
Cantor, Paul. 2008. "The Cause of Thunder: Nature and Justice in King Lear." In *King Lear: New Critical Essays*, edited by Jeffrey Kahan, 231–252. London: Routledge.
Carruthers, Mary. 1998. *The Craft of Thought: Meditation, Rhetoric and the Making of Images, 400–1200*. Cambridge: Cambridge University Press.
Casarella, Peter, ed. 2006. *Cusanus: The Legacy of Learned Ignorance*. Washington, DC: Catholic University of America Press.
———. 2008. "Cusanus on Dionysius: The Turn to Speculative Theology." *Modern Theology* 24 (4): 667–678.
———, ed. 2017. *Word as Bread: Language and Theology in Nicholas of Cusa*. Münster: Aschendorff Verlag.
Cassirer, Ernst. 1963. *The Individual and the Cosmos in Renaissance Philosophy*. Translated by Mario Domandi. Oxford: Blackwell.
Cavell, Stanley. 1999. *The Claim of Reason: Wittgenstein, Skepticism, Morality and Tragedy*. Oxford: Oxford University Press.
———. 2003. *Disowning Knowledge in Seven Plays of Shakespeare*. Updated Edition. Oxford: Oxford University Press.
Chambers, R. W. 1940. *King Lear*. Glasgow: Jackson, Son and Co.
Chrétien, Jean-Louis. 1990. *La Voix nue : phénoménologie de la promesse*. Paris: Editions de minuit.
———. 2004. *The Ark of Speech*. Translated by Andrew Brown. London: Routledge.
———. 2007. *Répondre : Figures de la réponse et de la responsabilité*. Paris: Presses universitaires de France.
———. 2013. "Essayer de penser au-delà de la subjectivité." *Critique* 790 (3): 241–253.**
Coleridge, Samuel Taylor. 2016. *Coleridge on Shakespeare (1811–1819)*. Edited by Adam Roberts. Edinburgh: Edinburgh University Press.

Bibliography

Colie, Rosalie. 2015. *Paradoxia Epidemica: The Renaissance Tradition of Paradox*. Princeton, NJ: Princeton University Press.
Cooper, Helen. 2010. *Shakespeare and the Medieval World*. London: Methuen Drama.
Corio, Anne Baynes, and Thomas Fulton, eds. 2012. *Rethinking Historicism from Shakespeare to Milton*. Cambridge: Cambridge University Press.
Cousins, A. D., and Daniel Derrin, eds. 2018. *Shakespeare and the Soliloquy in early Modern English Drama*. Cambridge: Cambridge University Press.
Cox, John D. 2006. "Was Shakespeare a Christian and If So, What Kind of Christian Was He?" *Christianity and Literature* 55 (4): 539–566.
———. 2007. *Seeming Knowledge: Shakespeare and Skeptical Faith*. Waco, TX: Baylor University Press.
Crawford, Jason. 2019. "Shakespeare's Language of Assumption." *Journal of Medieval and Early Modern Studies* 49 (1): 57–84.
Crider, Scott. 2009. *With What Persuasion: An Essay on Shakespeare and the Ethics of Rhetoric*. New York: Peter Lang.
Cross, Richard. 2008. "Idolatry and Religious Language." *Faith and Philosophy* 25 (2): 190–196.
Cubillos, Catalina M. 2012. "Nicholas of Cusa between the Middle Ages and Modernity: The Historiographical Positions Behind the Discussion." *American Catholic Philosophical Quarterly* 86 (2): 237–249.
Cummings, Brian. 2002. *Grammar and Grace: The Literary Culture of the Reformation*. Oxford: Oxford University Press.
———. 2013. *Mortal Thoughts: Religion, Secularity and Identity in Shakespeare and Early Modern Culture*. Oxford: Oxford University Press.
Cusa, Nicholas of. 1998–2001. *Complete Philosophical and Theological Treatises of Nicholas of Cusa*. Translated by Jasper Hopkins. 2 vols. Minneapolis, MN: Arthur J. Banning Press.
———. 2003. *Nicholas of Cusa's Early Sermons: 1430–1411*. Translated by Jasper Hopkins. Minneapolis, MN: Banning Press.
Danby, John. 1972. *King Lear: Shakespeare's Doctrine of Nature*. London: Faber&Faber.
Daniell, David. 2001. "Shakespeare and the Protestant Mind." In *Shakespeare Survey 54*, edited by Peter Holland, 1–12. Cambridge: Cambridge University Press.
Davey, Nicholas. 2019. "Experience, Its Edges, and Beyond." *Open Philosophy* 2: 299–311.
Dawson, Anthony, and Paul Yachnin. 2001. *The Culture of Playgoing in Shakespeare's England: A Collaborative Debate*. Cambridge: Cambridge University Press.
de la Taille, Maurice. 1930. *The Mystery of Faith and Human Opinion Contrasted and Defined*. Translated by J. P. Schimpf. London: Sheed and Ward.
de Libera, Alain. 1996. *La querelle des universaux: de Platon à la fin du Moyen-Age*. Paris: Seuil.
Diehl, Huston. 1997. *Staging Reform, Reforming the Stage: Protestantism and Popular Theater in Early Modern England*. Ithaca, NY: Cornell University Press.
———. 2008. "'Does Not The Stone Rebuke Me?': The Pauline Rebuke and Paulina's Lawful Magic in *The Winter's Tale*." In *Shakespeare and the*

Cultures of Performance, edited by Paul Yachnin and Patricia Badir, 69–82. Farnham: Ashgate.

Dobson, Michael. 2002. "Wilson Knight's Wheel of Fire." *Essay in Criticism* 52 (3): 235–244.

Dollimore, Jonathan. 1984. *Radical Tragedy: Religion, Ideology and Power in the Drama of Shakespeare and His Contemporaries*. London: Harvester Wheatsheaf.

Dollimore, Jonathan, and Alan Sinfeld, eds. 1996. *Political Shakespeare: New Essays in Cultural Materialism*. Chicago, IL: University of Chicago Press.

Donnini, Mauro. 2016. "Niccolò Cusano e la Retorica." In *Niccolò Cusano: L'uomo, i Libri, L'Opera: Atti del 52° convegno storico internazionale*, 301–323. Spoleto: Centro Italiano di Studi sul Basso Medioevo.

Duclow, Donald. 2004. "Life and Works." In *Introducing Nicholas of Cusa: A Guide to a Renaissance Man*, edited by Christopher Bellitto, Thomas Izbicki and Gerald Christianson, 25–56. New York: Paulist Press.

———. 2006. *Masters of Learned Ignorance: Eriugena, Eckhart, Cusanus*. Aldershot: Aldgate.

Dupré, Louis. 1990. "Nature and Grace in Nicholas of Cusa's Mystical Philosophy." *American Catholic Philosophical Quarterly* 64 (1): 153–170.

———. 1993. *Passage to Modernity: An Essay in the Hermeneutics of Nature and Culture*. New Haven, CT: Yale University Press.

———. 2006. "The Question of Pantheism from Eckhart to Cusanus." In *The Legacy of Learned Ignorance*, edited by Peter Casarella, 74–88. Washington, DC: Catholic University of America Press.

Dupré, Louis, and Nancy Hudson. 2002. "Nicholas of Cusa." In *A Companion to Philosophy in the Middle Ages*, edited by Jorge Garcia and Timothy Noone, 466–474. Oxford: Blackwell.

Dyrness, William. 2011. *Poetic Theology: God and the Poetics of Everyday Life*. Grand Rapids, MI: William B. Eerdmans.

Economou, George. 2002. *The Goddess Natura in Medieval Literature*. Notre Dame, IN: Notre Dame University Press.

Egan, Gabriel. 2015. *Shakespeare and Ecocritical Theory*. London: Bloomsbury Arden.

Elam, Keir. 1984. *Shakespeare's Universe of Discourse: Language Games in the Comedies*. Cambridge: Cambridge University Press.

Eliade, Mircea. 1964. *Shamanism: Archaic Techniques of Ecstasy*. New York: Pantheon.

Eliot, T. S. 1923. "The Beating of a Drum." *The Nation and the Athenaeum* 34 (1): 11–12.

Elton, William. 2015. *King Lear and the Gods*. Lexington: University of Kentucky.

Erne, Lukas. 2013. *Shakespeare as Literary Dramatist*. 2nd Edition. Cambridge: Cambridge University Press.

Estok, Simon C. 2011. *Ecocriticism and Shakespeare: Reading Ecophobia*. New York: Palgrave.

Evans, John. 1990. "Erasmian Folly and King Lear: A Study in Humanist Intertextuality." *Moreana* 27 (103): 3–24.

Evans, Malcolm. 1989. *Signifying Nothing: Truth's True Content in Shakespeare's Text*. 2nd Edition. London: Harvester Wheatsheaf.

Feerick, Jean. 2011. "Economies of Nature in Shakespeare." *Shakespeare Studies* 39: 32–42.

Felperin, Howard. 1992. *The Uses of the Canon: Elizabethan Literature and Contemporary Theory.* Oxford: Oxford University Press.

Felski, Rita. 2015. *The Limits of Critique.* Chicago, IL: University of Chicago Press.

Fernie, Ewan. 2002. *Shame in Shakespeare.* London: Routledge.

Flahiff, F. T. 1986. "Lear's Map." *Cahiers Elisabethains* 30: 17–33.

Foakes, R. A. 1993. *Hamlet versus Lear: Cultural Politics and Shakespeare's Art.* Cambridge: Cambridge University Press.

Fortin, René. 1995. *Gaining Upon Certainty: Selected Literary Criticism.* Edited by Brian Barbour and Rodney Delasanta. Providence, RI: Providence University Press.

Franke, William. 2012. "Apophatic Paths." *Angelaki* 17 (3): 7–16.

Frye, Northrop. 1991. *The Double Vision: Language and Meaning in Religion.* Toronto: University of Toronto Press.

———. 1995. "Recognition in *The Winter's Tale*." In *The Winter's Tale: Critical Essays*, edited by Maurice Hunt, 106–118. New York: Routledge.

———. 2000. *Anatomy of Criticism: Four Essays.* Princeton, NJ: Princeton University Press.

———. 2006. *Spiritus Mundi.* Brighton, MA: Fitzhenry.

———. 2010. *Northrop Frye's Writings on Shakespeare and the Renaissance.* Edited by Troni Y. Grande and Gary Sherbert. Toronto: University of Toronto Press.

Frye, Roland Mushat. 1963. *Shakespeare and Christian Doctrine.* Princeton, NJ: Princeton University Press.

Fulton, Thomas, and Kirsten Poole, eds. 2018. *The Bible on the Shakespearean Stage: Cultures of Interpretation in Reformation Engalnd.* Cambridge: Cambridge University Press.

Funkenstein, Amos. 1986. *Theology and the Scientific Imagination from the Middle Ages to the Seventeenth Century.* Princeton, NJ: Princeton University Press.

Gadamer, Hans-Georg. 2004. *Truth and Method.* Translated by Joel Weinsheimer and Donald G. Marshall. London: Continuum.

———. 2008. *Philosophical Hermeneutics.* 30th Anniversary Edition. Translated by David E. Linge. Berkeley: University of California Press.

Garber, Marjorie. 2005. *Shakespeare After All.* New York: Anchor.

———. 2013. *Dream in Shakespeare.* New Haven, CT: Yale University Press.

Gash, Anthony. 1998. "Shakespeare, Carnival and the Sacred." In *Shakespeare and Carnival: After Bakhtin*, edited by Roland Knowles, 177–210. Basingstoke: Palgrave.

Gatti, Hilary. 1989. *The Renaissance Drama of Knowledge: Giordano Bruno in England.* London: Routledge.

Gerlier, Valentin. 2015. "The Word of Love: Poetic Truth and Socratic Midwifery in Shakespeare." *Temenos Academy Review* 15: 71–90.

———. 2018. "Wonder, Adoration and the Ground of Language in Nicholas of Cusa." *Journal of Medieval Mystical Theology* 27 (2): 89–102.

Ghose, Indira. 2008. *Shakespeare and Laughter: A Cultural History.* Manchester: Manchester University Press.

Gillespie, Michael Allen. 2008. *The Theological Origins of Modernity*. Chicago, IL: University of Chicago Press.

Goldberg, Jonathan. 1988. "'Perspectives: Dover Cliff and the Conditions of Representation'." In *Shakespeare and Deconstruction*, edited by G. D. Atkins and G. M. Bergeron, 245–265. New York: Peter Lang.

Grady, Hugh, and Terence Hawkes, eds. 2007. *Presentist Shakespeares*. London: Routledge.

Graham, Kenneth. 1991. "'Without the Form of Justice': Plainness and the Performance of Love in King Lear." *Shakespeare Quarterly* 42 (4): 438–461.

Gray, Patrick. 2019. *Shakespeare and the Fall of the Roman Republic: Selfhood, Stoicism and Civil War*. Edinburgh: Edinburgh University Press.

Gray, Patrick, and John Cox, eds. 2014. *Shakespeare and Renaissance Ethics*. Cambridge: Cambridge University Press.

Greenblatt, Stephen. 1990. *Learning to Curse: Essays in Early Modern Culture*. London: Routledge.

———. 2001. *Shakespearean Negotiations: The Circulation of Social Energy in Renaissance England*. Oxford: Clarendon Press.

———. 2013. *Hamlet in Purgatory*. First Princeton Classics Edition. Princeton, NJ: Princeton University Press.

Greenblatt, Stephen, and Giles Guns, eds. 1992. *Redrawing the Boundary: The Transformation of English and American Literary Studies*. New York: The Modern Language Association of America.

Gregory, Brad S. 2012. *The Unintended Reformation*. Cambridge, MA: Harvard University Press.

Griffiths, Paul J. 2004. *Lying: an Augustinian Theology of Duplicity*. Grand Rapids, MI: Brazos Press.

Gross, Kenneth. 1992. *The Dream of the Moving Statue*. Ithaca, NY: Cornell University Press.

———. 2001. *Shakespeare's Noise*. Chicago, IL: University of Chicago Press.

Groves, Beatrice. 2007. *Texts and Traditions: Religion in Shakespeare, 1592–1604*. Oxford: Clarendon Press.

Grzegorrzewska, Małgorzata. 2019. "Shakespeare's Curtain: The Stage Revealed or the Stage Re-Veiled." *Cahiers Elisabethains* 20 (1): 1–10.

Gschwandtner, Christina M. 2015. "Creativity as Call to Care for Creation? John Zizioulas and Jean-Louis Chrétien." In *Being-In-Creation: Human Responsibility in an Endangered World*, edited by Brian Tranor, Bruce Benson and Norman Wirzba, 100–112. New York: Fordham Universiy Press.

Guite, Malcolm. 2012. *Faith, Hope and Poetry: Theology and the Poetic Imagination*. Farnham: Ashgate.

Hadot, Pierre. 1995. *Philosophy as a Way of Life: Spiritual Exercises from Socrates to Foucault*. Translated by Michael Chase. Oxford: Blackwell.

———. 2004. *Le voile d'Isis: essai sur l'histoire de l'idée de nature*. Paris: Gallimard.

Hamlin, Hannibal. 2013. *The Bible in Shakespeare*. Oxford: Oxford University Press.

———, ed. 2019. *The Cambridge Companion to Shakespeare and Religion*. Cambridge: Cambridge University Press.

Hardy, Barbara. 1997. *Shakespeare's Storytellers: Dramatic Narration*. London: Peter Owen.

Hardy, Daniel, and David Ford. 1985. *Praising and Knowing God*. Philadelphia, PA: Westminster Press.
Hart, Trevor, and Steven R. Guthrie. 2007. *Faithful Performances: Enacting Christian Tradition*. Aldershot: Ashgate.
Hartwig, Johan. 1982. *Shakespeare's Tragicomic Vision*. Baton Rouge: Louisiana State University Press.
Hassel, Chris. 1980. *Faith and Folly in Shakespeare's Romantic Comedies*. Athens: Georgia University Press.
———. 2007. *Shakespeare's Religious Language: A Dictionary*. London: Continuum.
Hayashi, Akie. 2008. *Shakespeare and the Sidney Circle: Giordano Bruno's Influence in Renaissance England*. Tokyo: Yushodo.
Hayes, Michael L. 2008. "'What Means a Knight': Red Cross Knight and Edgar." In *Shakespeare and Spenser: Attractive Opposites*, edited by J. B. Lethbridg, 226–241. Manchester: Manchester University Press.
Hayes, Thomas Wilson. 1987. "Nicholas of Cusa and Popular Literacy in 17th Century England." *Studies in Philology* 84 (1): 80–94.
Heffernan, Julián Jiménez. 2019. *Shakespeare's Extremes: WIld Man, Monster, Beast*. London: Palgrave.
Heilman, Robert. 1948. *This Great Stage*. Saint Louis: Lousiana State University Press.
Hillman, Richard. 1992. *Shakespearean Subversions: The Trickster and the Play-Text*. London: Routledge.
Höfele, Andreas. 2011. *Stage, Stake and Scaffold: Humans and Animals in Shakespeare's Theatre*. Oxford: Oxford University Press.
Höfele, Andreas, and Werner von Koppenfels, eds. 2005. *Renaissance Go-Betweens: Cultural Exchanges in Early Modern Europe*. New York: Walter de Gruyter.
Hoff, Johannes. Forthcoming. "Mystagogy Beyond Onto-theology: Looking Back to Post-modernity with Nicholas of Cusa." *The Brill Companion to Nicholas of Cusa*.
———. 2013. *The Analogical Turn: Rethinking Modernity with Nicholas of Cusa*. Grand Rapids, MI: Eerdmans.
Hoff, Johannes, and Peter Hampson. 2015. "Cusa: A Pre-Modern Postmodern Reader of Shakespeare." In *Theology and Literature After Postmodernity*, edited by Zoë Lehmann Imfeld, Peter Hampson and Alison Milbank, 115–136. London: Bloomsbury.
Holbrook, Peter. 2010. *Shakespeare's Individualism*. Cambridge: Cambridge University Press.
Holderness, Graham. 2016. *The Faith of William Shakespeare*. Oxford: Lion.
Holderness, Graham, Nick Potter, and John Turner. 1993. *Shakespeare: Out of Court*. Basingstoke: MacMillan.
Hopkins, Jasper. 1996. *Nicholas of Cusa on Wisdom and Knowledge*. Minneapolis: Banning Press.
Hornback, Robert. 2009. *The English Clown Tradition from the Middle Ages to Shakespeare*. Cambridge: D. S. Brewer.
Hughes, John. 2001. "The Politics of Forgiveness: A Theological Exploration of King Lear." *Modern Theology* 17 (3): 261–287.
Hughes, Ted. 1993. *Shakespeare and the Goddess of Complete Being*. Revised Edition. London: Faber&Faber.

Hunt, Maurice. 2004. *Shakespeare's Religious Allusiveness: Its Play and Tolerance*. Aldershot: Aldgate.

Hunter, Robert Grams. 1965. *Shakespeare and the Comedy of Forgiveness*. New York: Columbia University Press.

Imfeld, Zoe Lehmann, Peter Hampson, and Alison Milbank, eds. 2015. *Theology and Literature after Postmodernity*. London: Bloomsbury T&T Clark.

Izbicki, Thomas, and Christopher Bellitto, eds. 2002. *Nicholas of Cusa and His Age: Intellect and Spirituality*. Boston, MA: Brill.

Jackson, Ken, and Arthur Moratti. 2004. "The Turn to Religion in Early Modern English Studies." *Criticism* 46 (1): 167–190.

Jaffa, Harry. 1964. "The Limits of Politics: King Lear Act 1, Scene 1." In *Shakespeare's Politics*, edited by Allan Bloom, 113–145. Chicago, IL: University of Chicago Press.

Jasper, David. 2009. "The Study of Literature and Theology." In *The Oxford Handbook of English Literature and Theology*, edited by Andrew Hass, David Jasper and Elisabeth Jay, 15–33. Oxford: Oxford University Press.

Jensen, Phebe. 2008. *Religion and Revelry in Shakespeare's Festive World*. Cambridge: Cambridge University Press.

———. 2019. "Causes in Nature: Popular Astrology in King Lear." *Shakespeare Quarterly* 69 (4): 205–227.

Johnson, Kimberly. 2014. *Made Flesh: Sacrament and Poetics in Post-Reformation England*. Philadelphia, PA: Pennsylvania University Press.

Jones, David. 2017. *Epoch and Artist: Selected Writings*. London: Faber.

Kahn, Coppélia. 1986. "The Absent Mother in King Lear." In *Rewriting the Renaissance: The Discourses of Sexual Difference in Early Modern Europe*, edited by Margaret W. Fergusson, Maureen Quilligan and Nancy J. Vickers, 33–49. Chicago, IL: University of Chicago Press.

Kahn, Paul. 2000. *Law and Love: The Trials of King Lear*. New Haven, CT: Yale University Press.

Kahn, Victoria. 2014. *The Future of Illusion: Political Theology and Early Modern Texts*. Chicago, IL: University of Chicago Press.

Kaiser, Walter. 1963. *Praisers of Folly: Erasmus, Rabelais, Shakespeare*. Cambridge, MA: Harvard University Press.

Kastan, David Scott. 1999. *Shakespeare After Theory*. New York: Routledge.

———. 2014. *A Will to Believe: Shakespeare and Religion*. Oxford: Oxford University Press.

Kaytor, Daryl. 2015. "Shakespeare's Gods." *Literature and Theology* 29 (1): 3–17.

Kearney, James. 2012. "'This Is Above All Strangeness': 'King Lear', Ethics and the Phenomenology of Recognition." *Criticism* 54 (3): 455–467.

Kern Paster, Gail. 2004. *Humoring the Body: Emotions and the Shakespearean Stage*. Chicago, IL: University of Chicago Press.

Kerrigan, John. 2016. *Shakespeare's Binding Language*. Oxford: Oxford University Press.

Kirkpatrick, Robin. 2010. "Polemics of Praise: Theology as Text, Narrative, and Rhetoric in Dante's Commedia." In *Dante's Commedia: Theology as Poetry*, edited by Vittorio Montemaggi and Matthew Traherne, 14–35. Notre Dame, IN: Notre Dame University Press.

Knapp, Jeffrey. 2002. *Shakespeare's Tribe: Church, Nation and Theater in Renaissance England*. Chicago, IL: University of Chicago Press.

Knapper, Daniel. 2019. "'Thunderings, Not Words'L Aspects of Pauline Style in Pericles and *The Winter's Tale*." *Shakespeare Studies* 47: 169.

Knight, George Wilson. 1949. *Shakespearean Production: With Especial References to the Tragedies*. Harmondsworth: Penguin.

———. 1958. *The Sovereign Flower: On Shakespeare as the Poet of Royalism*. London: Methuen.

———. 1967. *Shakespeare and Religion: Essays of Forty Years*. New York: Barnes & Noble.

Kott, Jan. 1967. *Shakespeare Our Contemporary*. Translated by Boleslaw Taborski. London: Methuen.

Kronenfeld, Judy. 1998. *King Lear and the Naked Truth: Rethinking the Language of Religion and Resistance*. London: Duke University Press.

Kuzner, James. 2016. *Shakespeare as a Way of Life*. New York: Fordham University Press.

Laroche, Rebecca, and Jennifer Munroe. 2017. *Shakespeare and Ecofeminist Theory*. London: Bloomsbury Arden.

Leitch, Vincent B. 2014. *Literary Criticism in the 21st Century: Theory Renaissance*. London: Bloomsbury.

Levao, Ronald. 1985. *Renaissance Minds and Their Fictions: Cusanus, Sidney, Shakespeare*. Berkeley: University of California Press.

Levine, Caroline. 2015. *Forms: Whole, Rhythm, Hierarchy, Network*. Princeton, NJ: Princeton University Press.

Line, Jill. 2004. *Shakespeare and the Fire of Love*. London: Shepheard-Walwyn.

Lockart, Adrienne. 1975. "'The Cat Is Grey': King Lear's Mad Trial Scene." *Shakespeare Quarterly* 26 (4): 469–471.

Lothian, John. 1970. *King Lear: A Tragic Reading of Life*. Folcroft, PA: Folcroft Library Edition.

Lowenstein, David, and Michael Witmore, eds. 2015. *Shakespeare and Early Modern Religion*. Cambridge: Cambridge University Press.

Lupton, Julia Reinhard. 1996. *Afterlives of the Saints: Hagiography, Typology, and Renaissance Literature*. Stanford, CA: Stanford University Press.

———. 2005. *Citizen Saints: Shakespeare and Political Theology*. Chicago, IL: University of Chicago Press.

———. 2006. "The Religious Turn (to Theory) in Shakespeare Studies." *English Language Notes* 44 (1): 145–149.

———. 2009. "Renaissance Profanations: Religion and Literature in the Age of Agamben." *Religion and Literature* 41 (2): 246–257.

Lupton, Julia Reinhard, and Graham Hammill. 2006. "Sovereigns, Citizens and Saints: Political Theology and Renaissance Literature." *Religion and Literature* 38 (3): 1–11.

———, eds. 2012. *Political Theology and Early Modernity*. Chicago, IL: University of Chicago Press.

Lynch, William. 1975. *Christ and Apollo: The Dimensions of the Literary Imagination*. Notre Dame, IN: Notre Dame University Press.

Lyne, Raphael. 2007. *Shakespeare's Late Work*. Oxford: Oxford University Press.

MacIntyre, Jean. 1982. "Truth, Lies and Poesie in King Lear." *Renaissance and Reformation* 6 (1): 34–45.

Mack, Maynard. 1965. *King Lear in Our Time*. Berkeley: University of California Press.

MacNeice, Louis. 2007. *Collected Poems*. Edited by Peter McDonald. London: Faber.
Magnusson, Lynne. 1999. *Shakespeare and Social Dialogue: Dramatic Language and Elizabethan Letters*. Cambridge: Cambridge University Press.
Maillet, Greg. 2016. *Learning to See: The Theological Vision of Shakespeare's King Lear*. Newcastle: Cambridge Scholars Publishing.
Marcus, Leah. 2016. "King Lear and the Death of the World." In *The Oxford Handbook of Shakespearean Tragedy*, edited by Michael Neill and David Schalkwyk, 421–434. Oxford University Press.
Martin, Catherine Gimelli. 2004. "The Erotology of Donne's 'Extasie' and the Secret History of Voluptuous Rationalism." *Studies in English Literature, 1500–1900* 44 (1): 121–147.
Mayer, Jean-Christophe. 2006. *Shakespeare's Hybrid Faith: History, Religion and the Stage*. New York: Palgrave.
McCoy, Richard. 2013. *Faith in Shakespeare*. Oxford: Oxford University Press.
McDonald, Russ. 2006. *Shakespeare's Late Style*. Cambridge: Cambridge University Press.
McEachern, Claire. 2018. *Believing in Shakespeare: Studies in Longing*. Cambridge: Cambridge University Press.
McLuskie, Kathleen. 1996. "The Patriarchal Bard: Feminist Criticism and Shakespeare: King Lear and Measure for Measure." In *Poitical Shakespeare: New Essays in Cultural Materialism*, edited by Jonathan Dollimore and Alan Sinfeld, 88–108. Chicago, IL: University of Chicago Press.
McMahon, Robert. 2006. *Understanding the Medieval Meditative Ascent: Augustine, Anselm, Boethius and Dante*. Washington, DC: Catholic University of America Press.
McMullan, Gordon. 2007. *Shakespeare and the Idea of Late Writing*. Cambridge: Cambridge University Press.
Mentz, Steve. 2010. "Strange Weather in King Lear." *Shakespeare* 6 (2): 139–152.
Milbank, John. 1995. "Can a Gift Be Given?" In *Rethinking Metaphysics*, edited by L. G Jones and S. E. Fowl, 119–161. Oxford: Blackwell.
———. 1997. *The Word Made Strange: Theology, Language and Culture*. Oxford: Blackwell.
———. 2006. *Theology and Social Theory: Beyond Secular Reason*. 2nd Edition. London: Blackwell.
———. 2009. "The Transcendentality of the Gift: A Summary in Answer to 12 Questions." *Revista Portuguesa de Filosofia* 65: 887–897.
———. 2011. *The Stanton Lectures*. Accessed April 2020. http://theologyphilosophycentre.co.uk/2011/03/12/john-milbanks-stanton-lectures-2011.
———. 2015. "Fictioning Things: Gifts and Narrative." In *Theology and Literature after Postmodernity*, edited by Zoë Lehmann Imfeld, Peter Hampson and Alison Milbank, 215–252. London: Bloomsbury.
Miner, Robert. 2004. *Truth in the Making: Creative Knowledge in Theology and Philosophy*. London: Routledge.
Montemaggi, Vittorio. 2016. *Reading Dante's Commedia as Theology: Divinity Realised in Human Encounter*. Oxford: Oxford University Press.
Montrose, Louis. 1996. *The Purpose of Playing: Shakespeare and the Cultural Politics of the Elizabethan Theatre*. Chicago, IL: University of Chicago Press.

Moore, Michael E. 2013. *Nicholas of Cusa and the Kairos of Modernity: Cassirer, Gadamer, Blumemberg.* New York: Punctum.

Moran, Andrew. 2005. "Synaesthesia and Eating in *The Winter's Tale.*" *Religion and the Arts* 9 (1): 38–61.

Moretti, Franco. 2005. *Signs Taken for Wonders: Essays in the Sociology of Literary Forms.* Translated by Susan Fischer, David Forgacs and David Miller. London: Verso.

Mowat, Barbara M. 2003. '*What's In A Name?*': Tragicomedy, Romance, or Late Comedy? Vol. 4, in *A Companion to Shakespeare's Works*, edited by Jean Howard and Richard Dutton, 129–153. Oxford: Blackwell.

Neely, Carol Thomas. 1985. *Broken Nuptials in Shakespeare's Plays.* New Haven, CT: Yale University Press.

———. 1995. "*The Winter's Tale*: The Triumph of Speech." In *The Winter's Tale: Critical Essays*, edited by Maurice Hunt, 139–155. New York: Routledge.

Newcomb, Lori. 2001. "'If That Which Is Lost Be Not Found': Monumental Bodies, Spectacular Bodies in *The Winter's Tale.*" In *Ovid and the Renaissance Body*, edited by G. V. Stanivukovic, 239–259. Toronto: University of Toronto Press.

Nielsen, Melinda. 2016. "'Nothing Almost Sees Miracles/But Misery': Lucretian Philosophy and Ascetic Experience in King Lear." *Logos: A Journal of Catholic Thought and Culture* 19 (4): 101–116.

Nuttall, A. D. 2007. *Shakespeare The Thinker.* New Haven, CT: Yale University Press.

O'Connell, Michael. 2000. *The Idolatrous Eye: Iconoclasm and Theatre in Early Modern England.* New York: Oxford University Press.

Otten, Willemien. 2020. *Thinking Nature and the Nature of Thinking: From Eriugena to Emerson.* Stanford, CA: Stanford University Press.

Palfrey, Simon. 1997. *Late Shakespeare: A New World of Words.* Oxford: Clarendon.

———. 2015. *Poor Tom: Living King Lear.* Oxford: Oxford University Press.

Panagopoulos, Nic. 2017. "'All's with Me Meet that I Can Fashion Fit': Physis and Nomos in King Lear." In *Shakespeare and Greece*, edited by Alison Findlay and Vassily Markidou, 115–138. London: Bloomsbury Arden.

Parker, Patricia. 1996. *Shakespeare from the Margins: Language, Culture, Context.* Chicago, IL: University of Chicago Press.

Parvini, Neema. 2012. *Shakespeare and Contemporary Theory: New Historicism and Cultural Materialism.* London: Bloomsbury.

———. 2014. "The Scholars and the Critics: Shakespeare Studies and Theory in the 2010s." *Shakespeare* 10 (2): 212–223.

Pfau, Thomas. 2013. *Minding the Modern: Human Agency, Intellectual Traditions and Responsible Knowledge.* Notre Dame, IN: Notre Dame University Press.

Pickstock, Catherine. 1998. *After Writing: On the Liturgical Consummation of Philosophy.* Oxford: Blackwell Publishers.

———. 2005. "Duns Scotus: His Historical and Contemporary Significance." *Modern Theology* 21 (4): 543–574.

———. 2010. "Liturgy and the Senses." *South Athlantic Quarterly* 109 (4): 719–739.

———. 2013. *Repetition and Identity.* Oxford: Oxford University Press.

———. 2015a. "Matter and Mattering: The Metaphysics of Rowan Williams." *Modern Theology* 31 (4): 599–617.
———. 2015b. "Sense and Sacrament." In *The Oxford Handbook of Sacramental Theology*, edited by Hans Boersma and Matthew Levering, 658–673. Oxford: Oxford University Press.
Platt, Peter. 1997. *Reason Diminished: Shakespeare and the Marvellous.* Lincoln: University of Nebraska Press.
———. 2009. *Shakespeare and the Culture of Paradox.* Aldershot: Aldgate.
Power, Andrew J., and Rory Loughlane, eds. 2013. *Late Shakespeare: 1608–1613.* Cambridge: Cambridge University Press.
Prevot, Andrew. 2015. "Responsorial Thought: Jean Louis Chrétien's Distincive Approach to Theology and Phenomenology." *Heythrop Journal* 56 (6): 975–987.
Priest, Graham. 2002. *Beyond the Limits of Thought.* Oxford: Oxford University Press.
Quiller-Couch, Arthur. 1916. "Shakespeare's Later Workmanship: *The Winter's Tale*." *The North American Review* 203 (726): 749–760.
Raffield, Paul. 2010. *Shakespeare's Imaginary Constitution: Late-Elizabethan Politics and the Theatre of Law.* Oxford: Hart Publishing.
Read, Sophie. 2013. *Eucharist and the Poetic Imagination in Early Modern England.* Cambridge: Cambridge University Press.
Riches, Aaron. 2015. "The Shakespearean Music: Eliot and von Balthasar on Shakespeare's Romance and the 'Ultra-Dramatic'." In *Theology and Literature after Postmodernity*, edited by Zoë Lehmann Imfeld, Peter Hampson and Alison Milbank, 195–213. London: Bloomsbury.
Riquier, Camille. 2013. "Jean-Louis Chrétien ou la parole cordiale." *Critique* 790 (3): 196–211.
Rosendale, Timothy. 2007. *Liturgy and Literature in the Making of Protestant England.* Cambridge: Cambridge University Press.
Ruiter, David. 2007. "Shakespeare and Hospitality: Opening *The Winter's Tale*." *Mediterranean Studies* 16: 157–177.
Ryan, Kiernan. 2002. *Shakespeare.* 3rd Edition. Basingstoke: Palgrave.
Scarry, Elaine. 1985. *The Body in Pain: The Maing and Unmaking of the World.* Oxford: Oxford University Press.
Schalkwyk, David. 2002. *Speech and Performance in Shakespeare's Sonnets and Plays.* Cambridge: Cambridge University Press.
———. 2008. *Shakespeare, Love and Service.* Cambridge: Cambridge University Press.
Schreiner, Susan. 2010. *Are You Alone Wise?: The Search for Certainty in the Modern Era.* Oxford: Oxford University Press.
Schumann, Alex. 2014. *Rethinking Shakespeare's Political Philosophy: From Lear to Leviathan.* Cambridge: Cambridge University Press.
Schwartz, Regina. 2008. *Sacramental Poetics at the Dawn of Secularism: When God Left the World.* Stanford, CA: Stanford University Press.
———. 2016. *Loving Justice, Living Shakespeare.* Oxford: Oxford University Press.
Schwartz, Regina, and Vittorio Montemaggi. 2014. "On Religion and Literature: Truth, Beauty and the Good." *Religion and Literature* 46 (2–3): 111–128.
Screech, Michael. 1988. *Erasmus: Ecstasy and the Praise of Folly.* London: Penguin.

Shakespeare, William. 1996. *The Winter's Tale*. Edited by Stephen Orgel. Oxford: Oxford University Press.

———. 1997. *King Lear*. Arden Shakespeare 3rd Series. Edited by R.A. Foakes. London: Bloomsbury Arden.

———. 1998. *The Complete Works*. Revised Edition. Edited by Ann Thompson, Richard Proudfoot and David Scott Kastan. London: Bloomsbury Arden.

———. 2010. *The Winter's Tale*. Arden Shakespeare 3rd Series. Edited by John Pitcher. London: Methuen.

Shannon, Laurie. 2013. *The Accomodated Animal: Cosmopolity in Shakespearean Locales*. Chicago, IL: Chicago University Press.

Shaw, Gregory. 2014. *Theurgy and the Soul: The Neoplatonism of Iamblichus*. 2nd Edition. Kettering, OH: Angelico Press.

Shell, Alison. 2010. *Shakespeare and Religion*. Arden Critical Companions. London: Bloomsbury Arden.

Sherman, Jacob. 2014. *Partakers in the Divine: Contemplation and the Practice of Theology*. Minneapolis, MN: Fortress Press.

Shuger, Debora. 1988. *Sacred Rhetoric: The Christian Grand Style in the English Renaissance*. Princeton, NJ: Princeton University Press.

———. 2001. *Political Theologies in Shakespeare's England: The Sacred and the State in "Measure for Measure"*. Basingstoke: Palgrave.

Shupack, Paul. 1997. "Natural Justice and King Lear." *Cardozo Studies in Law and Literature* 9: 67–105.

Sinfield, Alan. 2006. "Review of Ewan Fernie's Spiritual Shakespeares (2005)." *Textual Practice* 20 (1): 161–170.

Smith, Emma. 2011–2017. *Approaching Shakespeare*. Accessed June 2019. https://podcasts.ox.ac.uk/series/approaching-shakespeare.

Smith, Matthew. 2017. "The Disincarnate Text: Ritual Poetics in Herbert, Paul, Williams and Levinas." *Christianity and Literature* 66 (3): 363–384.

Sommerville, C. John. 1992. *The Secularization of Early Modern England: From Religious Culture to Religious Faith*. New York: Oxford University Press.

Steffes, Michael. 2003. "The Ancient Greek Wild in *The Winter's Tale*." *Renaissance and Reformation* 27 (4): 31–51.

Steiner, George. 1961. *The Death of Tragedy*. London: Faber.

———. 1989. *Real Presences: Is There Anything in What We Say?* London: The University of Chicago Press.

Sterrett, Joseph. 2012. *The Unheard Prayer: Religious Toleration in Shakespeare's Drama*. Leiden: Brill.

Stirling, Kristen. 2018. "'As a Picture That Looks Upon Him, That Looks Upon It': Cusanus in Donne's Sermons." *American Cusanu Society Newsletter* 35: 7–14.

Strachey, Lytton. 1922. *Books and Characters*. New York: Harcourt and Brace.

Strauss, Leo. 1966. *Socrates and Aristophanes*. Chicago, IL: University of Chicago Press.

Streete, Adrian. 2009. *Protestantism and Drama in Early Modern England*. Cambridge: Cambridge University Press.

Tambling, Jeremy. 2015. "*The Winter's Tale*: Three Recognitions." *Essays in Criticism* 65 (2): 30–52.

Tanner, Kathryn. 1988. *God and Creation in Christian Theology: Tyranny or Empowerment*. Oxford: Blackwell.

Taylor, Gary. 2003. "The Cultural Politics of Maybe." In *Theatre and Religion: Lancastrian Shakespeare*, edited by Richard Dutton, Alison Findlay and Richard Wilson, 242–258. Manchester: Manchester University Press.

———. 2004. "Shakespeare's Midlife Crisis." *The Guardian*, 3 May. Accessed February 2020. https://www.theguardian.com/stage/2004/may/03/theatre.classics.

Taylor, Gary, and Michael Warren, eds. 1983. *The Division of the Kingdoms: Shakespeare's Two Versions of 'King Lear'*. Oxford: Oxford University Press.

Taylor, Kevin, and Giles Waller, eds. 2011. *Christian Theology and Tragedy*. Farnham: Ashgate.

Teilhard de Chardin, Pierre. 1961. *Hymn of the Universe*. Translated by Simon Bartholomew. London: Harper & Row.

Thomas, Alfred. 2018. *Shakespeare, Catholicism and the Middle Ages: Maimed Rights*. New York: Palgrave.

Tiffany, Grace. 2000. "Calvinist Grace in Shakespeare's Romances." *Christianity and Literature* 49 (4): 421–425.

———. 2018. "Paganism and Reform in Shakespeare's Plays." *Religions* 9 (7): 214.

Tillich, Paul. 1951. *Systematic Theology*. Vol. 1. Chicago, IL: University of Chicago Press.

———. 1954. *Love, Power and Justice: Ontological analyses and Ethical Applications*. Oxford: Oxford University Press.

Tolkien, J. R. R. 2006. *The Monster and the Critics and Other Essays*. London: Harper Collins.

Traub, Valerie. 2009. "The Nature of Norms in Early Modern England: Anatomy, Cartography, King Lear." *South Central Review* 26 (1): 42–81.

Traversi, Derek. 1969. *An Approach to Shakespeare*. Vol. 2. London: Hollis & Carter.

Travis, Peter. 1982. *Dramatic Design in the Chester Cycle*. Chicago, IL: Chicago University Press.

Utz, Richard, ed. 1995. *Literary Nominalism and the Rereading of Late Medieval Texts*. Lewiston, NJ: Edwin Mellen Press.

Vanhoozer, Kevin. 2014. *Faith Speaking Understanding: Performing the Drama of Doctrine*. Louisville, KT: John Know Press.

Vanita, Ruth. 2000. "Mariological Memory in *The Winter's Tale* and Henry VIII." *Studies in English Literature 1500–1900* 40 (2): 311–337.

Venard, Olivier-Thomas. 2002–2009. *St Thomas d'Aquin, poète théologien*. 3 vols. Geneva and Paris: Ad Solem.

———. 2009. "Literature and Theology: What Is it About?" *Religion and Literature* 41 (2): 87–95.

Voegelin, Eric. 1990. *What Is History? and Other Late Unpublished Writings*. Edited by Thomas A. Hollweck and Paul Caringella. Baton Rouge: Louisiana State University Press.

Vyvyan, John. 2013. *Shakespeare and Platonic Beauty*. London: Shepheard-Walwyn.

Waldron, Jennifer. 2013. *Reformations of the Body: Idolatry, Sacrifice and Early Modern Theater*. Basingstoke: Palgrave Macmillan.

Walsh, Brian. 2016. *Unsettled Toleration: Religious Difference on the Shakespearean Stage*. Oxford: Oxford University Press.

Ward, Graham. 2009. "Why Literature Can Never Be Entirely Secular." *Religion and Literature* 41 (2): 21–27.
Waterfield, John. 2009. *The Heart of His Mystery: Shakespeare and the Catholic Faith in England under Elizabeth and James*. Bloomington, IN: iUniverse.
Weil, Simone. 2002. *Gravity and Grace*. Translated by Emma Crawford and Mario von der Ruhr. London: Routledge.
Wells, Robin Headlam. 2005. *Shakespeare's Humanism*. Cambridge: Cambridge University Press.
Whalen, Robert. 2002. *The Poetry of Immanence: Sacrament in Donne and Herbert*. Toronto: University of Toronto Press.
Wilbern, David. 1980. "Shakespeare's Nothing." In *Representing Shakespeare: New Psychoanalytic Essays*, edited by Murray Schwartz and Coppélia Khan, 244–263. Baltimore, MD: Johns Hopkins University Press.
Williams, George Walton. 2002. "Invocations on the Gods in King Lear: A Second Opinion." *Shakespeare Newsletter* 51 (4): 89–106.
Williams, Rowan. 2005. *Grace and Necessity: Reflections on Art and Love*. London: Continuum.
———. 2014. *The Edge of Words: God and the Habits of Language*. London: Bloomsbury.
———. 2015. "Language, Reality and Desire in Augustine's De Doctrina." In *Theology and Literature After Postmodernity*, edited by Zoë Lehmann Imfeld, Peter Hampson and Alison Milbank, 115–136. London: Bloomsbury.
———. 2016. *The Tragic Imagination*. Oxford: Oxford University Press.
Wilson, Harold S. 1943. "'Nature and Art' in Winter's Tale IV, iv, 86ff." *Shakespeare Association Bulletin* 18: 114–120.
Wilson, Rawdon. 1995. *Shakespearean Narrative*. Newark: University of Delaware Press.
Wilson, Richard. 2004. *Secret Shakespeare: Studies in Theatre, Religion and Resistance*. Manchester: Manchester University Press.
———. 2016. *Worldly Shakespeare: The Theatre of Our Good Will*. Edinburgh: Edinburgh University Press.
Wind, Edgar. 1968. *Pagan Mysteries in the Renaissance*. New York: Norton.
Witmore, Michael. 2007. *Pretty Creatures: Children and Fiction in the English Renaissance*. Ithaca, NY: Cornell University Press.
———. 2008. *Shakespearean Metaphysics*. London: Continuum.
Wolfe (Tonning), Judith. 2004. "'Like this Insubstantial Pageant, Faded': Eschatology and Theatricality in The Tempest." *Literature and Theology* 18 (4): 371–382.
———. 2007. "Acknowledging a Hidden God: A Theological Critique of Stanley Cavell on Scepticism." *Heythrop Journal* 48 (3): 384–405.
———. 2015. "Hermione's Sophism: Ordinariness and Theatricality in 'The Winter's Tale'." *Philosophy and Literature* 39 (1a): 83–105.
Woodbridge, Linda. 1994. *The Scythe of Saturn: Shakespeare and Magical Thinking*. Chicago, IL: University of Illinois Press.
Woods, Gillian. 2013. *Shakespeare's Unreformed Fictions*. Oxford: Oxford University Press.
Yamaki, Kazuhiko, ed. 2002. *Nicholas of Cusa: A Medieval Thinker for the Modern Age*. Surrey: Curzon Press.

Yates, Frances. 2001. *The Occult Philosophy in the Elizabethan Age*. London: Routledge.
Ziebart, K. Meredith. 2014. *Nicholaus Cusanus on Faith and the Intellect: A Case-Study in 15th Century Fides-Ratio Controversy*. Leiden: Brill.
———. 2019. "Cusanus and Nominalism." In *Nicholas of Cusa and Times of Transition: Essays in Honour of Gerald Christianson*, edited by Thomas M. Izbicki, Jason Aleksander and Donald F. Duclow, 219–241. Boston, MA: Brill.

Index

Note: Page numbers followed by "n" denote endnotes.

acknowledgment: concept of 25–27, 92, 103, 140
Adelman, Janet 6, 103, 145, 176n54
Agamben, Giorgio 110
Andrewes, Lancelot 97–98
art: in Cusa 54–56, 61, 72; in Shakespeare 90, 97, 121, 122, 126, 134–135, 139, 147, 149, 151, 152, 158, 160–161, 164, 168–169, 170, 172, 174; see also nature, *King Lear*, *The Winter's Tale*
attention 54, 55, 59, 67, 68, 90, 96–97, 127, 167
Augustine 35, 47, 66, 69, 83n99, 96, 129n39

Baker, Anthony 36, 91, 121, 137
Balthasar, Hans Urs von 35, 136
Barthes, Roland 111
Beckwith, Sarah 9, 11, 12, 19, 25–27, 89, 97, 127, 146, 157
Bloom, Harold 118
Brook, Peter xviii, 116

call: phenomenon of xv, xix, 18, 62, 65–71, 76–77, 96, 116, 125, 162
Cavell, Stanley 26–27, 91–92, 107, 118, 143, 151, 158
Chrétien, Jean-Louis 66–71, 75–76, 96, 98, 167
Coleridge, Samuel Taylor 32, 96
Cox, John 7, 12, 68, 71–72, 90–91
Cummings, Brian 12, 69
Cusa, Nicholas of xvi, xix, 152, 156, 166, 167, 173; anthropology 62–63; coincidence of opposites 56, 60, 65, 72; and language 48, 53–59, 76–78; learned ignorance 29, 47, 48, 54, 56, 58, 111; and metaphysics of modernity 50–53; and science of praise 29, 48, 49, 59–65; and Shakespeare 27–30, 47–49

Dante Alighieri 36, 37
doxology xv, xvii–xviii, xix, 27–30, 50, 61, 62, 77, 78–79, 89, 98, 102, 108, 122, 125, 145, 157, 166, 167, 169, 173, 174, 181–186; and concept of self 71–75; and metaphysics of participation 28–29, 50; see also God; liturgy; praise
Dupré, Louis 50–53, 56, 60

Eliade, Mircea 114
Eliot, T. S. 114, 136
Erasmus, Desiderius 7, 48–49, 111–112, 148, 150

fiction xx, 17, 22, 113, 119–122, 150–152, 154, 156, 165, 172; see also *The Winter's Tale*
forgiveness 17, 22, 75; in the late plays 25–27; in *Lear* 23–25, 94, 99, 123–125, 126; in *The Winter's Tale* 151, 168, 174
Frye, Northrop 112, 144, 159

Gadamer, Hans-Georg xvii, 14–16, 17, 18, 25; and Cusa 41n80
gift: and language xv–xx, 20, 22–23, 27, 30, 36–37, 63, 66, 72, 73, 77, 106, 117, 124, 137, 138–139, 142–143, 144, 146, 154, 164–165, 181, 183; postmodern notion of 20; and theology 20–23, 24–25, 91, 156; see also doxology; grace; praise

God: names of 20, 35, 54–57, 60–62, 65, 93, 110–111; as praise itself xix, 64, 65, 78, 89, 109, 181, 185
grace xviii, 20–22, 25, 72, 90, 116, 136, 137, 138, 148, 152–153, 157, 166, 169–170, 172, 173, 182; as carnivalesque 148; and nature 24, 51, 53; as secular 'sublime' 34; as 'vocative superflux' 114–116, 184; of words xx, 18, 23, 36–37, 91, 95, 136–137, 138, 165, 172, 174; *see also* gift, language
Gray, Patrick 12, 43n117, 71, 72
Greenblatt, Stephen 8–9, 49
Gross, Kenneth 102, 108, 168, 169–170

Hoff, Johannes 27–30, 35, 48, 53, 57, 182
Hughes, John 23–25, 96, 102
Hughes, Ted 97, 98, 99, 100, 158–159

King Lear: concept of middle in 99–100, 105, 122; critical tradition 5–6, 70; curses in 102–109, 110, 122; gods in 90–91, 103–105, 127; justice 117–122; nature 70, 101–109, 118, 119; spatialisation in 93–95, 117, 121, 124; and weight of words 90, 92, 95–96, 100, 119, 125–127
Knight, George Wilson 4–5, 6

language: concept of 66; and dialogue 14–15, 54, 67, 69, 75–76; as embodied 16, 74–75, 92, 96, 184, 185; as hospitality 66, 75–78, 96–97, 163, 167; as listening 67–68, 75, 76, 96, 98, 167 (*see also* attention); as love 50, 62, 72, 90, 93–99, 100, 117, 122–124, 125–127; as medium of spiritual practice 35; and modernity 51–53; and nominalism 51–53, 54, 94–95; and postmodernity 27–29, 34, 153; as power xix, xx, 7–10, 12, 31, 71, 73, 93–95, 96, 99, 115, 127; shamanic 114–116; as silence 66, 75, 76, 95–97, 167; as symbolic 17, 32, 51, 90, 91–95, 100, 105–106, 108, 120–122, 123–125, 127; as vision 64, 77, 167, 181; *see also* doxology; gift; God; grace; *logos*; praise; Word

liturgy xix, 72–75, 98, 121, 136, 170, 184, 185
logos xv, xvii, xx, 14, 16, 20, 58, 67, 74, 89, 97–98, 100, 121, 127; and language 34, 51, 53, 117; *see also* Word made flesh
Lupton, Julia Reinhard 10–11, 12

matter: linguistic character of 16–17, 19, 74, 92, 108, 173; *see also* language, as hospitality; nature
metaphysics: doxological 182–183; of participation xvii, 18, 19–20, 28–30, 55, 60–62, 124–125, 151–152; potentiality and act 60–61, 82n74, 108, 144–145; of spatialisation 93–95, 108, 115, 118
middle: as Christ 100; as jointure of opposites 72, 99–100, 102, 105, 109–111, 116, 119, 122, 127, 164, 171, 172; as *metaxu* 30; in Psalms 100
middle-voice xx, 72–75, 116, 122, 124, 164, 184
Milbank, John xvii, 18–23, 61, 137, 156, 175n26

nature xx, 17–18, 62, 101; and art 55–56, 61, 64, 90, 121, 134–135, 139, 154, 159–165, 168–169, 171, 172; and grace 24, 51, 53; in *King Lear* 23–24, 70, 77, 90, 101–109, 118–119; and *natura* 101; in *The Winter's Tale* 141, 145, 147, 151–152, 158, 173–174; *see also* matter

oaths 100, 105–106, 110–111, 112, 115, 125, 140, 146, 147, 157, 165, 167; *see also* vows
ontology: analogical 19, 53, 95, 124–125; doxological 181; of forgiveness 24, 96; of power/violence xix, 19–20, 23–24, 60, 102, 112, 117, 122, 146, 178n105, 181–182

Palfrey, Simon 114–115, 143
paradox xx, 28, 30, 49, 59, 63, 99–100, 110–111, 112, 157, 169; as Christ 3, 58
Pickstock, Catherine xvii, 18, 72–75, 94, 124–125
poetics xx, xxi, 20, 181, 183; and ethics 20, 22, 26, 137, 173; and

Gadamer 15–16; New Historicist 7–9, 12; as praise 34, 36, 59–65; and Shakespeare 30, 32–33, 97, 127, 134–136, 152, 155, 172; and Thomas Aquinas 33–34; and Williams 17–18

postmodernity 5, 6, 20–21, 27, 28, 29, 34–35, 71, 72, 75, 153

post-tragic, the xvi, 12, 21–22, 25–26, 31, 43n123, 75

praise: in poetic tradition 49; as science xix, 29, 48, 49, 59–65, 74; *see also* doxology; God

prayer 68–69, 77, 172

redemption xv, xx, 6, 24, 26, 72, 73, 91, 111, 120; as aspect of language 26, 59, 76, 151

religious turn in Shakespeare studies, xviii, 10–13, 25, 181–182

Renaissance xviii–xix, 11, 14, 28, 49, 54, 70, 71–72, 74, 114, 182–183

response, phenomenon of xv, 16, 18, 19, 25, 26, 34, 65–71, 75–78, 96, 98, 101, 114, 125, 161, 163, 173, 181, 183, 185; and responsibility 26, 67–68, 72–75, 76, 163; *see also* call

repetition 22, 36–37, 73, 111, 124–125, 126, 141–142, 143, 146, 148, 149, 151, 152, 160

ritual *see* liturgy

Romance xx, 12, 25, 135–137, 151, 156, 159, 175n5; *see also* post-tragic

Schwartz, Regina 10, 11, 33, 120, 122, 124

Shakespeare, William: *As You Like it* 50; *Julius Caesar* 71; *A Midsummer Night's Dream* 32–33; *Sonnets* 29–30, 68, 96, 180n154; *Timon of Athens* 150; *Twelfth Night* 49; *see also King Lear*; poetics; *The Winter's Tale*

soliloquy: concept of 68–71

Steiner, George 30, 119

theology: and literature xvi, xviii, xix, xx–xxi, 3, 4, 27–28, 31–37, 181–186; natural 17–18

theurgy 72, 75, 149–150, 151, 169, 171–172, 180n153

Tillich, Paul 32, 120

Traub, Valerie 93–94, 118

Venard, Olivier-Thomas 33–35

vows 105, 109, 126, 150; *see also* oaths

Weil, Simone 90

Williams, Rowan xvii, 13, 16–18, 66, 113, 116, 136–137, 169

Winter's Tale, The 21–23, 137; and children 139, 143, 150, 151, 156, 160, 167; gift in 22–23, 138–139, 150, 151, 154; gods in 147, 149–150, 162–163, 166, 168; and grace 136, 137, 138, 148, 152–153, 157, 166, 169–170, 172, 173, 182; and innocence 141–142, 144, 145, 155, 156; and liturgy 75; and nature 141, 145, 147, 151–152, 158, 173–174; nature and art in 134–135, 139, 154, 159–165, 168–169, 171, 172; and tale/storytelling 134–135, 137, 143, 149, 150–157, 162, 165, 170–171, 172, 173, 174n3

Witmore, Michael 12, 156

Word made flesh xvii, xix, 3, 14, 20, 34, 35, 37, 50, 56, 57–58, 59, 75, 76–77, 97–98, 127, 173–174, 181, 183, 184; as human voice 67; as poetic 59; as poetic imagination 32–33; *see also* logos

Printed in Great Britain
by Amazon